Praise for

Learning to Fly

"I recommend this book only for those who are already of sound mind and constitution, because having just read this, I find that my adrenaline is flowing, my endorphins are thumping, and I am possessed with a weird desire to hurl myself off a cliff, possibly with a parachute or, God forbid, one of those winged batsuit contraptions. Buyer beware."

—J. Maarten Troost, author of *The Sex Lives of Cannibals*

"Alive, passionate, intense . . . about everything, Steph Davis climbs vertical slopes, drops out of planes, leaps off cliffs, and in the process teaches us all how to deal with the devastations, the fears, the challenges, and the joyous moments of life. Steph takes the reader on an emotional roller coaster full of highs, lows, and love, and it's contagious. You won't walk away unaffected."

—Rita Golden Gelman, author of *Tales of a Female Nomad: Living at Large in the World*

Learning to Fly

To Nate :)

A Memoir of Hanging On and Letting Go

Steph Davis

STEPH DAVIS

TOUCHSTONE

NEW YORK LONDON TORONTO SYDNEY NEW DELHI

Touchstone
An Imprint of Simon & Schuster, Inc.
1230 Avenue of the Americas
New York, NY 10020

First Touchstone trade paperback edition November 2015

TOUCHSTONE and colophon are
registered trademarks of Simon & Schuster, Inc.

Illustration Credits: Jimmy Chin, John Evans, Damon Johnston, Dean Fidelman, Tommy
Chandler, Brian Kimball, Jim Hurst, Krystle Wright, Alan Martinez, Heinz Zak, Chris Hunter,
Eric Perlman, Keith Ladzinski, Mario Richard, Lisa Hathaway, Jay Epstein.

For information about special discounts for bulk purchases,
please contact Simon & Schuster Special Sales
at 1-866-506-1949 or business@simonandschuster.com.

The Simon & Schuster Speakers Bureau can bring authors to your live event.
For more information or to book an event contact the
Simon & Schuster Speakers Bureau at 866-248-3049
or visit our website at www.simonspeakers.com.

Designed by Ruth Lee-Mui

Manufactured in the United States of America

3   5   7   9   10   8   6   4   2

The Library of Congress has cataloged the hardcover edition as follows:
Davis, Steph.
Learning to fly / Steph Davis.
p. cm.
1. Davis, Steph. 2. Women mountaineers—United States—Biography. I. Title.
GV199.92.D38A3 2013
796.522092—dc23
[B]   2012029998

ISBN 978-1-4516-5205-5
ISBN 978-1-4516-9833-6 (pbk)
ISBN 978-1-4516-5207-9 (ebook)

for Mario Richard

"Quand tu regarderas le ciel, la nuit, puisque j'habiterai dans
l'une d'elles, puisque je rirai dans l'une d'elles, alors ce sera
pour toi comme si riaient toutes les étoiles. Tu auras, toi, des
étoiles qui savent rire." —Antoine de Saint-Exupéry

je t'aime eperdument

I want to push myself to my limits, and if things don't work out, then I can give up. But I will do everything I can until the bitter end. That is how I live.

—HARUKI MURAKAMI

So I've started out for God knows where
I guess I'll know when I get there.

—TOM PETTY

Contents

The Roan Plateau of Colorado

*F*alling into dead air felt nothing like I thought it would. I'd spent much of my life trying not to think about it. It was my worst nightmare. After twenty years of going up rock faces and mountains, the idea of free-falling through the air was essentially x-ed out in my brain. Because you can't think about falling when you're climbing, or you won't go climbing anymore. In the few instances during my climbing career when my mind had flicked there, I'd yanked it right back. I figured if the big fall ever came, it would all be over, *wham,* just like that. I'd slip off. I'd start falling. A stab of panic. Then somehow I would just disappear or everything would go black or something. And that would be it. The end.

As it turns out, nothing could be further from the truth. You know you're falling for every millisecond of time your body is dropping through the air. You see the wall rushing past, the colors of the rock streak by, the ground coming at you. You see trees getting bigger, small rocks grow into giant boulders. Your brain knows exactly what's happening and where you're going: directly to the ground, faster and faster as you fall until you reach terminal speed, 120 miles per hour. And each of those milliseconds feels as long and full as some years.

Between my feet, a small runnel trickled toward the edge and scattered into clear, round droplets that cascaded into the air. The edge was square, like the front of a counter. I looked at my boots, coming right up to the end of the flat limestone, and then down past them. The wall dropped six hundred feet to meet a gray talus slope. The small rocks poured down to steep, rugged gullies and ravines, a thousand more feet rendered tiny by distance. The shift between the big view and the close-up view was disorienting, like refocusing a camera lens. I felt almost mesmerized and slightly vertiginous, watching the sparkling water balls drop out in space. I jumped.

The Perrine Bridge, Twin Falls, Idaho

Chapter One

Falling

I've been a rock climber for twenty years. So for two decades, I've been motivated by fear or pride, or both, not to fall. I would have picked myself as the second-least-likely person I know to ever go skydiving. The first being my mom.

First of all, I'm not a thrill seeker. Second, like any serious climber, I'm inherently cheap, and skydiving is expensive. Third, I don't prefer being scared. Falling, loud wind, cold air, hitting the ground hard . . . these are all things I also don't usually go out looking for. In the few years before the summer of 2007, I had become friends with several skydivers and base jumpers, and we all knew it would be a cold day in hell before I'd be sitting in a jump plane or standing at the edge of a cliff with them.

It's funny, though, how many times the thing you are least likely to do is what you find yourself doing. Or at least that's how it is for me. I grew up a studious, aspiring concert pianist with a master's degree in literature, then subsequently dropped out of law school to live in a truck and become a professional climber, so I've learned not to rule anything out.

Salt flats of the Great Salt Lake, Utah *John Evans*

My husband and I met in our early twenties, when we were both living out of cars and climbing as much as possible, waiting tables sporadically to sustain the traditional spartan, road-tripping existence of the climbing bum. Over the next twelve years, we traveled together, split up, reunited, climbed huge walls and mountains with ropes and without ropes, lived in vehicles, tents, and snow caves, and finally got married. We grew up together wildly and freely, challenging each other all along the way. Our life was pure adventure and self-invention, and nothing about it was safe.

I grew up in various suburbias in Illinois, Maryland, and New Jersey with one older brother and a cat, and my parents could never get their heads around my transformation from a model student into an itinerant climber. Though my ascents had quickly blossomed from basic outings into major ascents of big walls and peaks in Yosemite, Baffin Island, Pakistan, Patagonia, and Kyrgyzstan, they couldn't get comfortable with my non-usual lifestyle and nontraditional choices, even as climbing began to develop into a career. At the end of the day, I was still usually eating out of a camping pot, pulling a paycheck that must have seemed like a joke to someone who'd had every reason to bank on a lawyer daughter to match the doctor son.

To a climber, it looked like the dream life—married to my longtime partner, climbing big routes around the world, sponsored by a major outdoor-clothing company and a few other equipment manufacturers. And then, in 2006, my husband climbed a famous sandstone arch in a Utah National Park and a media uproar erupted in the outdoor world. It was just a hunk of sandy, crumbly sandstone, less than a hundred feet tall, surrounded by hundreds of miles of other, better rocks to climb, hardly a five-star route. But its shape made it a tourist attraction, and the Park Service had even glued and cemented it to hold it together and chiseled out steps in the slabs leading up to it. The Park Service was first annoyed by the climb and the media focus, then out for blood, and the media whipped up as much controversy as could be invented out of the situation.

The timing was unique. Climbers had just started to become active on the Internet through chat boards, populated by a prolific handful who used pseudonyms like *tradman* and *rokjock* rather than their names. Internet discussions on climbing forums, which started about climbing topics but regularly culminated in profanity, personal insults, and pornographic references, were a dominant form of communication. Both the real media and the chat-board addicts had a love/hate attraction to my husband, since his rebellious, mind-blowing ascents were characterized by a huge degree of daring and obvious unconcern for anyone else's opinion.

At first, somebody climbing up the iconic rock on the Utah license plate was a fun local-interest tidbit after the daily crimes, environmental disasters, and political feuds. But given an unusual lack of real news in the world just then, this story soon got legs. A professional climber climbing a rock that wasn't technically illegal to climb but was famous and in a national park provided an opportunity to rile up the Park Service. Voilà: an angle! The arch story catapulted from local Utah news channels to the Associated Press, CNN, NPR, and national magazines.

The media-driven "controversy" became progressively more elaborate in the following months. Incredibly, it just didn't seem to end, and everything we did or didn't do in response to the uproar only made it worse. The ensuing circus provided forum fodder for months. The chat boards recycled wildly embroidered versions of the story, mostly perpetuated by the same few Internet junkies, but which appeared far more concrete to onlookers than a group of scruffy guys shooting their mouths off around a campfire as in the good old days of the recent past. Before too long, the rock had ballooned into Utah's most cherished treasure, and the climbing of it was not only illegal but had caused untold damage. The publicity triggered the National Park Service, who already had a long-standing and habitual grudge against Yosemite climbers and my husband in particular, to mount a federal investigation of the climb and of him, apparently in hopes of finding some way to prosecute him for something now that they had been so publicly annoyed.

Ultimately, the NPS sent federal subpoenas to his, and my, sponsors, for no reason I could discern other than to inconvenience and possibly intimidate them, and months later they held investigative hearings before a judge in Salt Lake City. They seemed determined to find some way that a climber climbing a rock could be a prosecutable offense. In an immediate reaction that moved me deeply, our two smallest sponsors called to make sure we knew about the NPS's bizarre action and to express their indignation and offers of support. Much later, a third sponsor casually asked if things had settled down with all the arch nonsense, and that was the only thing they ever said.

In reality, there wasn't much of a controversy at all. The climb was not against any rules and didn't cause any harm to anyone or anything (except us), and much later the NPS finally gave up on the "investigation."

Their reactions stood in striking contrast to those of the two larger companies I had imagined to be true partners and even family, upon whose contracts we depended for our income—and who had not contacted us at all in the first few weeks after receiving the NPS subpoenas. The gear company that sponsored both of us was the first to bail. About a month after my contract had expired, my suspicions were confirmed by an awkward return call to the many messages I had left with the people I had known for years at the company. I was rather abashedly told that neither of our contracts would automatically be renewed as usual, for reasons that were impossible to explain, but which most assuredly had nothing to do with the arch thing. I had been with that company for twelve years, and the phone call was like a punch in the stomach. Financially, the loss of that contract wasn't life-altering, especially for climbers who were used to a no-frills existence, but it wasn't ideal. It was the big clothing company we truly depended on financially.

Even in the midst of the turmoil, I sensed that this time of my life was a rare opportunity I might otherwise never have, to see things for what they really were, professionally and personally. Years later, when my life wasn't exploding around me, I would be able to see it as the most valuable learning experience of my life, and I would even find myself giggling occasionally when I reflected that I had never even climbed that crumbly little rock.

The arch debacle, as I called it, reached its height of strangeness when both of us were dumped by our main clothing sponsor in the early spring of 2007, not long after the federal subpoenas went out, in a single phone call.

My marriage, never a place of safety, was not a refuge in this unpredictable time and was unraveling as fast as my career. We were both shell-shocked and had no resources or experience in dealing with an escalating PR disaster. We were just a couple of climbers who were far more comfortable on the side of a rock, and every reaction we had seemed to be wrong. Abruptly losing our jobs and our surrogate family for something that didn't make sense to us was almost impossible to wrap our heads around. It seemed like solid rock had turned to water beneath our feet without explanation.

To top it all off, I was scheduled to travel across the country and to Europe for a book tour, which started just three weeks after I was terminated by my main sponsor. Over the last year, I'd got the idea of collecting the eclectic stories and essays I'd written about climbing and living the climbing life and putting them together into a book. The Mountaineers, a well-established climbing club and publishing group in Seattle, had taken me under their wing, coaching me through my first stab at making a book. In between days spent on El Cap and travel to South America, I'd written a few more stories and compiled them all into a book I titled *High Infatuation: A Climber's Guide to Love and Gravity*. Now I was anxious and grieving, and the feelings I'd written about so naturally of living a simple, pure climbing life, seemed almost alien to me, as if they'd been written by someone else. The bottom had dropped out.

Traveling around the country, trying to recapture that simple infatuation for audiences of devoted climbers, seemed nearly impossible. But I was caught between a rock and a hard place. I felt that since I had all my arms and legs, I had no acceptable reason not to honor my commitments. Though I'd been left high and dry, in no way was I going to do that to someone else. It was against my principles. Canceling wasn't an option. I was going to go through with the tour and do a great job, if only because that was what I had agreed to do and people were depending on me to be there. But making a string of public appearances before my community, being on display just as my professional life had come unglued, was guaranteed to be on the list of hardest things I'd ever done. Endurance mode was something I knew well, from long alpine routes and big-wall climbs, perhaps the thing I was best at. I moved doggedly forward, all emotions on standby. When I allowed myself to feel at all, I felt sad that on the debut of my first book, something every writer dreams about, I was struggling just to keep myself together. Several of the prescheduled book readings were in the stores of the company that had just terminated me, which made the experience excruciatingly surreal.

Halfway through, in a Hampton Inn on the second day of a three-day tour through the Northwest, I sat at a mahogany-veneer desk feeling

worn-out and hopeless and isolated. I didn't know if I could do this anymore. I called my older brother, Virgil, an ER doctor, and broke down.
My husband had been unreachable for weeks. He didn't pick up his cell
phone and wasn't answering e-mails. Somewhere between Seattle and
New York, he disappeared into the backcountry of the Sierras, leaving
me a message that he didn't want to communicate, maybe ever. While
I'd been traveling through cities, steeling myself to stay strong in public, he had sequestered himself in Yosemite, refusing to deal with any of
the external world, which was his way of circumventing the anger and
frustration he was struggling with. A highly independent individual with
elemental views of right and wrong, he couldn't tolerate the situation.

By the time I figured out that the silence was a severance, I was flying
from Boston to Denver and then to Italy. Fletcher, the Heeler-mix dog
from a Navajo reservation I'd had for ten years, was also in California
with my husband during the six weeks of my nonstop travel.

Normally, Fletch and I were nearly inseparable. On top of everything

Messing with Fletch in
Hueco Tanks, Texas

else, living without her was unbearable. Until I was finished with my book tour, I had no way to physically address any of it.

As a climber, I'd never had much spare meat on my bones, and by now I'd lost ten pounds and was relying on coffee for energy. When my travel was finally over, I dropped everything and went to California to track down my husband, get my dog back, and fix this mess. Reuniting with Fletch was an enormous relief, but my husband proved to be a little harder to find. If I hadn't lost my mind yet, the weeks of virtually stalking him, asking sympathetic but uncomfortable friends for sightings, and sitting at trailheads or in parking lots for hours, in hopes of just finding him, finished the job.

Driving into Tuolumne out of Yosemite Valley

The marriage was obviously in its death throes, but I wasn't ready to give up. As ethereal as the relationship had become, I didn't think I could handle any more loss. I'd never been unable to fix something in the past, but lately I'd been finding myself unable to fix anything. Beyond that, purely out of principle, if this was really the end of our marriage, after all this, I felt entitled to at least a conversation. Finally, a few days before my fifth wedding anniversary, I sat in El Cap meadow before the person I'd considered the other half of myself for so many years, trembling and sobbing in sorrow and defeat as he repeated forcefully, with no room for doubt, that he didn't want to deal with anything, including me. Even I could see there wasn't any glue in the world that could fix it. It was done.

In a short time, I was without a marriage, without a paycheck, and pretty much without a career. In a life defined by risk and uncertainty, almost all of my anchors were gone. I'd never had a linear concept of time or even seen the point of one. But June 2007 became a temporal landmark. On June 22, two days before my wedding anniversary, I understood at last no more pieces were left to pick up. I drove out of the valley with tears smearing the insides of my sunglasses and Fletch lying quietly beside me, and with nothing else I used to think I had.

Chapter Two

First AFF skydive with Brendan and a second jump master

As Yosemite Valley receded behind my blue Ford Ranger, I leaked a steady flow of tears through all of California and most of Nevada. Fletcher leaned her head on the armrest, under the cloud of my sadness. I was desperately thankful to have her back. I didn't know where to go or what to do.

Usually there was no decision to be made—since the age of eighteen, I was either going climbing or getting other things done so I could go climbing. But for the last few months, climbing had become hard. I was lackluster, dull. I tried to force myself to get out, thinking the joy would come, but I had no energy and it was hard to join in with friends. I'd found myself walking to the cliffs alone, free soloing up the rock without a rope, climbing with death consequence. In those moments of climbing up with no safety systems, no equipment, no partner, nothing between me and the earth if I let go, I felt a kind of peace. On the ground, I returned to miserable—hopeless and anxious until the next time I mustered the energy to step alone into the vertical, with nothing but the soothing, simplistic sensation of rock in my hands and under my feet.

Moab home

My mind traveled through memories as Nevada receded in the rearview mirror. My home in the quirky desert town of Moab, Utah, was my haven, a paradise of red cliffs, green river water, and white mountain peaks. Finally craving a home base more solid than my truckbed, I'd slowly renovated a 1968 doublewide in a quiet neighborhood just off Main Street, transforming it into a place to relax and recharge between trips, with the simple luxuries of a bed, a shower, and a garden. I loved my home. But right now going there seemed unspeakably desolate.

I passed Green River, Utah, and watched the signs come up for Crescent Junction, the Moab exit. I kept driving, letting them slip into the rearview mirror. Suddenly nothing was clear. I had no idea where we were going.

Rifle, Colorado, just east of Moab, was also a refuge. I liked life there, camping in the aspen groves and climbing the steep, well-protected limestone routes in the cool, creekside canyon, enjoying the extreme physical effort and the relaxing safety of the sport climbing, as well as the community of inspiringly fit friends who were guaranteed to be there during the summer season. Rifle was the first place I'd ended up after dropping out of Boulder Law School, the climbing area where I had decided once and for all to become a climbing bum. But climbing strenuous, gymnastic routes seemed like too much effort now. Even just thinking about it drained me.

I watched the exit sign come up for West Rifle, the sign that usually sent a shiver of anticipation through me, knowing I was only a half hour away from Rifle Canyon. I kept my foot on the gas pedal, truly without a plan now.

The truck was pointed east toward the Colorado Rockies, where I had first learned how to live in the mountains and where I had climbed long granite faces so many times in my early years of climbing. I'd spent two blissful years in Fort Collins, teaching writing to college freshmen, writing a master's thesis on mountaineering literature, and climbing as much as possible. When the degree was finished, I waited tables and climbed in Estes Park, Colorado, for the summer, made a five-day attempt to be a law student in Boulder, and decisively moved into my car to become an itinerant climber. Later on, I made a base in the Utah desert, then got pulled even farther west to Yosemite by El Cap and marriage. But the front range of Colorado was my first adopted home, the first place I chose on my own.

I reached for my cell phone and dialed. In the whirlwind of the book tour and all of the drama and trauma of my failing marriage, as well as the normal flow of long-term friendships in the climbing and jumping communities, months had slipped by since I'd spoken to my friend Brendan. He had barely got out his happy hellos when I burst out, "Brendan, I want to learn to skydive. Can you teach me if I come to Boulder? Tomorrow?"

Like many jumpers, Brendan had made a nomadic career in skydiving. For decades he had been working as a tandem master, taking thousands of people out of planes at drop zones around the world, depending on where he felt like living, which was currently Boulder. He was a seasoned and early convert to base jumping, the more extreme version of jumping from fixed objects, which grew from skydiving in the late seventies. Originally dubbed B.A.S.E. jumping, for "building, antenna, span, earth," the objects that can provide enough altitude for flight without the aid of an aircraft, the acronym is now often depunctuated and lowercased to make it easier on the eyes. Brendan had made hundreds of base jumps from cliffs, antennae, bridges, and buildings. And, having worked in every aspect of the industry for decades, he was also a certified skydiving instructor.

Now I was calling him out of the blue, telling him I wanted to go through Accelerated Free Fall training, to become a skydiver.

Brendan at the G Spot exit, Moab, Utah

After an impressively shocked silence for a couple of seconds, Brendan immediately recovered his bearings and asked only one thing: What time could I be there? I gave him a brief overview of where I was, in every sense, and he insisted that I not worry about anything. He would be delighted to train me to skydive, we could start tomorrow, and we would meet in the morning at his local coffee shop, Vic's.

I'd met Brendan a few years before while a group of base jumpers from Utah, Colorado, and California were mentoring a handful of climbers who had become interested in base jumping. Brendan was a good friend of my husband's, and the two of us hit it off immediately. He was a wiry, athletic, kidlike jumper in his early fifties who tended to dash rather than walk, when going anywhere. We were of similar size and build and recognized in each other an intensity of focus mixed with tenderheartedness. Brendan was also an avid trail runner, which is a little unusual in jumpers, who are typically more hungry for adrenaline than for exercise, and we had done one memorable and fast-paced twelve-mile run together in the Moab desert.

Around that time, I had gone on a tandem jump in Moab, my first experience of skydiving. I didn't know a thing about what was going on. I was simply strapped to the front of a friend who owned the local skydiving operation, with several of my jumper friends crammed along for the occasion in the tiny plane. I didn't know what to expect, but quickly found everything about it deeply unpleasant, starting from the moment the door of the little Cessna opened ten thousand feet above the desert earth. The sound and the blast of cold wind vividly threw me into the sensations of fighting through Patagonian storms, shouting words that got ripped away by wind, sleet, and snow while rappelling on soaked, tangling ropes that blew sideways and wrapped heart-stoppingly around snag points on sheer granite faces.

My friends appeared to be sucked out the door, one by one, with huge grins on their faces, giving me a thumbs-up as they dropped out. I found it terrifying to watch them fall out and down. When they were all gone, I was facing the open door of the plane, the cold air screaming past. I grabbed the doorframe, instinctively trying to save myself from falling out, like a cat with its feet braced and sliding on the sides of a bathtub. The large tandem master on my back felt heavy, pushing me out the door of the plane. My hands broke free from the metal frame with the hopeless feeling of fingers peeling off rock, and then I was free-falling, speeding face to the earth with the added weight of a heavy person on my back. As a free solo climber who often ascends vertical rock faces without a rope, the feeling of free fall was the stuff of my worst nightmares—physically, a sensation I equated with death.

When the canopy finally opened, everything slowed to a sedate, floating pace in the suddenly quiet air. I felt first relieved and then quickly bored, since I saw this sort of bird's-eye view all the time from the tops of cliffs and mountains without being strapped to the front of someone like a sack of potatoes. As we came in to land, the ground rushed up fast. All I could think about was breaking an ankle and being unable to climb or run or do yoga or house projects for months. The slight wind died just as the parachute came to the ground, and we landed on hard-packed dirt with a strong thump, giving me a good whack on the butt as we dropped hard. Shaken and overwhelmingly glad it was over with nothing broken, I swore to everyone present that I would never jump again.

I very much respected my new friends, whose base-jumping and sky-diving obsessions both baffled and impressed me. As the years went by, it became something of a joke for us that jumping was far too scary and I would never do it, because they found climbing to be hard and scary.

Despite all this, Brendan, a highly experienced tandem master with an unusually considerate and reassuring personality, took it almost as a personal mission to get me to try another jump, and to like it. Being the only person on the planet who had completely hated a tandem sky-dive experience, I was apparently an irresistible challenge. Brendan was convinced that the feeling of trust I would have with him would make everything different, since skydiving is almost all about mental state. After pondering my extreme aversion to the experience, I had developed a theory. When it comes to life and death, I'm used to relying on myself. Aside from the fully reasonable climber's fear of falling, I suspected that my main fear had come not so much from lack of trust of the particular tandem master I was jumping with, but from knowing I was not in control of the situation. Falling out of a plane was a potentially life-threatening situation where I was an incompetent passenger with no chance of saving myself if I had to. Those were the elements of my ultimate nightmare, and in retrospect I realized I could never have liked it.

I never wanted to skydive again, but if I somehow did, I decided I would not do another tandem jump. Instead, I would enroll in an Accelerated Free Fall course where I would train to become a skydiver on my own. As an AFF student, I would skydive by myself, wearing my own parachute, deploying it, flying it, and landing it on my own. I would learn how things worked and what to do. Not that I would ever want to.

But now, with one phone call to Brendan, everything had just changed. More important, this dramatic, completely unanticipated change had come from me, from my own decision. That hadn't happened in a long time. In a few hours I would be in Boulder, and I would be falling through the air. For the first time in a long while, I was looking forward to tomorrow.

Now, from a safer place, I can see the edge I was standing on then. It's not so surprising that on the day of my fifth wedding anniversary I would be crouched in the open door of an airplane, thirteen thousand feet above the Colorado plains, about to jump out. That coincidence of timing really wasn't. I was fortunate to have a true friend in Brendan, who would do everything in his power to keep me safe and make the experience purely symbolic. Like every longtime jumper, he'd seen too many tragedies where emotion-fueled impulses became final on impact.

I met Brendan at Vic's Coffee in the morning, where he tactfully asked only a few questions about my last few months and what my plans were for the summer, and we drove to the drop zone with Fletcher squeezed between us in the front of my truck, looking slightly affronted that Brendan was sitting in her spot. He was scheduled with a tandem customer first thing in the morning, but I was kept busy in the office filling out stacks of papers and release forms and making the first of the hefty AFF course payments.

The Mile-Hi Skydiving Center is quartered in three lofty airplane hangars, side by side, just outside Boulder. The drop zone boasts a fleet of jump planes ranging in size from a Cessna to a King Air to a twin-engine Otter, all painted white with the purple and yellow Mile-Hi stripes and furnished with long benches instead of seats and roll-up Plexiglas doors mounted into the wall of the body. The oval runway, surrounded by open farm fields, leads toward the Longs Peak Diamond, a sheer granite rock face on the most famous fourteener of the Rocky Mountain range. Every summer day, the jump planes carry skydivers on a twenty-minute ride to thirteen thousand feet above the ground and come back down empty, while parachutes fly from the sky toward the windsocks planted in football-field-size landing areas. I had been to two other skydiving operations, in California and Utah. When I walked in the door of my third, I could see that all drop zones are in some ways alike, a familiar haven for skydivers, no matter where in the world they might be.

Straight across from the front door, the entire side of the hangar was open to the tarmac, where a few small planes were parked in front of a facing hangar. The high-arching walls inside were decorated with skydiving posters, pennants, and video screens. Flat, office-grade carpets covered the cement floor, where bright parachutes were laid out in rows, the lines stretching out behind them to open backpack-like containers. Some people stood with canopies over their shoulders, arms buried in the nylon, expertly folding and smoothing the panels. Others were lying flat on top of parachutes, tucking their arms down the sides of the fabric, pressing the air out to get them small enough to fit back into the containers.

Skydivers packing at Mile-Hi drop zone

Student jumpers, suited up in purple-and-yellow Mile-Hi jump-suits with huge round altimeters on their wrists, watched the skydiving instructors explain how they should fall through the air and steer the parachute. Tandem customers, there for a onetime taste of free fall, sat in chairs with nylon body harnesses buckled over their shorts and T-shirts, while the tandem masters walked over with huge, double-size parachute rigs on their backs, like turtles.

The experienced "fun jumpers" were easy to pick out in formfitting jumpsuits in bold colors that would make most rock climbers cringe, and slick, wraparound sunglasses. They wore compact, sleek skydiving rigs and had an air of relaxation wound with excitement. Most had small digi-tal instruments on their helmets or wrists and expensive-looking video cameras attached to their carbon fiber helmets. Overall, the fun jumpers and professional skydivers were a pretty flamboyant bunch, with their big, tinted skydiving goggles or sunglasses, multiple piercings, tattoos, dyed hair, shiny helmets, and snug, embroidered jumpsuits. These "up jumpers" moved in and out of the hangar constantly, watching videos of their last jumps, packing their tiny parachutes, seemingly conditioned to finish just in time to catch the next planeload. Inside, the hangar buzzed with energy, wildness, and adrenaline. Watching, I understood immedi-ately that this world was a distant cousin of the climbing world. An ex-pensive, octane-fueled cousin, but certainly a relation. Just like a climber, a jumper could go anywhere, find a drop zone, slip into the community, and be at home. These skydivers looked a little more wild-eyed and, at least fashion-wise, far less inhibited than climbers, but they all clearly had the wild spirit that I valued.

With so much to look at, I was surprised when Brendan dashed over to me, having already landed with his tandem customer. He grabbed the AFF checklists and the *Skydiver's Information Manual* (*SIM*), which he'd insisted on buying for me, and led me off to a small room in the hangar. As soon as the door closed, I was transported from the bustling energy of a vibrant drop zone to the flat, white silence of a tiny classroom. We sat at a desk, going through page after page of the *SIM*, the 229-page bible of skydiving. After decades in the sport, Brendan knew such abstruse facts as "pilot of an unpressurized aircraft is required to breathe supplemental oxygen above 14,000 feet MSL" as automatically as he knew his own name. For a nonjumper (or whuffo, the skydiver's shorthand for nonjumpers, thanks to the stereotypical, rather unanswerable "What do you do that for?"), it is a truly overwhelming pile of information. This thick book represents a large chunk of the knowledge in an experienced skydiver's brain, and at the moment the only thing in it I knew was that you need a parachute. And an airplane.

Being understandably concerned about my current state of mind, and having a vast, multidecade knowledge of every possible nuance or potentiality in the sport of skydiving, Brendan was unable to gloss over anything during our one-on-one AFF ground school. I also tend to ask for further explanation of any detail that confuses or interests me, especially when it seems extra-important, like when learning how to fall out of an airplane. Most people find this annoying, but Brendan ever patiently digressed into lengthy detours from the basic points to answer all of my questions, most of which led to more digressions. So instead of the standard four hours of ground school leading immediately into the airplane for the first jump, our session ended up lasting the whole day at the drop zone, continuing on the drive back to Boulder, through the evening with Thai food at Brendan's house, over coffee at Vic's the next morning, and then most of the next day at the drop zone. At this point in my two-day, full-immersion AFF ground school, my brain was starting to overload. Finally I said, "Brendan, I'm losing my mind, we just need to jump." Brendan was starting to look almost as nervous as me, obviously starting to picture all of the same worst-case scenarios I was, as well as a few more.

Brendan got me equipped with a huge student parachute, altimeter, jumpsuit, and helmet, then began going through the more pragmatic questions of how to jump out of the plane, get my parachute out, and steer it to the earth. Basically, to pass my first AFF level, I needed to get in the open door of the moving Otter with Brendan and a second AFF instructor, then jump out while arching my back as much as possible, the most stable position for the human body in free fall. I needed to check the huge altimeter dial on my wrist to keep track of how close I was getting to the ground and to check the horizon to make sure I wasn't upside down or something. I would also need to reach back to the right, back corner of my skydiving rig and touch the small ball on top of the pilot chute that was folded in there and make sure I felt it—practice touches for when it was actually time to toss out the pilot chute and let it fly out into the air and yank out my parachute.

At fifty-five hundred feet above the earth, I would wave my arms to signal Brendan and my other instructor to let go of me and move away. Then I would reach back for real this time to pull the pilot chute out of its sleeve and throw it out into the air. All of that would take about fifty seconds. I would then be on my own, hoping the canopy opened correctly and without any problems. If there was a malfunction, heaven forbid, I would need to figure out what it was and how to fix it—or decide to pull the cutaway handle to chop it away and pull the other handle that would deploy my reserve parachute.

With some radio direction from Brendan, who would already be on the ground watching, I would then steer my parachute toward the giant landing field and pull the brake lines down hard at the right moment to flare the canopy and stop its forward speed exactly as my feet touched the ground. All of which is harder than it seems it should be when you're filled with adrenaline and need to accomplish it in under one minute because you are falling through the air at 120 miles per hour. I was nervous about failing the jump, for the obvious reasons, but also because each of these AFF jumps costs a lot of money, despite Brendan's refusing to accept his instructor's portion of the cost. Failing an AFF level would mean having to repeat that jump, which meant paying an extra $220 to try it again instead of moving on to the next jump. So far it was all extremely stressful.

Outside by the runway, Brendan and I waited, along with twenty other skydivers, a mix of tandems and experienced fun jumpers, for the twin engine Otter to land. The plane came in and taxied off to the side, and we all hurried over, walking behind the tail to give the large, spinning propellers a wide berth (naturally, someone has been hit by a propeller at some point in the history of skydiving), sheltering our eyes from the powerful blast. The propeller seemed loud and close, blowing my hair wildly as I climbed up the four-step metal ladder into the open side of the plane, just behind the wing. The clear, Plexiglas door was rolled up inside the plane, and two wooden benches lined the plane's body. The jump pilot sat up front looking at a clipboard, waiting for everyone to pile in. I was the only student on the plane, sitting in the front near the pilot with Brendan and my other instructor, feeling glad to be far from the open door. It was physically reassuring to be wedged in among the other jumpers, shoulders and thighs pressed between the two people next to me.

The video guys had flat-topped helmets clamped tightly under their chins to bear the weight of both a large video camera and a full-size digital still camera with a lens mounted on top. They looked like something from *A Clockwork Orange* with their small, round camera sights, rigged on a tiny, jointed metal arm directly in front of one eye. Everyone was rowdy and exhilarated, making jokes, reaching over shoulders to pan camera lenses into each other's face.

Jumpers riding to altitude in the Otter

The tandem customers, each sitting beside a tandem master, were a little more conventional-looking, equipped only with wide-strapped body harnesses instead of parachutes. They seemed nervous yet exhilarated in the midst of this colorful group, and many of them had come with a friend or two, so they smiled and laughed at one another, anticipating the rush.

The plane taxied slowly at first, then accelerated madly until it tilted up from the ground, climbing into the air directly toward the Rocky Mountains. Some of the skydivers grew calm, closing their eyes to visualize the routines they were planning to do in formation during their fifty seconds of free fall. Others got more wild and rambunctious as the plane climbed, whooping, laughing, and performing elaborate fist-bumping, hand-slapping routines with their buddies. Many of them did this all day, every day, for work as tandem masters or cameramen, and they were genuinely lit up.

I grew up flying in small airplanes with my dad, an aeronautical engineer who worked for Cessna, and I always experience an exhilaration in my chest at the moment a plane lifts off, even on a commercial flight. It's one of my favorite moments. Despite my anxiety, as always my heart rose as the wheels left the ground. I was going up.

I watched the altimeter on my wrist, as the dial pointed from one thousand to two thousand to three thousand feet. I've spent a lot of time at thirteen thousand feet and above, but always with solid stone under my hands and feet. From the windows, the earth got smaller and smaller as the dial climbed, and I started to feel doubt. As a free solo climber, when trying extremely difficult or dangerous movements on rock for the first time, I try it first with the safety of a rope. This way I can work out the difficult moves and make calculated decisions about my ability to do them in a more dangerous scenario. I was nervously realizing that there is no rope in skydiving. The only way I could do my first skydive was to actually do it and hope I didn't mess up. I was not convinced I could do this new thing perfectly, first go.

The pilot leaned back and said something about wind and numbers to Brendan, and he shouted it out through the plane. Everything seemed to happen quickly. Someone threw the door up, and cold air rushed in the gaping side of the plane. The engine cut slightly, changing the frequency of the sound. People shuffled over and disappeared out the open door in rapid succession, as though they were being sucked out into the air.

Brendan leaned toward me and shouted, "Students aren't allowed to jump when the winds are gusting above twenty-five miles per hour on the ground. We'll have to ride down." It had taken Brendan and me so long to organize that we'd gone up just in time for the daily late-afternoon weather buildup. I slid sideways on the bench as the plane banked sharply, engines roaring back to full speed, and seemed to dive straight toward the runway. I looked out the window by my head, watching the landing strip grow before us until the wheels bumped down. I felt an intense mix of extreme relief and anticlimax as the propellers wound down into sudden silence. We hopped out the door of the empty plane, a four-foot drop onto solid ground, as the other jumpers' canopies came in to land in the field beside the runway. It felt a little weird to be watching them float out of the sky, standing with my unused parachute still packed away inside the heavy rig on my back.

Back in the hangar, Brendan told me not to worry because the storm cells would quickly pass, and we would be able to go back up once the winds had calmed again. I went out to my truck to check on Fletch. She was denned up underneath it, hiding from the dark clouds. I sat on the tailgate and called my brother, Virgil, in Arcata, California. An ER doctor and avid surfer, he'd started skydiving the year before. Virgil had been a strong and motivated rock climber for ten years, but had been slowed down by chronic-overuse shoulder injuries, which weren't aggravated by skydiving or surfing. In typical style, he had quickly become a jumping fanatic and was already fairly advanced, traveling to various drop zones to jump during vacations and long weekends.

Virgil cheered me up with his usual gentle logic, helping me get some perspective larger than the pencil point of reality my focus had narrowed into. It occurred to me that I had actually done the plane-ride portion of my first AFF jump, so now I would have less newness to absorb all at once on the second trip. I suddenly felt much more at ease. The sky was turning from gray to blue, and the winds were dropping down. I walked back inside to get my rig back on.

The buildup of anticipation started all over again, as it does all day at a drop zone, and we climbed into the plane. But I felt prepared and ready this time. Everything was the same—the rowdy, animated group of jumpers, the plane slowing audibly at thirteen thousand feet, the door sliding open to let the air rush in. One by one, people disappeared out the door. It was my turn. I looked at Brendan and the second instructor and hopped out the door into the cold air, feeling its force pushing on my limbs as though holding me up. I went through the drill we'd rehearsed for this skydive, making eye contact with both, arching my back as hard as I could. The air caught my lips as I smiled, blowing the skin of my cheeks into rippling waves, and holding my body with an almost comforting push from below. I checked the altimeter on my wrist, touched the pilot chute on the skydiving container behind my back, and looked at the altimeter again, surprised by how much time seemed to be left.

Suddenly it read four thousand feet. I tossed the pilot chute and let it

Flying over Longmont, Colorado

catch the wind, to pull the main canopy into the air. The parachute blossomed out above me. I was on my own in the quiet air, floating under my own parachute, looking at the open fields below. The winds had come up again, and it dawned on me that my giant student parachute wasn't moving forward enough to fly to the main landing area.

I knew a story of a recent AFF student, also a climber, who had been badly injured by trying to make it back through winds and ending up in a ditch bordering the drop zone. I was above a field just on the other side of that very ditch, being pushed back from the landing area by a strong east wind. The flat, open landing zone was inviting and enormous, the size of a couple of football fields. But I didn't want to come up short and end up in that ditch. Though the helmet was covering my ears, I could hear the wind moving around, keeping me from going forward. My heart started to beat harder. I scanned the ground, trying to figure out how high I was by how small the trees looked.

I needed to let go of trying to make it back and focus on landing safely on the other side of the ditch in the green field, away from the fence line. The ground rushed up before me as I got closer, but I could see the field was flat and free of obstacles. The tall grass looked soft. Brendan's voice came over the radio clipped to my chest strap, telling me to flare. I yanked down hard on both steering toggles, bringing my arms straight down to my thighs to pull down the back of the parachute in a flare, and met the ground lightly as the canopy draped down around me. I stood in the bright green grass about a quarter mile from the main landing area, down and safe, with a huge, real smile on my face. Whatever else had happened or was happening in my life had been shut down for this space of time. I was awash in feelings of freedom and lightness, sensations I hadn't been sure I'd ever feel again. If this was what heroin felt like, I understood immediately how people dropped their lives into it. Free soloing took the edge off things, dulled them. Skydiving made me feel good—better than good. I knew one thing without a doubt. I would not stop doing this.

Chapter Three

Brave New World

Tracking over Longmont, Colorado *Jay Epstein*

I opened my eyes and tipped my head back against the sofa arm in my friend Brad's apartment. The shadows shifted across the high ceiling as light crept through the tall window sheers. Fletch was still asleep on her fleece blanket next to me, paws twitching. I felt quiet, emotionless. It was the mind-set I cultivated for long routes in the mountains, a kind of climbing I'd specialized in for many years. Being a naturally ebullient person, I'd learned over time to enter a state of detached efficiency when climbing for hours or days in dangerous, unforgiving environments, thousands of feet off the ground. It was the way I'd found to endure storms, fatigue, fear, and hunger while climbing at the edge of my limits, without being controlled or weakened by emotions. Out of the danger zone, safely back in civilization or base camp, my natural self revived. It was strange to be nowhere near a mountain, locked into the alpinist's mind, machinelike.

I was too ashamed to talk about it, but I'd spent a lot of time sifting through ways to end things in those desolate weeks in California. A climber in Yosemite, surrounded by sheer drop-offs and walls, shouldn't have to look too far for a way out. Plenty of big cliffs in Yosemite were staring me in the face. Though I hated myself for even fantasizing about hurtling off one, every minute felt relentlessly bleak and painful and I couldn't see any relief. But the worst part was that I simply couldn't do it. Sixteen years of climbing, avoiding falls at all cost, had rendered me incapable of stepping off a cliff edge into free fall. I was more viscerally afraid of falling to my death than I had been before I became a climber. I hated myself for that too. Every other option I came up with seemed too violent or horrible, or too difficult in the actual details, which was also kind of pathetic. I hated myself for being so weak, in every way, and I was above all disgusted with myself for giving in to what I saw as self-indulgent depression. My so-called problems were nothing compared with the real suffering that I knew millions of people and creatures were actively enduring, so I found it ridiculous and even offensive to be wading in a swamp of self-pity and anxiety. That intellectual self-chastisement didn't snap me out of my mind state—it just made me despise myself more for my lack of mental strength, for my petty, egocentric inability to get it together. I'd always been hard on myself, a trait that made me relentlessly improve at things. Now it relentlessly tore away at my remnants of self-esteem.

The things I'd been most afraid of losing—my life partner, my support system, my career, everything I believed to be my past, present, and future—I'd lost. I hated feeling miserable, hopeless, and isolated day after day, merely living because I lacked the courage not to. It seemed like I'd never be able to get anything back in control, including my mindset. The prospect of feeling this way for the rest of my life was almost unbearable. But I had Fletch back now, and she needed me. In the last few weeks, the black thoughts had turned to gray, and dullness was much easier to endure. Numbness worked, a way I knew to keep on through cold and fear, whether on a mountain or inside my mind.

Skydiving was a life preserver I could grab on to. The intense mix of feelings, from standing in the open door of the Otter to screaming through the cold, open sky, had poured directly into the void that seemed to be consuming me. In those moments the void felt as if it were inside me, rather than the other way around, and if nothing else, I felt compelled to plunge back into three-dimensional space just to see it again, to feel around for the boundaries of my reality.

I watched Fletch sleeping next to me, the rise and fall of her breathing, her thick white and black and brown fur, and thought about my house in Moab, my sofa and kitchen, my bed, my garden on the automatic drip system I'd made for it through trial and error. I wondered what my (ex?) husband was doing in California, and my mind started to wander through painful, swampy questions of what he technically was now or how normal people actually got divorces. I stood up and pulled on my shorts, set my sleeping bag in a corner, and straightened up the sofa cushions. Fletch led me to the high counter separating the kitchen from the living room and stood next to her nylon dog-food sack by the front door. Her crunches seemed especially loud in the quiet room as I waited for her to finish breakfast and lap up some water. We slipped out and walked down the wooden steps into the cool morning air of a Boulder July.

I drove the few blocks to Vic's Coffee and crossed the street to Ideal Market, the quintessential local organic grocery store, to grab a spring roll, a peach, and bottled water for lunch. Fletch put her nose out the window, smelling the wind as we cruised down the flat twenty-mile stretch from Boulder to Longmont. A mile from the airport, canopies floated high over the fields, Longs Peak hanging in the distance like a movie backdrop. I felt my heart jump a little, with a sudden urge to be there right now. Things were happening without me. I stepped on the gas and drove fast to the airport turnoff, crunching over gravel past the hangar to the grassy field nearby. I grabbed a clean T-shirt from my duffel bag—the same clothes I'd thrown together before driving out to California a month ago—and changed behind my open truck door. I tugged out the heavy bag of skydiving gear and set up Fletch under the truck with her water dish and a long piece of rope clipped to her harness, purely for appearances, since we both knew she could easily slip out of her harness anytime she chose. "I'll be back in a little bit, girl. You hang out." She ducked under the tailgate, gave me the slightly put-upon glance, scratched a little at the grass, and curled up with her head on her paws.

I walked into the hangar, dropped my bag by the wall near Brendan's stuff, and walked into the office holding my Visa. I slid it over the counter. "Hi, Emily," I said to the girl standing at the manifest counter. "I'll put two hundred dollars on my account."

It's impossible to emphasize enough how financially shocking skydiving is to a climber. A Mile-Hi jump ticket went for $22. In grad school, that was more than half my weekly food budget. When I was waiting tables and living out of my truck at climbing areas, a weekly rest day in town ran about $2.50 for laundry, $6 for breakfast at a diner, $10 to restock groceries, and $3 for thrift-store purchases. At the Mile-Hi drop zone, $22 bought thirteen thousand feet of altitude, which took two minutes to burn through. I'd easily jump through my $200 credit in two days. It was such an incomprehensible amount of money by dirtbag climber standards that buying jump tickets somehow felt like spending Monopoly money—too outrageous to be real. Climbers pay close attention to the price of ramen noodles and chunk light canned tuna. Here I was surrounded by skydivers wearing equipment worth more than my vehicle who didn't seem to think about it at all as they spent hundreds of dollars a weekend.

I couldn't stand wasting money almost out of principle, a trait that was only magnified by living on a teaching assistant's stipend in grad school, and then a hand-to-mouth climber/waitress existence in my car. Although I'd never earned a lot of money, I'd been a disciplined saver all my life, careful to keep a reserve cushion and to stay out of debt. To me, having enough money in the moment meant freedom, and having some money saved for the future meant stability. Working to maintain that balance was important to me. I had a few credit cards, habitually paid in full every month, and some money saved. I'd babysat steadily since the age of twelve, until I was old enough for real jobs. I'd never been without some type of work from then on, whether as a video-store clerk, a teaching assistant, or a climbing guide, and then finally as a sponsored athlete, work I took as seriously as any other. I seemed to be spending more money than I could ever have imagined, and to make it worse, I didn't have a job. But whatever. Funny enough, I didn't care. The future no longer seemed like a priority, and the present seemed to happen of its own accord. Whether I ran through my reserve cushion or racked up credit card bills didn't mean anything to me right now, for the first time in my life. I didn't think much about my sudden shift from conserving money to spending it with no concern and no income, beyond a some-what intellectual interest in the astounding price of everything. At the drop zone, and even just eating in the city of Boulder, I felt as if I were on another planet where everyone was rich and it didn't matter what any-thing cost. But this planet was fine.

Emily passed back my Visa card and the curling receipts with an in-candescent smile that was impossible not to return. A practicing attorney, Emily spent all her spare time at the drop zone, doing everything from working at the manifest, where jumpers bought tickets and turned them in for jumps, to coaching new jumpers, and like most of the women at the drop zone, she always looked gorgeous. She wore low-cut T-shirts and expertly applied makeup. My idea of a beauty routine was being clean when possible. Around other climbers, I felt self-conscious for taking a second to smooth down my hair in the rearview mirror after wearing a hat pulled over my face all night. Here I was starting to feel that habitual disregard for my appearance was perhaps not the way to blend in. I scribbled my name on one credit slip, crumpled the other one into a ball, and dropped it in the trash. "Thanks, Emily! Can I get on the next load?"

Emily checked the computer screen by the open manifest window, with twenty-one jumpers listed for the next planeload. "There's one spot. Is it just you? What's your number, Steph? Oh, wait, I have it, never mind. Otter Nine, fifteen minutes. Have fun!"

In three weeks, I'd gone from knowing nothing about skydiving to being a regular at the drop zone, walking in every day with my own gear, and being able to pack it and jump by myself. I'd decided to commit to buying equipment even before I finished my seven AFF training jumps; I could start "saving" money on rentals as soon as possible by buying my own gear. I'd found a suitable used container and parachute for sale in the skydiving classifieds the first day I looked, and I just went ahead and bought it.

It was the right size for me, in good condition, and pretty. The Mirage container was a striking combination of red and purple, my two favorite colors, and the Spectre parachute was black, teal, and purple. The canopy was smaller than a student parachute but still oversize for my body weight at 170 square feet, which was appropriate for a new jumper without any canopy skills yet. It was good gear, and Brendan assured me I wouldn't need to upgrade it for years. Twenty-five hundred dollars was a pretty big chunk of change to part with, about what I'd consider a reasonable price for a car. But just like my vehicle, I intended to take care of this rig and drive it until the wheels fell off, hopefully for the rest of my life. And now I wouldn't be spending $30 on rental gear for every single jump. Now all my money was going directly into those $22 jump tickets. Compared to the $1,400 I'd spent in two days on my seven AFF training jumps, followed by several $52 jumps with rental gear, it seemed pretty reasonable. At least on this planet.

I bent over my skydiving rig and turned on the AAD, the automatic activation device, the tiny computer that tracks altitude and fall speed so it can deploy the reserve parachute for you in case you get too close to the ground without opening your main parachute. The digital numbers raced backward over the flat display until it finished at 0 with a piercing *beep beep beep*. I strapped the big metal altimeter to my left wrist, like a giant wristwatch, and hoisted the rig onto my back, stepping into the dangling leg-loops and cinching them tight on my thighs through massive buckles. Skydiving gear seemed heavy and ridiculously overbuilt from a weight-fanatical climber's perspective. But then skydivers don't carry anything up. That's what planes are for. I buckled the wide chest strap, picked up my helmet and goggles, and walked out to the pickup truck in front of the hangar, ready to drive around the runway to the plane.

Riding the trailer around the runway to the jump plane

The pickup was hitched to an open flatbed trailer lined with weathered packing carpet, the sides corralled in by wooden planks. I climbed up and sat on the edge, squinting in the sun. I could see Brendan and the other tandem masters inside the other hangar, tightening the buckles of tandem harnesses on their passengers. The other up jumpers started to stroll out to the trailer, many of them buckling their chest straps as they walked. I looked around for Emily and her husband, Kiwi, hoping they would be on this load. I liked seeing Emily's bright face and quick smile as she joked and talked with everyone around her. Seeing Emily's vibrant energy somehow made me feel a little lighter.

Brendan walked out of the hangar, turtlelike with the giant, double-size tandem rig on his back, and hopped onto the trailer, holding out his hand to his tandem customer to help her up the high step. He sat across from me, smiling with his eyes crinkled almost shut as the trailer pulled off, now crowded around all three sides with jumpers and tandem passengers. I craned my neck to check on Fletch, still curled comfortably under my truck, as we drove around the hangars toward the runway.

"What jump is this, Steph?"

"This is number forty-one."

"What has it been, three weeks since your first AFF jump?" Brendan said. "What are you going to do on this one?"

"Hmm. Let me see. Wait, I think I'll track!" I said, smiling slightly. "You know that's all I do, Brendan."

"I know. Well, tracking is the first step to flying a wingsuit. And base jumping."

"Yeah. I guess. I just like it."

As with climbing, or any other sport, skydiving has many specialized subsets. In just the last few decades skydiving has developed by leaps and bounds from the early days of round, silk parachutes. Jumpers quickly grow accustomed to the unnatural feeling of jumping out of a moving airplane and focus their attention on refining their body control during free fall. Once the basic skills of reading an altimeter, deploying the parachute, and steering it to a safe landing have been mastered, skydivers have a full gamut of technical skills to cultivate and practice.

The most traditional type of flying is called belly flying, or relative work (RW). Skydivers fall with their belly down in a deep arch, the most stable free-fall position, and try to dock; that is, grab one another's hands or ankles to make group formations—all in the forty-five seconds they have while speeding toward the earth. Teams of four to eight jumpers, like the army's Golden Knights, spend months rehearsing together for competitions, perfecting a precision routine as they switch positions with one another during free fall. Other jumpers try to set big-way records, forming rings or multilayered stars in the air with hundreds of bodies, before breaking away in time to pull parachutes safely and float to the ground.

The belly fliers do lots of "dirt diving"—rehearsing their planned routines and docks on the ground and scooting around on small, wheeled dollies, so they can perform the sequence correctly while free-falling at 120 miles per hour.

The latest generation has evolved to free flying. Bored with the belly-to-earth position and the RW routines, free fliers zoom around one another like spirits while sitting or standing in the sky, or turned straight head-down to the earth, making their fall rate even faster. Free flying is extremely acrobatic and takes a lot of practice to refine. Many jumpers train in a commercial wind tunnel, a round, glass-sided room above a high-powered fan, which simulates the wind blast at terminal speed. This way, they can practice skydiving without even jumping out of a plane, dedicating all their attention to holding and flying a sit or head-down position without having to stop and deploy a parachute or worry about racing gravity, since they will never reach the ground inside the wind tunnel.

At the other end of the spectrum are wingsuit fliers. Wingsuiters wear a special nylon suit, sometimes called a squirrel suit, with arm and leg wings. The suit slows the jumper's downward speed dramatically, converting it into forward speed, and actually allows the jumper to fly like a small airplane. In a wingsuit, a jumper can choose where to fly, change the forward speed and fall rate, and fly through the air in flock formation with other wingsuiters. The suit adds another dimension to flight, but it also restricts normal movement. Wingsuit fliers must learn stability in the air so they don't go spinning out of the sky, and they also need to learn how to deploy the parachute with their arms semibound up in the wings and be able to get out of the zipped arm wings quickly if any problem occurs with the parachute on opening.

Tracking—soaring straight through the air like Superman—is also like flying, but without a wingsuit. Jumpers sometimes do tracking dives together, flying around in the sky like a flock of birds. But in a wingsuit a jumper can stay in flight for over twice the time.

The free fliers fall the fastest, the belly fliers the second fastest. Trackers and wingsuiters have the slowest fall rate. So the jumpers exit the plane in order of how they will be jumping, to lower the odds of anyone's falling through anyone else's open parachute—free fliers first, belly fliers next, then tandems, then trackers, then wingsuits.

After I'd demonstrated my basic body control with the required belly-flying maneuvers to graduate from AFF, I'd started to track on every single jump. Unlike most skydivers, who want to try many different skills and practice new maneuvers with others, I wasn't interested in doing anything else or expanding my skills as a skydiver. I just wanted to fly, for that one weightless minute of time streaking through the sky. It felt like nothing I'd ever experienced.

We hopped off the trailer and walked over to the Otter, which was waiting with the engine running hot. I shielded my eyes from the propeller blast and turned away from the hot fumes of jet fuel as I climbed up the four-step ladder into the open door near the tail. In the plane, I bent my head and shuffled all the way into the front, pressing into the corner of the bench behind the pilot. Brendan slid in across from me with his tandem customer. The other tandems piled in, pushing against my shoulders, then the belly fliers, then the free fliers.

I closed my eyes as the Otter climbed, imagining my body speeding straight as an arrow through the sky, the cold air slicing clean around me. Jumpers started to jostle around, putting on helmets and goggles, powering on video cameras, giving one another fist bumps with gloved hands. I opened my eyes and checked my altimeter. Ten thousand feet above the ground. I tucked my hair up under the back of my helmet and pulled the small bungee cord on the side of my plastic goggles tight. They started to steam up immediately. I tipped the bottom edge open a little, letting some air in. Brendan reached over and gave me a little palm slide and fist bump and shuffled toward the door with his tandem passenger. I watched the free fliers bunch up in front of the door. They locked eyes, rocked their heads back and forth at one another in a one-two-three exit count, and dropped out into the sky in a sit position. The tandem passengers got all wide-eyed as they tumbled out into the air, strapped to the front of the tandem masters, one after another, the cameramen smiling straight into their faces from behind the crazy-looking camera helmets as they followed them out.

I was alone at the door now. The cold air roared as I stood in the open plane with both hands clutching the silver bar on the top of the door, ducking my head to keep from hitting it. I looked at the oval runway thirteen thousand feet below. I knew the pilot was waiting for me to exit so he could turn sharply and dive toward the drop zone. I looked up at the wing outside, arched my back, stretched my arms behind me, and stepped off the solid metal floor and into the sky.

The air seemed to hold my body the minute I left the door. I fanned my arms back by my sides like a snow angel and stretched my legs out

Tracking with Jay at Mile-Hi *Jay Epstein*

straight with my toes pointed hard, flying through the sky like Superman. It felt fast, like being a race car. The cold air rushed over my cheeks and mouth, tearing spit out when my lips parted, making my eyes tear up behind the tight plastic goggles. It rushed loudly past my ears under the thin helmet. Longs Peak sat straight ahead of me, high in the horizon. I almost felt like I could fly straight to it. I turned my head slightly to the left and tipped my wrist up to check my altimeter. Nine thousand feet. I turned left and flew south, watching the green fields below me, the tiny houses and roads like models in an architectural mock-up. Six thousand feet. I turned left again, flying east, starting to see canopies in the air below me. Three thousand feet. I reached back and felt the firm leather of the hacky-sack handle stitched to the top of my pilot chute and yanked it from the spandex sleeve at the bottom of my container into the air behind me. The pilot chute inflated and jerked my parachute out of the container, swinging my body from flat to vertical as the canopy bloomed out above my head into a massive rectangle of air-filled nylon, the thin parachute lines stretching straight from my shoulders to the canopy like an enormous cat's cradle. Everything went quiet.

Bright canopies zigzagged below me. I watched the first one touch down, landing to the west, and set up for my box pattern at the west end of the landing field. I checked my altimeter: one thousand feet. I flew straight, made a right-hand turn at five hundred feet, and made another right turn at three hundred feet for my final leg, heading into the wind in the same direction as everyone else. I flared the canopy, pulling my arms down as my feet touched. My parachute floated down, crumpling blousily to the grass. Suddenly everything was still, quiet, and finished, with just the sound of my fast breathing. I felt a dizzying mix of exhilaration and pride at having fallen out of an airplane thirteen thousand feet above the earth and then impossibly survived. I'd streaked across the sky like a falcon, floated down to earth like a dandelion seed. My whole body tingled.

I coiled up the lines, tossed the parachute over my shoulder, and walked across the big, flat field to where Brendan had landed with his tandem passenger. She was covered in smiles, like everyone else. The jumpers gathered around the flatbed, tossed their unpacked parachutes into a fluffy mound in the center of the flatbed, and vaulted onto the side planks. The truck accelerated and bounced on the dirt road next to the runway. The Otter sped down the tarmac beside us, overtaking the trailer and lifting into the air with the next load of jumpers. I watched it get smaller in the sky, seeming to disappear into Longs Peak as we drove around the curve at the west end of the runway. I felt the wind on my face, my canopy pooled over my feet, my shoulders jostled by the people sitting next to me. I felt light.

In Longmont, I had three friends who knew me before I appeared in their world at the drop zone—Brendan, Jay, and Chris. I liked that they didn't ask me about anything other than here and now, because here and now was working for me. I liked the intense, fun-loving energy around me, the feeling of being part of a group. Even more, I liked being a stranger to the new friends I was making in this new world. I'd been embedded in the climbing community for so long that I had no anonymity anywhere I went in it, which was especially uncomfortable with the current, low state of my life and my mind. Here I didn't know anything or anyone, and no one knew anything about me except what I offered, which wasn't much. I liked being a beginner, being brand-new. When I was at the drop zone, I felt clean and hopeful. Maybe my new friends asked Brendan what my story was, why I'd appeared one day and was virtually living at the DZ with no signs of having anything else to do. Maybe they didn't. As long as they didn't ask me, I didn't care. As a rule, I didn't like talking about myself anyway. A lot of skydivers have complicated stories, I'd been finding. When I let myself think about my own story, I got a hollow, sick feeling in my stomach. My mind flicked back to those moments in El Cap meadow and I felt like throwing up and crawling under the truck with Fletch, until I urgently pushed it out and draped the gray cloud layer back over my thoughts. Here, in this world of open sky, exhilaration, and new everything, I had better things to think about.

The trailer stopped at the hangar and everyone hopped off, buzzing into the different sections of the DZ. I carried my parachute in, dropped it on the flat carpet, and walked backward from it, letting the lines uncoil from the daisy chain I'd looped them into, then stepped out of the harness and let the rig fall to the floor. I was already boxed in by other unpacked rigs spread in lines down the floor. I grabbed a milk jug filled with sand and set it on my container, to keep it from sliding forward as I picked up the lines and followed them down to the parachute. I had the lines hooked on my shoulders, with the fluffy parachute draped down the front of my body and my arms buried in the folds, when my older brother walked in, six feet tall and lanky, with his messy dark hair and easy smile.

I dropped my pack job back on the floor and rushed over to Virgil as he wove around the parachutes stretched between us on the packing carpet.

We hadn't seen each other in months. I could tell by the strength of his hug that he was relieved to find me in one piece and appearing emotionally stable to boot, surrounded by jumpers and parachutes.

"Did you just get here?" I asked, stepping back to look up at him.

"Yeah, I got a car at the Denver airport, and I have a job interview tomorrow at the Colorado Springs hospital. So I can do a few jumps today."

"Can you believe we can jump together?!" I exclaimed, almost unable to believe this was real.

Virgil was older than me by two years. Like me, he tended to be self-deprecatory and quick to smile, exuding an air of somewhat scholastic

Steph and Virgil at Mile-Hi

athleticism. He was astonishingly driven, though calm and gentle at the same time—the perfect temperament for an ER doctor. Like most people who knew Virgil, I was somewhat in awe of his intelligence and generous nature. He never had a bad word to say about anyone and was always willing to offer medical advice or care to our many injured athletic friends. He was continually being promoted and asked to teach at the university hospitals where he worked, which suited him, since he was basically unable to stay still.

Only a year before, I'd suggested to Virgil that he should take up skydiving. We'd both started climbing sixteen years before, though I'd been at college in Maryland and Virgil in Missouri. While I'd started off on safe, established climbs at local crags, he'd juggled med school with first ascents of unnerving, unfriendly routes in Missouri and then Tucson during his residency at the university hospital. Thwarted by recurring shoulder injuries, he'd reluctantly turned from climbing to downhill mountain biking and snowboarding, and then cold, lonely surfing in Arcata, California, where he'd moved with his wife. He kept getting hurt crashing his mountain bike or surfboard, and I suggested, half jokingly, that skydiving might be a less injurious sport for someone like him, who went 100 percent all the time, between twenty-four-hour ER shifts. At least people didn't seem to get chronic overuse injuries when jumping, I'd pointed out, and as far as I could tell, they only impacted the ground when they seriously messed up.

Virgil had plunged headfirst into skydiving, literally, racking up big numbers of jumps and traveling to drop zones around the country. He got briefly addicted to free flying in wind tunnels, which many jumpers referred to as "the crack pipe," since it was so easy to burn through money in two-minute chunks, and now he wanted to move to a place that was more accessible to skydiving, skiing, and snowboarding. Virgil began taking trips to interview at hospitals around the Colorado and Utah area, and I couldn't wait for him to move. I'd missed him during his last few years in Arcata, a remote town hours away from anything, on winding, mountainous roads, which seemed to require a full expedition to visit. When I'd started AFF, I'd fantasized about becoming a jumper and being able to share adventures with my brother again the way we had when we climbed together. Now it was really happening.

"Let's get on a load, I can be ready in a minute," Virgil said. "What should we do?"

"Do you want to track?" I smiled.

"So you haven't tried to sit-fly at all?"

"A couple of times. I'm really bad at it. I love tracking!"

"Let's do a couple of tracking jumps, and then we could do a sit jump. You can just try to hold a sit and I'll stay with you."

"Okay," I said.

My dad had grown up fascinated with motorcycles, taking them apart and rebuilding them, riding to college engineering classes through the Michigan winter. He'd sold his best street bike to buy my mother an engagement ring, but had continued to ride in three-day enduro races while my brother and I were both in diapers until my mother put her foot down and ordered him to quit. He began designing radar systems for Cessna, which required him to learn to fly the planes himself, much to my mother's chagrin. On family vacations we piled into a four-seater Cessna along with our cat, who was always airsick. My dad flew the tiny plane from New Jersey to Missouri, where he had a small cattle farm and could work on the buildings, machinery, and fields from sunup to sundown, both my parents' idea of a relaxing vacation.

My brother and I didn't like going to Missouri. We didn't share my parents' enthusiasm for recreational farmwork. I wanted to stay home and go swimming with my friends or read books. But my dad had kept his favorite enduro bike and it stayed at the farm. This relatively small bike (for a six-foot adult) had a double-size yellow plastic gas tank and had been my dad's most cherished racing bike back in the day. To start it, you mounted the seat, stood your foot on the small metal kick pedal, and jumped down on it with your full body weight. If you were a skinny twelve-year-old, not kicking it hard enough resulted in getting kicked back hard on your calf and shin while the engine coughed.

We were both allowed to ride the motorcycle around the farm to check fence lines. Virgil and I loved checking fence lines. Since I couldn't generally start the bike, despite persistent jumping on the kick-starter, with only bruises on my leg to show for my efforts, I mostly rode behind Virgil as he tore across fields and through trees. We frequently ended up sandwiched on the ground with the revving dirt bike on top of us, and I'm not sure how either of us never got seriously hurt.

At fourteen, my brother was also deemed old enough to drive the smaller tractor while I stood behind him on the platform so we could collect rocks to fill ditches. When rock-collecting with the tractor, in a few incidents the tractor nearly tipped on both of us. Naturally we didn't tell our parents about any of it. The climbing adventures we'd had together after college were often similarly more than we'd bargained for. But we always managed to scrape our way to the top with just a few harrowing incidents along the way that were funny from the safety of hindsight.

Our tracking jump went perfectly. I flew through the air next to my brother, almost fighting back tears at how wonderful this moment felt, wondering how it could even be real. We quickly packed and rode the trailer out for the next load.

"How do you want to do this?" I asked, as the truck curved around the end of the runway toward the plane.

"We can get in the door together and then squat down like you're sitting, and then we'll lock our knees and grab arms. So then we'll exit and get stable like that, and then let go and try to hold the sit. I'll stay with you, so you can just try to sit."

Virgil had been free flying for months already and had spent hours in the wind tunnel practicing his sit flying. I'd tried it twice with a group of skilled free fliers and found it surprisingly hard to keep my body sitting up in the strong-moving air without being tossed backward or sideways to the belly-to-earth arch that was the skydiver's default stable position. The fifty seconds went by fast, and I could see why people got addicted to the tunnel to learn how to control their bodies.

We boarded the plane last, sitting right by the door since we would be getting out first for our sit jump. The Otter climbed quickly, and the shouts of "Door! Door!" started up from the crowded jumpers farther down the bench. Virgil bent to grab the bottom of the Plexiglas door, sliding it up into the curved ceiling so the cold air could rush into the plane. I sat, watching the fields get smaller, at the edge of the open doorway, encased in the noise from wind and engines, and starting to shiver in my long-sleeved T-shirt. The tandem guys were always too hot and yelling for the door to be opened as soon as the plane was up, but I liked being tucked back in the warm corner near the pilot, away from the cold wind blast. I was relieved when we got to ten thousand feet and Virgil slid the door shut again.

At thirteen thousand feet the plane slowed slightly and the yellow get-ready light came on by the door. It switched to green, and Virgil threw the door up again. I squatted as though sitting in an imaginary chair, facing him. We locked our knees and grabbed each other's forearms and launched out of the plane. We were still upright in the air together until Virgil let go of my arms, as we'd planned. I popped backward like a champagne cork. I fought to get upright again, then tumbled backward and spun down through the sky, struggling to get sitting. As the seconds stretched out, I felt frustrated that I couldn't get back into the seated position. I had been taught to get into a stable position before throwing out my pilot chute, and I knew that if I threw it out while I was spinning out of control in two directions, I could get spun up in the bridle and even wrapped in the lines of the canopy. I'd also been taught to keep altitude awareness and to deploy at three thousand feet. I gave up on the sit, arched my back almost into a backbend, and finally stopped spinning. A little dizzy, but finally stable, I looked down at my altimeter for the first time since I'd started cannonballing. I was less than fifteen hundred feet above the ground. Instantly, I threw out my pilot chute as hard as I could. I was nine hundred feet above the ground when the parachute opened completely. It had all happened in less than forty seconds.

I landed just fine and started slowly coiling up my lines. Virgil appeared in front of me, looking deeply upset.

"What happened? Why did you pull so low? Are you okay?"

"I'm fine. I was open just below one thousand feet, it was fine. I just couldn't get the sit to stay. Anyway, I had the CYPRES too."

"Do you realize your CYPRES fires just below one thousand feet?

You could have had both your main canopy out and the reserve out at the same time, and that can put you into a downplane."

"Oh." I hadn't thought of that. I remembered Brendan's showing me pictures from the AFF manual about a malfunction where both parachutes are out at the same time, and somehow they push away from each other, driving the jumper into the ground. "But it didn't. I'm fine."

"Did you just not check your altimeter?" Virgil pressed.

"No, I was spinning pretty hard and I didn't realize how long it was. I thought I could get back to sitting, and I guess I lost track of time."

"Look, I have two audible altimeters, just take one. You should have one anyway, so you're not relying on just your wrist altimeter."

I was confused. Virgil seemed rattled to the core, and I'd almost never seen him so upset before. I knew what kinds of stomach-turning accidents and injuries he saw every day in the ER, and he was typically unflappable. "Why are you so upset? I'm totally fine!"

"You were dropping like a cannonball, and I was watching you go down below me even after I pulled. It's really bad to see your sister looking like she's about to crater into the ground right in front of you. That was not good. You need to use this audible in your helmet."

"Okay. Sorry. I'll get you another one if I take yours, though."

We were quiet as we rode the trailer back to the hangar. Without discussing it, we both packed and manifested on the last load of the day, for another sit jump. This time, we both sat in the air, I deployed my parachute at three thousand feet, and everything was fine. We stood around the landing area, drinking beer with a few of the other jumpers, watching the sunset over Longs Peak. Virgil had recovered his good spirits, and I was relieved to see him chatting and laughing with the others. I watched the colors streak and shift in the sky, thinking of how just a short time before I had been up there, just a thousand feet overhead, plummeting out of control toward the ground where I was now standing safely with a beer in my hand. Strangely, I felt no emotion at all. Not fear, not relief, not the weak, shaky feeling you get when you've just missed a car accident. True, I had had the CYPRES to fire my reserve for me, but it could also have given me a double-parachute malfunction. I hadn't felt afraid during the jump, which made sense, because things were happening so fast. But I should have felt all of those emotions when standing in the grass with my canopy draped in front of me, when I was miraculously safe on the ground, realizing how close I'd come to hitting it. I'd been in some close calls while climbing and had always subsequently been overcome by a deep sense of disquiet, understanding I'd just missed serious injury or death. But I felt absolutely nothing, all the way inside and out. Just nothing. It was strangely liberating.

Chapter Four

Cutting the Cord

Eldorado Springs, Colorado

In Boulder most things could be found at the right coffee shop at the right time. I almost always met my friend Christian at the Italian-style Amante on sunny mornings. A famous climber and quintessential Boulder local, Christian was elegant, brilliant, and warm, with European verve. He had a boutique-style climbing-clothing company, kept intentionally small, a few historic houses in town, and several dogs he'd adopted from the pound.

Christian also had a rustic cabin just outside Eldorado Canyon, a historic climbing destination about ten miles from Boulder. Many of Christian's legendary climbing feats had taken place on the slick and devious sandstone prows in Eldo, and he hadn't been able to resist buying the little cabin when the opportunity arose. He mainly just liked having it, but kept it rented to climbers or outdoorsy guys to sustain the expense, the most recent of whom had disappeared without a clear return date. Brad was a generous friend, I told Christian over my strong Italian coffee, but at a certain point he'd need his living room back. I showed no signs of going home and was starting to think I needed a semitemporary living situation instead of a couch. "Maybe you should check out Just Rite," Christian suggested. "If you like it, you can rent it for a while. We can work something out." It sounded like the ideal solution.

Christian gave me a key and directions to Eldorado Springs, an eclectic grouping of trailers, cabins, and opulent vacation homes at the mouth of the canyon. I hadn't climbed much in Eldo, but I knew just where the place was. The houses sat tightly along the creek below the spring itself, where you could fill water jugs for twenty-five cents a gallon. The thought of actually living there was a climber's dream come true. I swallowed the rest of my coffee fast, and Fletch and I set off.

The city streets gave way to open space and farm fields, the deep brown, anvil-like Boulder flatirons and buttresses of Eldorado Canyon rising up to the west. We turned up the narrowing road that led to the mouth of the canyon, where pavement became dirt just before the park entrance. A wooden bridge over the creek, just wide enough for a car, led to a cluster of close-built cabins. I spotted the small, hand-carved sign nailed to the dark siding, JUST RITE, and pulled into the steep dirt drive in front. Flagstone steps led to a door on the side facing straight into the neighbor's, a few feet away.

The rock steps were set much steeper than normal ones, and Fletch was clambering more than scampering up them ahead of me. For years, we had run on trails together, Fletch zooming around everywhere. I'd already downshifted from runs to walks in the last year, and now hills were starting to get difficult for her little legs. I felt a cold stab of anxiety as she strained hard through her shoulders to bring her back legs up the last step. She was only twelve. I wasn't expecting her to really be "old" for another seven years at least. It had never occurred to me before that Fletch might die, and now that it had, I considered it a pretty outlandish idea. But seeing her struggle like that raised the slightest shadow of doubt in my certainty. Fletch sat on the summit of the landing and looked up at me with her customary wide grin.

Just Rite, just outside of Eldo

I unlocked the rough wooden door with the tingly feeling of stepping into an old, empty structure. The door opened into one room dominated by a funky, sandstone fireplace, and several multipaned windows relieving the dark wood paneling. Just past the fireplace, a counter split a galley kitchen from a small eating space. There was a fridge. And a shower, with a door opening directly into the living room. Just beside it I found a closet-size toilet with a window that looked straight across the walkway into the neighbor's. Fletch and I nosed around, opening cabinets. The recent climber had left all the essentials: an armchair, a floor lamp, a small kitchen table and chair, a few cups and plates, a mattress in the loft, and an impressive array of kitsch.

I scaled up the wood ladder to the loft, using the sandstone fireplace for extra footholds. It seemed like you had to be a climber to live here, or at least if you wanted to sleep in the loft. I mantled over the top and stretched out. A wood-framed window opened onto the grassy hillside behind the cabin, and the roof came down at a sharp angle from my head to my toes, a clear sheet of Plexiglas epoxied into the slanting ceiling just above my face. It was an airy place to sleep, beneath roof beams and sky. There was just enough room for the small mattress. But Fletch would get the whole downstairs to herself and she wasn't much of a cuddler anyway unless we were sleeping in the truck. It was 100 percent just right.

As if the cabin weren't perfect enough, it sat just a stone's throw away from the entrance to Eldorado Canyon and a lifetime supply of rock climbing. I'd climbed in Eldo only a few times, and now I could just walk up the road and be there in minutes. Though I'd been absorbed in jumping in the last five weeks, I hadn't completely stepped away from climbing. I'd never be able to do that.

For seventeen years, climbing had been as much a part of me as breathing or walking. I'd been eating outside on a concrete wall on an unseasonably beautiful February day in my freshman year at the University of Maryland, with my mountain bike propped beside me, when a rugged guy approached. He looked exactly like a former Airborne Ranger turned wolf biologist, which he was. He'd exchanged to Maryland from Wyoming through a university program and was having trouble finding like-minded companions in this urban area. His name was Kevin. Since my lunch partner was a mountain bike, I apparently looked like a good candidate for outdoor activity, and he suggested we go rock climbing. I'd never heard of rock climbing. It was 1991, and extreme sports weren't as mainstream as they are today. I'd spent most of my childhood in New Jersey reading books and playing the piano, and poking around the woods a little. I had never been exposed to outdoor sports, though I'd recently started mountain biking, maybe because it was a bit like riding my dad's old enduro bike. I also liked taking it apart and cleaning the gears and replacing the bearings, something that had to be done after almost every ride on muddy East Coast trails.

On such a beautiful day, doing anything outside sounded more appealing than going to calculus class, and naturally I was curious. What better way to find out what rock climbing might be than to go and do it? Kevin took his Volkswagen Vanagon to a small, unintimidating cliff not far from the campus, called Carderock. We walked through the woods for a few minutes to the edge, and he tied a rope to a tree trunk and tossed it over. We followed the trail down through a gully in the center of the cliff band to the flat area below, where his rope hung down the slabby face to the ground. Kevin showed me how to tie into the end of the rope while he belayed me from the other end, and how to stand on my feet and puzzle my way up the low-angle face. He lent me his special rock shoes, only three sizes too big for me, and his chalk bag, to tie around my waist and use to keep my hands from sweating and slipping off. I was transfixed by all of it—the forested rock walls beside the Potomac River, the game of stepping up from one little rock bump to the next, the odd feeling of the tiny holds under my fingers, this unknown world of knots and ropes and rigging. I scrabbled my way to the top of a few short, simple climbs, and that afternoon my life changed course completely.

Within a year, I had student-exchanged to Colorado State in Fort Collins, following in Kevin's footsteps by applying to the interuniversity exchange program. I quit playing piano, which I'd practiced daily since the age of three, and dropped all my music classes. My budding interest in mountain biking fell by the wayside too. Everything was subsumed by the greedy fire of climbing, an intense blaze that seemed to engulf all my thoughts and allowed little time for anything else. Five years later, I tucked my master's degree in literature into the trunk of my grandmother's Oldsmobile, next to my other few possessions, and started waiting tables to earn money for season-long climbing trips. With all the passenger seats out, I had room to sleep in there and even cook with a camp stove.

Living out of Grandma's Oldsmobile at Indian Creek, Utah

It wasn't anything like what my parents had imagined for my future, and they were adamantly unsupportive of my unconventional, most likely dead-end, life choices. My brother was diligently laboring away in med school, though he had coincidentally discovered rock climbing at the same time. I was living out of the Oldsmobile in campgrounds in Yosemite, Moab, and Hueco Tanks, Texas, while scholarship offers to PhD programs and law schools piled up in my PO box. I was frankly terrified at my rebellious decisions, my parents' unequivocal disapproval, and the feeling of speeding along a road to nowhere and beyond. But my urge to climb was stronger than my fear of becoming a bag lady. It was stronger than anything, and although I was almost as convinced as my parents that I was ruining my life, I found myself unable to step off the path once I'd stepped onto it. It was almost as if I didn't have a choice.

I loved rock climbing, tying into a rope and heading up a vertical face, creating my own web of safety by placing different pieces of metal climbing gear into cracks, allowing the natural features of the stone to guide me. I quickly learned of the many different facets of climbing, from bouldering difficult moves a few feet off the ground with no equipment beyond a pair of rock shoes, to full expedition-style ascents of mountains and giant walls, which required months of time and every type of gear from tents to ice tools to thousands of feet of rope.

Then there was the purity and simplicity, and the seductive danger, of free soloing—climbing high off the ground without a rope. Within my first years as a climber, I chose easy climbs on clear, perfect days and set

Outer Limits, Yosemite *Dean Fidelman*

out alone to taste the freedom of moving over stone with pure freedom. No rope, no equipment, no partner, just the clean air and my hands and feet on the rock. It wasn't something to do all the time or to an extreme, but it sometimes felt right, like trail running alone with all the time and space in the world to soak in the sky, the earth, my own breath, and my emotions. I relished the absolute focus of free soloing, knowing that every move I made counted more than anything else in the world at that moment.

As much as I was drawn to increase my strength and skill on pure climbing difficulty, I was also attracted to the complex knowledge needed for bigger climbs. I spent winter months living in Hueco Tanks, the best bouldering area in the States, where I threw myself again and again at difficult moves never more than fifteen feet off the ground, and the summers in Yosemite or Colorado, learning how to work with the full gamut of climbing gear and big wall techniques on multipitch routes up long granite faces.

I came to love the Longs Peak Diamond, in Estes Park, Colorado, during these early years. Most people reach the summit of Longs on the Keyhole Route, a hiking trail that snakes up the mountain and around its west side. Though considered a "hiking" trail, the Keyhole is a serious endeavor. The rapid gain in altitude and the exposed scrambling make Longs Peak one of the more coveted fourteeners among the hiking/mountaineering crowd. The Diamond itself is the sheer wall on the east side of Longs, a thousand-foot face of granite that sits above a six-hundred-foot subwall called the North Chimney. For climbers willing to

The Longs Peak Diamond

carry their equipment for three hours up to the glacier at the foot of North Chimney and take on more than a thousand feet of strenuous climbing at thirteen thousand feet, climbing the Diamond is an equally coveted outing. Once I'd learned how to lead up cracks and place protection gear, and how to manage ropes on several pitches of climbing in more user-friendly locations, the Diamond had become an irresistible dream.

I was twenty-two the first time I climbed the easiest route up the face, the Casual Route. I had a few years of rock-climbing experience, and none in the mountains, but I was with my friend Craig, an excellent and highly accomplished climber. The route's name was somewhat misleading because any climb on the Diamond was not exactly casual, but since the rest of the routes became progressively even more difficult, the first ascensionists had dubbed it so with a wink and a nod. We left Fort Collins in the night, the standard protocol for avoiding afternoon lightning storms on the highly exposed face, and entered the dark forest for hours of quiet hiking up to the mountain.

The time slid by faster in the darkness as we made our way through the steep, canopied pine forest, and then the trees stopped abruptly and spat us out into the open night. Shooting stars dropped from the sky and I stumbled on the rocky trail, unable to keep my eyes on my feet. When the Diamond emerged through the dawn, still far away, it loomed bigger and steeper than any wall I'd ever seen, striking me with the physical force of a loud orchestral chord. That moment of awe stayed pressed forever into my mind, almost like a first childhood memory.

The "casual route" was a significant undertaking—requiring us to start our ascent at twelve thousand feet after the dark hours of hiking up, by climbing unroped together up the North Chimney. This climbing was not hard, but we had to ascend about six hundred feet of free solo terrain, watching out for loose or wet rocks through some surprisingly steep sections. We emerged on the top of the chimney onto Broadway Ledge—a sloping outcrop that splits the Diamond. On this sharply angled and deceptively meadowlike ledge, one could easily stumble on a loose rock or skid on an icy slab and tumble eight hundred feet to the glacier below, a tragic slip that had claimed more than one experienced climber.

Craig and I started climbing in a cold mist, the rough stone scraping my hands as we hurried up pitches of vertical crack climbing and face traversing up the sometimes slick granite. When the clouds lifted high on the route, I was dazzled by the vertical pink-and-gold granite. The gray, creased snowfields below seemed to lap against the walls like frozen waves. I felt vulnerable and small. But I liked the sense of urgency, of climbing on the edge. I struggled up chimneys, following behind Craig as he belayed me from above, fighting hard through the bulging crux section at the top of the wall, gasping for breath in the thin air.

When we topped out from the Diamond's face at Table Ledge and scrambled up the final several hundred feet of easy terrain to the summit, we stood at about fourteen thousand feet, higher than I'd ever before been. The air was thinner, adding to the fatigue, and we had a long way to go down. But more than the exhaustion, I felt giddy and lighthearted, in love with this wall and this mountain and everything about it, the same infatuation I'd felt the very first day I went rock climbing with Kevin, back in Maryland.

We descended the north face of Longs, picking our way down and over talus and boulder fields, back to the steep, rocky trail we had come up in the dark. In daylight now I saw thick clumps of purple and white columbines, light-tipped pine shrubs, and granite steps of all colors. It was one of the most beautiful places I had ever been.

I was wiped out for days after the Diamond, and elated. I had never experienced a day so demanding. I wanted more. I wanted to master this kind of climbing and know that place closely. There was so much to learn.

For the next several summers, I spent many days on the Diamond, bivying at its foot like a pilgrim in a rock shelter below the North Chimney. I grew more comfortable with the environment and intimately familiar with the landscape—knowing the best water sources and descent routes, the exact feeling of each granite edge I grasped to climb up the North Chimney. The mandatory 3:00 a.m. alpine starts to get up and off the face and the summit before the regular summer-afternoon lightning storms became less painful, somehow satisfying.

I also met my future husband, Dean, high on the vertical face of the Diamond in those long-ago summer days. It was July and I was twelve hundred feet up on the wall when a climber appeared beside me on the route I'd climbed the day before. He moved quickly, with aggressive confidence, looking around somewhat wildly for the anchor. He was obviously a strong rock climber somewhat out of his element on this alpine wall, wearing tights, a hot-pink windbreaker, and an air of urgency. A little amused, I pointed up and left to the cluster of nylon slings about thirty feet away, and our routes diverged. The next day we bumped into each other again at the local breakfast café down in town and decided to climb together the following week. We stayed up there for four days, each day climbing a harder route up the face, lying shoulder to shoulder in the small rock shelter every night. It was another beginning that would change everything.

In the spring and fall, I waited tables in Moab, Utah, a mecca of sandstone crack climbing and desert towers, living in the Oldsmobile while I saved my tip money for the next climbing season.

Moab was an easy place for a climber to get by. The unpretentious little town was sustained by tourism and outdoor recreation, from four-wheeling to river rafting, and it was rich in free camping spots along the Colorado River, where a girl living in a Cutlass Ciera could sleep quite happily. An easygoing, live-and-let-live atmosphere pervaded the community of locals, a mix of Moab natives, ranchers, artists, and outdoor folks. Every second I spent in the Utah desert reinforced my conviction that it was my destined home, a place that had everything I needed, including the opportunity to earn money in the restaurants to travel to other climbing dream destinations. Eventually I bought a rickety travel trailer, and my best friend, Lisa, let me park it in her large dirt driveway, just above Main Street.

Lisa, a six-foot-tall, blond bartender and wildlife biologist, was the heart of Moab's climbing social scene. She lived surrounded by dogs, friends, and visitors, in a remodeled henhouse that she called the Bird

Shack. Her door was literally always open, which meant there were typically at least three random climbers to be found on her couch at any time, sometimes to her chagrin. That's where I met Fletch.

Lisa, the heart of Moab's climbing scene

Fletch was mostly Heeler, though it was always fun to try to imagine what else she was. A lot of people thought she had some corgi, or some husky, or some Akita, or some beagle, or some coyote in her. She was a striking little tricolored res dog, from the Navajo lands in Arizona—the best, most beautiful, smartest dog in the world, in fact. Fletch was originally plucked from the Navajo res as a starving pup by the girlfriend of Jimmie Dunn, a famous desert climber. Betsy brought her to Moab, where, like all itinerant dogs and climbers, she was fostered briefly by Lisa, but was then gradually adopted by Lisa's friend Scott. Scott always said if he ever got a dog, he wanted to name it after those Chevy Chase movies. Lisa christened her Betty M. Fletcher, to make it work, and everyone else called her Fletch.

I'd never had a dog before and wasn't sure how I felt about them. I'd endured lots of barking, charging, lunch-stealing dogs at the crags, and I saw them as generally a nuisance. Scott was also living in Lisa's driveway, in a travel trailer, but he was a hardworking construction man and inflexible about the moral imperative of disciplining a dog to be good and to mind. Fletcher gradually won my heart by being generally unobtrusive and impeccably behaved, thanks to Scott's diligence. She was also uncannily intelligent and an excellent running/climbing companion. Before too long, I was sharing custody of Fletch with Scott, who was usually at a job site all day and happy to have me provide her with extra exercise and adventure. After about a year, he took off for a trip that started with an electrician contract in Antarctica, continued with freelance construction work in New Zealand, and had no fixed end date. Scott made me purchase Fletch for a dollar, so the deal would be made fair and square, and promise I'd never leash her unless it was for her own safety. Deciding to commit to such a responsibility was terrifying. But I already couldn't imagine life without Fletch. I gave him two dollars.

The next season, I started working as a climbing guide in Moab instead of as a waitress and quite suddenly began to get a little financial support from a climbing-clothing manufacturer—the same one that would ultimately drop me over the phone many years later. I'd been putting my heart and soul into climbing for eight years, to the exclusion of anything else, and some of my climbs were getting noticed by the climbing world. Being a decent-looking girl was a plus, and pictures of me started to pop up in the small climbing magazines. The sponsorship pay was modest, to say the least, but it gave me the freedom to live in my car full-time and travel, my dream come true.

The next seasons brought trips to the Karakoram, Baffin, and Kyrgyzstan, and then to a time when I was obsessed with El Cap free climbing, spending my summers in Yosemite, living on a three-thousand-foot granite wall. Fletch would go off and stay with one of her many friends for a couple of months here and there when I left the country, rejoining me on my return in the pickup truck I'd bought used from a friend when the Olds finally died. We'd spend our days climbing and hiking and our nights cuddled together in the truck bed under a sleeping bag. Always a little solitary by nature, and increasingly isolated and consumed by my climbing drive, I grew deeply bonded to this intelligent little dog. We seemed to be able to read each other's thoughts, and we had conversations. Fletch and I were more like partners or comrades than anything else, and before long we were two halves of a whole.

A proper home for two, the back of the Ford Ranger *Eric Perlman*

The wild guy I'd met that July on the Diamond entwined into my life too, though not nearly as smoothly as Fletch. Over the next twelve years, we traveled, split up, reunited, split up and reunited some more, got married, and then split up for good. But more than anything else, we climbed, with a devoted ferocity. We were both absolutely driven, intensely passionate, and impatient with anything that got in the way. For many winters we made the pilgrimage to hostile granite peaks in Argentine Patagonia, both together and apart, where the storms and the intensity of the mountains seemed to match our own tempestuous dynamic. In almost every way, we grew up together. Though we were puzzlingly incompatible, we seemed destined to travel on a parallel path through life, pushing and pulling, always connected by a stretched thread, always knowing we would come back together in the end. Until now.

Fletch and I moved into Just Rite immediately. I nested a little, splurging on some coffee cups and throw pillows at a Boulder thrift store, and put away my few clothes on the open shelves in the wall. It took just a few days to get used to waking up in the loft with blue sky above my face, stopping for a morning coffee in Boulder, driving out to the drop zone to make some skydives, and coming back to cook a simple meal. One evening I stood in the kitchen, stirring some kale in a frying pan as Fletch crunched her dinner in the glowing orange light, and realized that I felt content. Normal. Good. I smiled. I was in a strange place with no idea where I was going, and everything had changed. But I felt like me.

On the last day of July, I woke to the sound of the creek bubbling and birds chirping outside. I looked down at Fletch curled on her bed, propped up against a pillow, as light came through the windowpanes. It had been over a week and we were settled in. It was time I did a quick climb in Eldo. I slipped out with a pair of rock shoes strung to the cord of my chalk bag and walked up the dirt road to the park entrance. No one was in the entrance booth this early, and I walked the few hundred yards to the Bastille, the most famous rock formation in Eldorado Canyon. A crack-riddled buttress of unusually compact, slick sandstone, it started right off the edge of the dirt road above the creek. You could reach out and touch the first holds as you walked by. The Bastille Crack was the most classic route on this most famous rock tower. Though the climbing was close to vertical on the Bastille Crack, the good holds and plentiful cracks made it an enjoyable, relaxing free solo for locals and advanced climbers.

The canyon was empty and quiet at dawn, the air cool and fresh. I stepped off the ground, grasping the square, positive rock edges. I climbed slowly, carefully, as always when climbing without a rope. I relished the feeling of being in control of every muscle in my body, every thought in my head. I passed the first anchor and kept going, following the obvious path up the cracks that led me higher and higher. Physically, I was totally unfettered with no weight to carry—no harness, no slings, no carabiners, no rope. I didn't have to stop to place gear into the rock and clip my rope into it. I was the lightest I could be, not weighed down by any equipment. The climb took half the time it would with a partner, since I never had to belay someone else to me, and I could simply climb without stopping or messing with equipment. My mind followed my body, lifting into the freedom, the complete reliance on myself, all filling my entire being with good feelings. Two months ago, I'd been finding what could only be called relief, rather than pleasure, from climbing this way. In these weeks of skydiving and falling into a new life, I'd lost much of the weight I'd been carrying. I felt more at ease, simply happy at times. My natural buoyancy was returning. People were starting to comment again on how my wide smile mirrored Fletch's. As I climbed, I felt no fear, no sadness, no ache, just a sense of lifting rightness.

Free soloing is often perceived as extreme or crazy. I'd always done it in a very careful way. My style was to solo as if I were going for a pleasant hike, never pulling through at-my-limit hard moves hundreds of feet off the ground without a rope. I'd seen people free solo like that, and I considered it reckless and not smart. If I went to a climb that was too close to my top climbing ability and started up it with no rope, I would certainly be hit by fear. I didn't want to feel scared, my physical ability impaired by feelings of fear. I flatly drew the line at free soloing anything I considered at all difficult and would choose moderate, classic routes as my overall ability increased year after year. Rather than breezily sashaying up faces the way I would with a rope, I climbed with an extreme style of deliberate movement, each foot placement ultra-calculated, each handhold chosen with intention. I moved smoothly up the Bastille Crack and noticed again the unusual sensation I'd had since I'd started free soloing more and more in the last few months. I felt abnormally casual and almost fully relaxed, with no deep, inner voice keeping tabs on every movement I made. I'd been free soloing for fifteen years, but it had become completely different now. The difference was that the thought of falling held no fear for me. It wasn't that I wanted to fall. I didn't feel that black sense of half wanting it. That seemed to be over now. I truly didn't want to fall. It was just that I wasn't concerned about it. I didn't have the slightest feeling of anxiety or doubt as I climbed. This uncon-cern and lack of fear made me feel truly free in a way I'd never experi-enced before. It felt delicious.

I crossed over the top of the Bastille and scuttled my way down the backside onto the well-built trail that led me back to the base by the road where I'd left my shoes. I slung my chalk bag and rock shoes over my shoulder and strolled home to the cabin, where Fletch was still in bed.

That day, as I slipped from the jump plane and flew toward Longs Peak, a thought sprang into my mind, seemingly out of nowhere. As I stood packing my parachute in the hangar, the idea grew more tangible, more urgent, repeating in my mind. I wondered if it had been there all along, from the moment I'd let the truck keep driving toward Colo-rado in June. In some ways it seemed so obvious as to be inevitable. I would free solo the Diamond. For years, the Diamond had floated in my thoughts, an apparition in the sky as I'd first seen it. Now it floated before me every day as I soared in the air, again a breathless beginner in a high place. It was time to go back.

The next morning I woke at 2:00 a.m. Fletch woke for breakfast in the dark and curled back into bed. I drove up to the Longs Peak parking lot under bright stars, thinking about Kieners, the easy alpine route that ascends snow gullies and rock ledges up the left side of the Diamond. While hanging on the wall at belay stances, waiting for my partner to climb, I'd often watched parties kicking steps up the Lamb Slide, the first snowfield of Kieners. It looked pretty fun. But I just never got around to climbing it, always pulled away by the sheer rock face of the Diamond itself.

I kept a pair of light, strap-on crampons and a small ice tool in my truck, since you never know when you might need them. I could strap the crampons to my running shoes, and one ice tool would surely be enough for the moderate angle of the snow gullies. Today I would scramble up Kieners as a scouting day, a training mission to get back up to higher elevation, and a prelude to my bigger plans. I wanted to get up there, to get a look at the Diamond, and start thinking about what it would actually take for me to climb such a big, forbidding face alone, without a rope. Memories of all those past Diamond days came rushing at me as I drove up the winding roads through through the darkness. I couldn't believe I'd waited so long.

I parked in the dark among the other handful of cars in the lot—hikers who were prudently getting an alpine start to avoid the consistent afternoon thunderstorms on the Keyhole Route. My tiny pack held only the crampons and the short tool, a liter of water, and a couple of Clif bars. I slipped into the dark forest.

It was funny how much shorter and less strenuous the trail seemed now, more than a decade since the last time I'd hiked its sharp switchbacks. The crisp smell of pine and the sounds of rushing water over rocks followed me as I walked. I recognized certain wizened trees and lichen-painted rocks as they came into the circle of my headlamp. I emerged from the forest at 5:00 a.m., dawn light just illuminating the east face of Longs. It was a moment I remembered as viscerally as a scent, the face-to-face confrontation with that stunning vertical wall. It was every bit as beautiful as I remembered, the giant kitelike face, blended with pale green, gray, beige, and pink, set into a valley of snow, boulders, and clear water. I wondered what had taken me so long. Being here felt more right than it ever had before. I fought back waves of emotion but let the tears roll down my cheeks as I stepped rhythmically up the granite blocks of the trail, watching the Diamond grow before me, just as it always did in my mind's eye.

By 6:00 a.m. I was sitting below the Lamb Slide snow gully, strapping the crampons onto my sneakers, much to the surprise of two young Russians who had come properly prepared with boots, ice tools, and a rope. I wished them a good climb and set off up the snow, light and quick with my empty little daypack. The snow was just right, firm but grippy, and I zigzagged comfortably up the long tongue until it met a rocky ledge system high up on the peak. I followed the ledge, scrambling at times, and reached another snow gully. I was on the left edge of the Diamond's face, and I could see the rock well. It looked fairly dry, without any snow on the small shelves, in perfect condition for climbing, as far as I could see. I marched up the snow and took the crampons off at the Staircase, the final few hundred feet of rocky steps I'd gone up so many times before to the top of the Diamond. I skirted over the high face on shifting talus to descend the opposite side. I passed another surprised party who were climbing up the North Face with a full kit of ropes and climbing gear as I scooted down past them to Chasm View.

From Chasm View, I descended boulders and talus to the main hiking trail, feeling light and energized, completely in my element for the first time in months. I'd be at the parking lot in an hour. It had been thirteen years since I'd first climbed the Diamond. To free solo it now would

Climbers starting up the Kieners Route, Longs Peak

somehow be coming full circle for me. In a vague way, I had the sense that being able to climb that forbidding face alone, with no one to help me or keep me safe, would somehow free me from the past, or at least free me to live my present. I felt strongly that I needed to do it. I needed to live that experience.

Climbers on the North Face, descent route

With the what and why of my destiny suddenly settled, my mind snapped into analytical mode, as it had done so many times before when I'd dreamed up a climbing project. Though I'd scanned the face of the Diamond from my distant view on Kieners today, I needed to make sure the cracks were dry and free of snow. I also needed to see how I felt on the crux section of the Casual Route, which I remembered as being strenuous and rather insecure. I needed to climb the route with someone else, using a rope, before I committed to this idea of free soloing the climb. The pieces quickly fell into place. My seemingly random appearance in

Boulder suddenly appeared so inevitable and so clear. I felt the familiar, though long-damped, fire inside. I had a project.

I got back to Eldorado before noon, so Fletch and I headed out to the drop zone. I walked in to see a lanky fun jumper stepping into his gear. Jacob was young, a photography student at the University of Colorado, who had been in the military for a few years and decided that freedom was more appealing. He had started skydiving about a year before and was anxious to start base jumping. He looked like a climber, with a tall, extremely thin frame, and as I chatted with him, I discovered that he indeed had some experience climbing.

"You should let me know if you want to go out and climb something," he said. "I'd like to start getting back into it."

"Do you feel like going up to the Diamond? I'd really like to go climb the Casual Route soon," I said.

"Definitely! I've never been up there. When do you want to go?"

"How about the day after tomorrow? We'd have to get a super-alpine start."

"Absolutely," Jacob said, "I'm up for anything."

At 1:00 a.m. we met in the dark parking lot of Vic's in Boulder. We took two cars up the winding roads to Estes Park because I was planning to stay up there after we climbed. I'd told Jacob about my ultimate intentions, and he looked surprised but made no comment, obviously having learned in the military to keep his thoughts to himself.

We walked up the familiar trail with light packs. The Casual Route was no longer as daunting a climb as it had been for me at age twenty-two, so I had packed the barest minimum of climbing gear and a thin rope. I'd also brought a small sleeping bag, a camp stove, and a little food to spend the night in the rock cave. We reached the base of the North Chimney, below the Diamond, at 6:00 a.m. under clear blue skies. There had been a light snow, and the Diamond was gorgeous with little white patches on the face. Chasm Lake sparkled in the high valley of talus and snow behind us as we scrambled over the cold granite together, ropes and gear on our backs. I savored the feeling of clean, thin air in my lungs, and the slightly giddy mind state of higher altitude.

Jacob and I clicked, even more than I had expected. As a climber, he proved to be easygoing and competent. He had downplayed his skill and speed, which were considerable, and I was delighted by his artless blend of razor-sharp humor and candid sweetness.

We cruised up the rock smoothly, enjoying the positive granite edges and the vertical cracks. Though climbing the Diamond was strenuous, most of the climb now felt fairly straightforward, thirteen years after my first trip up the route with Craig. I had brought the minimum of protection devices, partly because that was my custom nowadays on long routes, but partly because I wanted to intentionally test myself for a free solo by relying on as little gear as possible to reduce the fall, should I slip off. Climbing with the rope stretching far below me, leaving myself open to a big fall if I slipped, was obviously much less dangerous and scary than climbing with no rope at all. But it was a controlled way to taste the feeling of being more exposed to danger, withholding the safety of placing gear as I climbed, but knowing I could lean back on the crutch of gear if I needed it.

I took my time in the crux section at the top, memorizing which holds to grab and the most secure body movements. I resisted the precaution of setting a piece of gear to protect the hardest moves. I lingered in the middle of the crux, looking down to fully register the impressive exposure below me, training my eyes, brain, and emotions for when the security of the rope was gone.

We climbed quickly and efficiently and reached the top of the Diamond before 10:00 a.m. We made our way down the shifting, boulder-filled slopes with gear and rock shoes hanging from our harnesses, chatting and laughing. We slid down the final snow gully and ended up in front of the granite cave where I'd left my camping things. We dropped the gear and rope in a small pile, then had nothing else to do.

We both got a little quiet and I said, "Thanks so much for climbing." Jacob looked uncertain. All at once, his tall, lanky frame and tousled, sandy hair made him seem young, a little vulnerable. I knew we were both thinking of the slight possibility of not seeing each other again, but at the same time not really believing in it. He stood there for a minute and finally just gave me a quick, firm hug and turned to walk down the trail alone. I felt a little pang as I watched him go.

"I'll call you tomorrow," I shouted after him.

Alone in the bivy cave, I went about my usual evening and morning bivy routines: prepacking my espresso maker and putting it next to the stove, the lighter, and my headlamp, all within reach, where they'd be easy to find in the dark, stuffing a Clif bar inside each of my climbing shoes and placing them next to my chalk bag and my windbreaker. I ate some miso soup and listened to music for a while and set my alarm. I put the watch on a small rock near my ear so I wouldn't miss the sound if I burrowed too deeply into my sleeping bag hood. I was tired from the climb, but a little wired, and it was only four o'clock. It was like trying to go to bed before Christmas. I wanted to sleep, but I mostly just wished it would be morning already. I gazed out at the rocky ridgelines in the distance, thinking of the hours I'd spent lying in this cave beside my estranged husband, talking softly about the shapes in the rock outcroppings against the skyline—the little polar bear walking uphill, the kicking feet, the bent old man. This was the first cave we'd shared together, and then there'd been so many nights and days in caves like this, on top of El Capitan and Mount Watkins, below Half Dome, Cerro Torre, and Fitz Roy, pressed shoulder to shoulder.

At 2:59 a.m. I woke and checked my watch. Twenty seconds later the alarm rang. I lit the stove, propped up in my bag, and drank coffee in the dark, then set off for the first snow tongue to the stretch of talus below North Chimney. In the circle of my headlamp, I grabbed the first familiar holds, pressing my climbing shoes against granite slabs, and started to climb. It was still dark as I reached Broadway Ledge. I was way too early. I huddled on the ledge alone in an alcove, feeling small and cold. I watched the glow of sunrise in the sky, out in the distance to the east. Time passed. I was getting too cold. I needed to move. I paced around the high ledge in my snug rock shoes and my thin windbreaker with the hood cinched tight around my face, trying to generate heat. Finally the weak dawn light leaked onto the ledge. I blew on my hands and rubbed my feet. The light gathered a little strength.

I stood below the first pitch of the Casual Route and looked up at the thousand feet of granite that stretched above me. I closed my eyes and breathed deeply, entering my climber's mind. Nothing else mattered except for the here and now on this clean dawn wall in the half-light. It was time. I grasped the chilled granite edges and stepped up onto the first footholds, leaving the safety of Broadway Ledge behind. My feet were numb and cold, making it hard to feel the smaller edges under my shoes. I struggled to relax as I climbed. The muscles in my back and arms felt a little sore from climbing the route the day before and doing all the rope work of belaying on each pitch. The sun gathered strength as I climbed, starting to create warmth finally. My muscles relaxed and everything felt better.

I climbed slowly, making sure every move was solid and secure, and gradually warmed up, the climbing becoming easier and more fluid. After the long traverse pitch, climbing almost straight left for fifty feet, I stopped at a big ledge to pull off my shoes. I rubbed my feet and got the feeling back. The long dihedral pitch of hand jams and finger locks was as enjoyable as climbing can be, and I started to become more aware of the sensations, and to open my focus to take in where I was. I noticed other parties around, climbers to my right on Chasm Wall, to my left on the Diamond, and small dots walking on the snow below. It was a perfect

High up on the Casual Route, Longs Peak Diamond

Diamond day, with crisp air, blue sky, and the first puffy clouds moving in already.

The cirque fell away beneath me until I reached the stemmed-out stance below the bulging crux of the climb. I stood with my shoulders tipped back slightly, one hand buried in a crack, feet stemmed out a little, the wall dropping away a thousand feet below my rock shoes. I started to reach high for a side pull with the other hand, making sure the other was still securely jammed into the crack before I let go to take it. I hesitated. I heard the beat of my heart pounding, loud inside my ears. With no warning, my mind instantly cartwheeled into images of my body falling down the wall, impacting Broadway, and tumbling for another thousand feet to talus and snow on Mills Glacier. Like an onslaught of invading enemies, tension, paralysis, and weakness rushed into my limbs. I froze in position, like a rabbit in the headlights of a truck. I knew that I had to move, immediately, before my panic took over completely, but I had to move with control or I would definitely fall and die. Shaking, yet clamping down on the holds through sheer instinct to survive, I fought through the panic and climbed to the safer, vertical terrain. Physically, I'd just exerted twice as much effort as I needed and I was drained, but I still had more climbing to do.

The holds became large and positive again. Lactic acid flowed out of my muscles. Energy flooded back into my body as the adrenaline flooded out, making me feel almost euphoric. I breathed out and kept climbing to the final traverse, and then to Table Ledge. I'd made it. It was seven forty-five.

I retrieved the running shoes I had tied in a grocery bag and wedged in a crevice the day before and headed up the south ridge over the top of the Diamond. I sat for a few minutes, empty, looking out at Chasm Lake and at the mountains spreading into the distance into somber grays, greens, and blues. It had happened so fast. I had just lived one of my greatest dreams and just tasted my greatest nightmare. I felt sated and a little staggered. More than that, I was confused. I didn't understand how fear could have hijacked me, when I'd been almost immune to it for so long. A stream of thoughts, emotions, and memories washed through me as I walked slowly across the top of the Diamond to the North Face.

For the first time, I saw what I'd been doing for the last four months, though it had probably been simple to see from the outside all along. I had always had a healthy respect for fear, as a climber and as an alpinist. I saw it as something necessary, something that could keep me alive. I believed I had come to understand it and had developed my own methods to use it as a tool, rather than being controlled by it. As events in my life had suddenly spiraled out of my control, my fears had seemingly inevitably come to pass one by one and I had become hopeless, expecting the worst to happen from here on out. I'd allowed myself to become ruled by fear and anxiety, something that came as a real shock to acknowledge. I could almost understand how my husband had shied away from my infectious anxiety, as he struggled with the same fears himself. For me, the disintegration of my marriage had been a tipping point. It had left me immune to fear in a way I had never been. Perhaps this strange imperviousness had come from a surrender because I finally gave up, something I'd never done before. I'd studied and tried to practice Buddhist teachings and Sufi principles, but now I was starting to live the liberation that had eluded me before. When death holds no more fear and when you've lost the things most precious to you, there's nothing more to be afraid of.

So getting scared on the short crux of the Casual Route was confusing. It did show me that I wasn't free soloing from some death wish. And it also showed me that my immunity to fear was not impenetrable. Maybe I hadn't turned fearless. Maybe I'd just turned numb with the self-preservation instinct of locking out all emotions. Maybe being numb was fearlessness. I wasn't sure about any of it. But I saw now what I was doing here in Colorado. I suddenly saw my life in the most elemental terms. Freedom had always been my greatest priority in life, and fear was the only thing that could keep me from it—the thing that had almost seduced me into giving up on life completely. I needed to get control of fear, completely, and figure out what was going on with it. It had progressively, insidiously been destroying my life and destroying me, and I wasn't going to be a slave to it any longer. Fear and I were done.

At Chasm View, I leaned out and looked across the sheer face of the

Diamond and at the parties still halfway up the wall. The clouds were turning gray already and building. The other climbers would probably get caught in the afternoon thunderstorm, a little early today, while I'd be safely down from the mountain.

When I was a teenager living in New Jersey, my piano teacher was a tiny woman who'd been a Juilliard scholar. I would sit at her Steinway grand piano and cringe slightly as I dropped a note through the most technical section of a Mozart fantasia, hoping she wouldn't notice. The sound of the grand piano was so lavish, so rich, compared with the small upright I played on at home, that I wanted to get through the fast strings of notes

Climbers on the Diamond, seen from Chasm View

into the orchestral chords, to hear them filling the room. I also hated making mistakes. Failing. I could feel her sharp eyes drilling into my shoulder blades at the first error, and her inevitable shrill voice rang out behind me, *"Fix it!"* With a sigh, I stopped the lush flow of sound. It wasn't enough to fudge through the piece to the end. I couldn't go on unless I played it perfectly. I could still hear her voice in my mind. Free soloing up the Diamond and surviving it wasn't good enough. I hadn't played it perfectly. I had to fix it. I needed to solo this route again, as many times as it took until I learned how to control my fear and erase it completely on my own terms. I would fix it. I hopped from boulder to boulder, across the ridge, over the Camel, and down the gully to my bivy cave, then past Chasm Lake and all the way back down to the green world.

I hiked up again on a windy, stormy morning, knowing the east face would be sheltered once I reached Mills Glacier. The cirque was empty and the air was still. I had the whole place to myself. Except for the clouds rolling overhead, and the strong west wind (which might explain the lack of people), it was perfect. I looked up at the looming, dark face, streaked with wetness from heavy rain the day before, knowing the route could be wet and possibly slippery at the crux, where I'd been overcome by fear in perfect conditions a few days ago. But I had complete faith now that my safety or peril was utterly dependent not on the conditions or the climb itself, but on what I did with my mind. I made a conscious decision to stay entirely relaxed, from start to finish, no matter what.

As I started the second pitch, raindrops struck my face. I immediately started to downclimb, knowing I was close enough to Broadway to get back there safely. I knew I could climb back down the North Chimney in a waterfall if I had to. But fifty feet down, the rain stopped. Just as quickly, I climbed back up, a little amused as thoughts of the eensy-weensy spider popped into my mind.

The beautiful little snow patches I had enjoyed seeing on the face two days ago had melted. As I traversed way left, my hands dunking into big edges filled with water, I focused all my attention on maintaining a rising mind state. I was warm and relaxed, totally happy and calm, alone on the quiet face.

High on the route, the thin vertical cracks were soaked. I coated my fingertips with chalk and wedged them securely into the seeping cracks, climbing in guarded, wet-rock style as the chalk turned into something that resembled mayonnaise rather than a drying agent. After many years in the mountains and on big walls, I was no stranger to wet rock. As long as the holds were sharp-cut and positive, I knew I could climb up them without slipping off even if they were running with water. For a moment I considered what I might do if the flaring finger slots in the crux section above were also soaked, because it would be almost impossible to climb those, but I reasoned that the steeper cracks should be dry. Anyway, worrying about it at this point in the route was pointless; I was fully committed.

I got to a stance below the crux and wiped the chalk slime off my hands onto the backs of my thighs, dipping back in the bag to cake my hands with dry powder. I was in luck. The jams and footholds in the bulge were dry, and the climbing felt like nothing. I climbed through the steep section slowly and confidently, feeling the way I wanted to feel— deeply relaxed, calm, and self-possessed.

At the top, I sat for a while and watched the clouds roll over, until raindrops started falling on me. In a quiet, euphoric state, I thought more about fear. I should have been much more nervous soloing the Diamond on this stormy day with water running down the wall. Instead I felt totally comfortable, relaxed and confident, enjoying the touch of the pink-and-gold granite and the positive edges and cracks under my hands and feet. I'd been almost amused by the threatening clouds and the wet rock. I believed with all my heart that I would reach the top safely. My goal was almost unrelated to succeeding on the route; after all, I already had. Rather, all my energy was focused on climbing it right, fearlessly, with relaxation and good feelings.

As I scrambled down the North Face, the brooding sky opened into heavy rain. I smiled as my thin wind jacket turned transparent and began sticking to my shirt. I knew this lifting feeling. It was the feeling of a beginning.

Chapter Five

The Edge

Zipping into the gray sparrow suit

August in Boulder felt like the point of a corner. It was still the height of summer, but I could almost smell autumn in the first morning chill. The drop zone had the magical atmosphere of life purely in the present, the sharp focus of flying through the air and the upbeat energy of the other jumpers. Boulder had been good for me. I'd landed here two months ago, lost and helpless, uncertain of where to go and what to do. Now I was filled with direction and energy. I felt stronger than I'd ever been, and curiously fearless, but at the same time more vulnerable. I was more guarded than before and maybe less quick to trust, but I felt keenly how kind people were to me, how much others helped me out of simple goodness. In Boulder, in a bigger city than I'd ever lived in, I'd discovered how nourishing it could be to become part of a whole. In this way, as in seemingly every other, I was a late bloomer. I still sought solitude and quiet space on my own and with Fletch, but now I understood the power of community, of both being and having a support system.

But the Diamond had got me thinking about the future. And thinking about the future brought me around to the thought of going home. Though it would be easy to stay here in Boulder forever, in this simple, carefree existence, my real home and my real life were six hours west, in Moab. I couldn't live in a fantasy world forever. But more than that, I didn't need to.

I could see, though, that I'd become addicted to jumping every day, the seductive mix of abandon and control. Emotionally, I felt dependent on it. I wasn't sure what would happen if I went home to Moab and quit jumping cold turkey. A town of five thousand, Moab had Skydive Moab, a small tandem skydiving operation that ran during the tourist season, but no big, bustling drop zone like Mile-Hi. Their Cessna 182 had room for two customers clipped to their tandem masters, and fun jumpers didn't pay enough to get the plane up in the air. What Moab did have was cliffs. Lots and lots of cliffs. For a skydiver, that didn't mean much. For a base jumper, a four-hundred-foot cliff meant just enough altitude to free-fall for two seconds, open a parachute, and land.

If skydiving was the last thing I'd ever thought I'd be doing, base jumping was even more last. Rock climbers generally don't feel an instant kinship with base jumpers. At first glance, the two pursuits could hardly seem more opposed. Climbers spend almost all their time trying to climb up walls, and the rest of the time training for strength and technique. Falling off is the worst thing that can happen and is usually bundled up with death, injury, or failure at the least. While watching climbing has been compared to watching paint dry, base jumping seems made for YouTube. Base jumpers aren't so interested in the finer points of getting to the top. For them, the whole point of being on a cliff is to fall off it and once it begins, it's over in seconds.

Climbers and base jumpers tend to hang out in high places, and I had encountered some base jumpers on the same cliffs I was climbing. But despite the obvious differences between climbing up walls and jumping off them, I saw many parallels between the two games of gravity. Like climbers, base jumpers live in a fringe, almost countercultural, community. They often drop out of real life, traveling the world in search of altitude. They are both small user groups and not politically powerful, and thus become almost the scapegoats of national park restrictions. Even more than climbers, jumpers feel most alive when tasting risk in a daily existence defined by survival.

Still, as a climber, watching someone leap out from solid earth into air is perhaps the ultimate taboo. Nothing could be more drastically opposed to climbing or more terrifying to a climber than the thought of running off the edge of a cliff into free fall. My mind could barely wrap around the idea, and I didn't even like thinking about it.

The first time I saw a base jumper flying a wingsuit, I thought I had just seen someone die. I was perched on a small ledge fifteen hundred feet above the ground on the side of Half Dome in Yosemite National Park, close to the top of the sheer northwest face. The overhanging summit block sat just two hundred feet above us, and I could see the curious ravens poking their heads out. My husband and I had free climbed the route, starting at first light. I was feeling a little sleepy as I fed out the rope, when suddenly the sound of a large falling object tore through the air. Instinctively I flattened myself against the wall. I'd been grazed by huge blocks of ice and rock before. In another split second, my brain registered the sound as something bigger and slower. It sounded like a body.

Base jumpers had jumped past me before while I was climbing, on El Cap or in Moab, and the distinctive sound of a falling body was always immediately followed by the loud crack of a parachute opening. The canopy would blossom out and float through the air while climbers on the wall whooped and cheered. But the bang didn't come. I leaned out from the wall and looked. I almost thought I saw a silver shape in the air, but I blinked and saw nothing. Seconds went by. The sound never came. I looked out into the distance, toward the valley floor, over the expanse of green trees and gray talus slopes, and saw only empty air. Gripped by dread, my brain tallied the falling body, no parachute opening, nothing to be seen—it could mean only one thing: the base jumper had fallen to his death on the granite boulders fifteen hundred feet below us. My stomach clenched.

Above me, my husband was laughing and shouting, "Did you see that? That was amazing!" I climbed up the last two pitches in a daze, feeling nearly sick. I sat on the top of Half Dome, hollow and stunned, immune to the blue, green, and gray panoramic views of Glacier Point, El Capitan, Mount Watkins, Clouds Rest, and Tenaya Canyon. Death was not new to me, after years of alpine and rock climbing, but to be here virtually watching that jumper's last moments of life filled me with grief.

Dean was talking fast, not making sense to me. Since I knew next to nothing about base jumping, I had never heard of wingsuits. I had only seen regular base jumpers in the past, opening their parachute after a few seconds of free fall near the cliff face. Apparently, special nylon suits enabled the wearer to fly out from the wall for an amazing distance through the air before opening a parachute. The jumper had been in a wingsuit and had flown out from Half Dome, way across the valley floor, much farther and lower than I had thought to search for an open parachute. My husband had known what he was seeing the whole time. While I was searching for a parachute that never opened, he had watched the winged man rocket through the air from the top of Half Dome all the way to Mirror Lake in the valley floor.

I was emotionally wrung out. The descent felt even longer and more tiring than usual as we made our way down the cables on the rounded granite shoulder of Half Dome and then the nine miles of trail back to the valley floor. They were tedious hours of downhill walking compared with the birdman's two minutes of glorious flight through the sky.

When I thought of that day, I remembered the sick feeling in my stomach as tears poured from my eyes, making it hard to see the granite footholds on the wall, and then the mixture of relief and anger I'd felt when I realized I'd gone through all that emotion for nothing. In the end, when I thought about the birdman, I just felt upset.

In recent years I'd met several people who'd learned to skydive solely so they could start base jumping as soon as possible, including my husband. And I had made several friends who were dedicated base jumpers. I'd learned a lot about the mechanics and the methods of jumping, just by being around them. In Moab, I'd watched them run off the edge of the cliff right in front of me, and it was disturbing.

Now, against all likelihood, skydiving had pulled me into the air. Though pretty short on skydiving, Moab was loaded with cliffs, a mecca for base jumping. And walking to the top of a cliff didn't cost a thing. Base jumping was starting to seem . . . practical.

It was a strange thought, but it did make sense. Most base jumpers believe a person should do the bare minimum of a hundred skydives before learning to base jump. And I had two good friends who actually taught first base-jump courses. If I got the requisite skydiving experience by the end of September, I was sure they would let me join one of their courses. Used base gear is much cheaper than skydiving gear, and if I just found a rig, I'd be able to fly as much as I wanted from the Moab cliffs just outside my house without ever buying a jump ticket. Rather than being a geographically inconvenient money pit, jumping would become a normal outdoor pursuit, like climbing or running.

Now, though I would have sworn it was the last thing I'd ever do, even more last than skydiving, I wanted to learn to base jump. And I wanted it badly. For a few months, I'd been consciously forcing myself to live in the present, shutting off my fearful, sad thoughts of the past or future. Now the future seemed full of promise, as it always had before. I had direction, a major goal, both in climbing and in jumping. This was the life I knew and had always lived, the energy of being caught by inspiration and swept into the passion of a big project. Now everything I was doing and would do became a piece of a growing whole, a flagstone that needed to be turned and examined to see where it would best fit into the pathway I was building toward my dream.

It's funny how many times in life I've found myself rolling full steam ahead toward something I was sure I'd never do. Whatever might happen in life, whether I liked it or didn't like it, I could know one thing for sure: it would change. There was absolute certainty in uncertainty, in some ways an enormous comfort.

It made me see that I should never rule anything out, never assume I'll have the same desires or goals in the future as in the present, never close myself off from any possibility, no matter how outlandish it might seem at first. No matter what I'd done or thought or been before, I didn't have to be anything or stay any way now, and I had the endless possibility to be anything I imagined. The one thing I could always count on was that I would change, as much as everything else would. And rather than use my energy fighting it, I could embrace it and use that energy to fly. Somehow I'd never truly understood that until this summer. It was so simple and so liberating.

In past years, I hadn't taken much interest in the nuts and bolts of base jumping, though I'd become familiar with it. For a whuffo, my knowledge of base jumping had become pretty deep just from being around my jumper friends.

While skydiving is regulated and even fairly mainstream, base jumping has always been perceived as somewhat renegade. In the early years of base jumping, base jumpers were blackballed from drop zones, and many drop zone owners were known to get furious at the sight of a base canopy spread out on the packing carpet. Somewhat like vampires, base jumpers teach one another how to base jump, and survival is often a matter of luck until a jumper has gained more experience. Most experienced base jumpers will avoid mentoring anyone, but those who do traditionally insist that an aspiring jumper make hundreds of skydives first. No one wants to be responsible for someone's death or injury, and it's notoriously difficult to make hungry, new jumpers understand just how serious things can get when a jump goes wrong. Though base jumping doesn't seem to require much athleticism or skill at first glance, an enormous wealth of knowledge and experience is required to make it out of an emergency situation, and that, in a nutshell, is the problem with base jumping and new jumpers. The incidents of fatality and serious injury are frequent and expected in base jumping, especially in the first year before a jumper has gained any real experience and usually knows just enough to get into trouble.

However, many highly skilled base jumpers who are pushing the envelope of safety also consistently die in numbers that would be unheard of in other sports. Perhaps the common thread with base jumping is severe consequences from pushing one's limits. At any given time, there are probably fewer than two thousand active base jumpers in the world.

Less visible and even more unique is the core group of extremely experienced jumpers jumping since base began in the eighties. They value "conservative" decision making and a more low-key approach and, on the whole, are much less prone to accidents and death.

In the eighties, when base jumping was in its infancy, Carl Boenish coined the acronym B.A.S.E. for "building, antenna, span, and earth"—the objects jumpers use to leap from. A jumper who had made at least one jump from all four objects could write to Carl and receive the next base number. Brendan, I knew, was B.A.S.E. #391, the low number his badge of longevity in a notoriously dangerous sport.

A prospective base jumper traditionally had to gain acceptance by local jumpers, come along on base-jumping missions as "ground crew," and gradually earn entry into the community before entering the sport. Now, twenty years later, people could sign up for a first base-jumping course and take a more direct route to starting to jump. But many jumpers remained clannish, as I'd seen firsthand.

It didn't take much knowledge of the sport to understand that base jumping was a lot more dangerous than skydiving. I left the jump plane thirteen thousand feet above the ground, with almost a minute of free-fall time to get stable in the air and deploy the parachute. I also had a second, reserve parachute, in case of a problem with the first parachute, and a small computer connected to it that would automatically deploy the reserve if I was still in free fall when I got a thousand feet above the ground. So I could do everything wrong or even pass out, and my parachute would still open. Since the drop zone's landing area was the size of several football fields, the odds were good that I'd end up in a flat, grassy place, even if I failed to fly the parachute or didn't have the skills to land where I wanted to.

Base jumps range mostly from two hundred to four thousand feet tall. When jumping from a two-hundred-foot cliff, a person will hit the ground in less than four seconds. So base jumpers have only one parachute, and they have to deploy it at precisely the right second before they run out of altitude. Base jumpers also have to avoid actually hitting the object they've jumped from. And compared with the giant, grassy airport fields, the places where I had seen base jumpers landing looked like booby traps, full of rocks, bushes, and trees to hit.

I knew that falling into dead air from a still object felt very different from being supported by the rush of wind from the moving plane. When I stepped out the door of the plane, the wind caught me and held me until I reached terminal speed at 120 miles per hour. Many of my friends at the drop zone laughed about their first balloon jumps, how they'd fallen head down from the edge of the basket before regaining the force of the air at terminal velocity. It required a different type of body control to stay stable through the soft air when leaving the edge. I had no idea what that would feel like, falling with the full sensation of dropping through still air. There wasn't any way to find out, except by jumping from a balloon or a helicopter, before experiencing a base jump for the first time.

Many base jumps are so low that a jumper never even reaches terminal speed in the free fall. Cliffs eight hundred feet or less are usually referred to as subterminal. Twelve hundred to four thousand feet gives enough free-fall time to reach terminal speed before needing to deploy the parachute, so these are often called terminal jumps. A terminal jump can be done with a wingsuit, more than doubling the amount of time the jumper has in the air. With a wingsuit, the jumper can also fly far from the cliff, as I had seen on Half Dome.

I also knew that packing a base parachute was much more complicated than packing a skydiving parachute, and that it could take an hour to do it perfectly. When jumping with a single parachute and no backup systems, it was absolutely crucial for the chute to open immediately and correctly. I hadn't yet had a parachute malfunction in skydiving, but malfunctions were common, and I'd learned the cutaway procedures in AFF. Basically, if the parachute didn't open right or if the lines were twisted and I found myself as low as fifteen hundred feet above the ground, I had to pull the two handles on the front of my skydiving rig. The first handle would release the bad parachute, sending me back into free fall, and the second handle would pop out the reserve parachute, which could be repacked only by a master rigger. The packing method for reserve parachutes was almost the same as the one used by base jumpers, an intricate sequence of perfect folds and creases for this parachute that could not fail.

Though my knowledge of base jumping was limited, I could see that if I wanted to learn, I'd need to keep skydiving as much as I could, and I should also do some jumps from a helicopter or a balloon to feel the difference of jumping into dead air, as from a still object. I'd also need to learn how to pack a base rig. And get one. And somehow, I felt, the Diamond and I weren't quite finished with each other.

My bank account was telling me I couldn't stay in Boulder past August, especially since my current income wasn't enough to sustain me even at home in Utah, where the cost of living was so much lower. It was a strange situation. My few smallest sponsors still had me on retainer. But that income added up to a total that was well below poverty level, just not enough to make it. This was not sustainable. Should I hang in there and work toward rebuilding my climbing career, or should I just walk away from it all, look for a teaching job or something entirely new? I didn't have a clear answer. I'd need to sort this out when I returned to my real life, in just a few weeks. September would be a perfect time of year to go home to the desert anyway, having missed the blistering heat of a Moab summer. I realized with a start that I had a lot to get done. Two months ago, I'd felt aimless, unsure of how to fill my time or where to go. Suddenly I was wondering how I could possibly get everything done here in just three weeks. Time seemed to be speeding up. I had a lot to look forward to, so many things to plan. I felt ablaze with thoughts and ideas. I dug out my pocket calendar from the glove compartment of my truck and opened it to August and September. For the first time since I'd come to Boulder, I actually needed to think about what day it was and what I'd be doing next month. And I needed to talk to Chris, Jay, and Brendan.

My friends Chris and Jay were also part of the tight group of skydivers-cum-base-jumpers at Mile-Hi. I'd known Chris for a few years, since he was one of the base jumpers who also climbed now and then. Chris worked as a video flier, following the tandems out of the plane and flying right in front of them with a heavy video camera on his head. Most people who were doing a tandem skydive considered it a once-in-a-lifetime experience and wanted to buy a ten-minute souvenir video of their jump.

As soon as the canopies opened in the air, the tandem team slowly floated down under a massive 360-square-foot canopy, and the video flier's job was finished. Chris's canopy was a tiny rectangle of nylon, one-quarter of that size, which allowed him to speed through the air and swoop to a landing at speeds of up to 60 miles per hour. Swooping with a tiny sport canopy is highly addictive for some skydivers, and tragically lethal for many. For cameramen who jump all day, every day, for a living, swooping tiny canopies is a way to add some bonus exhilaration to each work jump, since they're basically off the clock as soon as a tandem parachute opens. To me, safely landing in the right place under my parachute twice the size of those sport canopies was exhilarating enough. Every time I saw a camera flier or fun jumper come screaming in, skimming the ground with a toe, knees cocked, and ready to run, I cringed.

I hadn't seen anyone smash into the ground yet, but I'd heard about plenty of people who had. Broken legs, femurs, pelvises, backs, and necks were, sadly, common in swooping accidents. For me, the parachute was something I needed to get me safely to the ground after I was done flying through the air, and that's all I asked of it. With less than two months of skydiving experience, it was still challenging for me to consistently land on my feet even with my oversize canopy, and though I could generally steer myself to the big circle of pea gravel at the landing area, I also missed it sometimes when the wind changed. Swooping small canopies seemed like a good way to get hurt or die, and I wasn't even putting it on the list of things I'd never do. But for swoopers, it was the whole point of jumping. And having the skill to land such a tiny canopy safely was obviously a huge advantage for base jumpers, whose lives often depend on maneuvering a parachute safely into a tight, rugged landing spot. Though I found it slightly nerve-racking to watch my friend come screaming toward the earth, Chris had impressive skill with his small sport canopy. He never seemed to miss a load and sometimes didn't even return to the hangar between jumps. I often saw him swooping across the front edge of the landing zone and running to the trailer, where he'd exchange his unpacked rig for a packed one and then run over to the plane to film the next tandem customer.

Jay was rarely at the drop zone because he was almost always hard at work at the Mexican restaurant his family owned in downtown Boulder. Curly-headed and compact, Jay was full of high energy and an unapologetic workaholic. He would grab a couple of hours here or there to drive out to Mile-Hi, get into his wingsuit or freefly suit, and do a couple of skydives, zipping off as soon as he landed. Unlike most people, who would like to go on trips if it weren't for all the planning, Jay loved organizing base jumping trips to exotic locations, coordinating helicopter rides and foreign travel for a group of friends. Seeing his friends enjoy themselves was a huge source of pleasure for him. The best way to hang out with Jay was at his restaurant, since he could socialize while bartending and load his friends up with margaritas.

Jay, Chris, and Brendan were apprehensive but hardly surprised when I walked into the restaurant that night, sipped down half the margarita Jay had just made me, and told them I wanted to learn to base jump as soon as I'd done a hundred skydives. They'd heard it before, more than once.

"Steph, I don't think Jimmy and Marta are going to even let you join their course with such low skydiving experience," Jay said.

"In the next few weeks, I'll have more than a hundred skydives. That's the minimum they ask."

"I know, Steph, but you have to keep in mind that you've been really accelerated. Most people don't go through AFF and do a hundred jumps in two or three months. It does take a while for things to soak in. Jimmy and Marta are your friends, and they don't want to see you rush things and break yourself. They might not want to take that responsibility. It's different than a stranger signing up for their jump course."

As always, my thoughts were written all over my face. I forced myself to keep quiet.

"On the other hand, jumping every day does make you pretty current," Brendan offered, looking pointedly at Jay. "And you've skydived every day since you showed up here at the end of June."

"Exactly," I said. I looked at Chris. He wasn't saying anything. "What?"

"Honestly, Steph, I think it's rushing things," Chris said. "But you are supercurrent, and you're also not the average new skydiver. You're really good at your sport. You know how to deal with high-pressure situations and you're used to handling gear. If Jimmy and Marta are willing to let you join a first jump course, it would be the best way for you to start jumping. But it's really pushing things, which isn't the best approach."

"It's serious, Steph. You have to know how many people get hurt or die base jumping. It has to be something you really want to do," Jay persisted. "For yourself."

"Jay." I was kind of offended.

I wanted their honesty, of course, but I didn't like being told I should slow down. I'd never slowed down in my life, and as far as I'd always seen, forging full steam ahead was the way to get things done. As alpinists always say, "Speed is safety." I knew I was inexperienced with only two months of skydiving behind me. But I did believe that my advanced climbing skills helped me in this new discipline. And as far as I could see, I was doing everything right with my skydiving as a background for base, practicing only tracking with my body and accuracy of landing with my parachute every day. If I kept practicing these skills and then learned how to base jump from my highly qualified friends, surely I could learn the right way, the safe way.

"Look, Steph, I just don't want to see you rush into base jumping. You should get on the Internet and look at the base boards. It lists every fatality and how it happened. It's pretty scary. Even with tons of experience people go in. It's not like skydiving," Jay said.

"Okay, Jay, I will. But will you teach me how to pack a base rig? Brendan says you have the best packing method, because his pack jobs are kind of a mess." I smiled at Brendan. "I actually did talk to Jimmy and Marta, and if I have a hundred skydives and I learn how to pack, I can join a course they have in October. That's what they said. And I'll have way more than a hundred jumps by then."

"Well, that's true. Jay packs much better than I do," Brendan said with a grin. "But mine always open."

As much as Jay had reservations about me jumping, it was almost physically impossible for him to refuse to help a friend.

"Okay," Jay said, surrendering. "Let's do it tomorrow."

Jay came to the drop zone the next day with two of his base rigs, which were identical. Brendan teased him endlessly for owning nine base rigs, because he wouldn't part with any of them though he didn't take a lot of vacation time to go and use them.

Jay laid the canopies out on the carpet with the lines stretched straight to the empty containers, just like an unpacked skydiving rig. Though these canopies were much bigger than most skydiving parachutes, the containers were much smaller because they held only the single parachute, with no reserve chute taking up half the space. He pulled out five orange-tipped metal Pony clamps and some pull-up

Packing a skydiving rig

cords, thick grosgrain ribbons used to thread the curved closing pin through the closing loop after the parachute was stowed inside the container flaps.

A skydiving container is held shut by a single curved closing pin attached to the bridle, which will slide out with no resistance when the pilot chute is thrown into the air and yanks on the bridle, opening the container and pulling the main parachute into the air.

A base container is a pared-down system, but it has two closing pins attached to the bridle. The canopy is attached to multiple lines that run to risers, four wide straps coming up from the container above the shoulder straps. The container itself, when empty, is simply a piece of sturdy fabric with four flaps and leg-loops and a chest strap sewn to it. When the canopy is neatly packed into a tight square, the flaps wrap around it and are held shut by the two closing pins sewn onto the bridle, twelve feet of flat webbing that connects the pilot chute and the main parachute. When the jumper throws the pilot chute into the air, it inflates, pulling out the bridle. The bridle pulls the slick curved pins out of the small closing loops and yanks the parachute out of the container, where it will inflate with air. The jumper is suspended from the lines and the risers below the flying wing. When everything goes right, the system is beautifully simple.

When falling through the air toward the ground, you do not have much time to figure things out or fix them, and impact almost always results in bodily damage. The problem with jumping from an object instead of an airplane is that the object is always around to hit too. With no backup systems, the parachute has to open on time, perfectly, and also pointing in the right direction. Many accidents in base jumping happen when a parachute opens facing the wall and the jumper fails to turn it around in time. Base jumpers use an origami-like system for folding the parachute into a small square, with each fold calculated to result in a perfect, on-heading opening. Most people have slightly different packing methods, some using many clamps to hold the fabric in place as they work, some using none. No matter what, all packing methods are designed to make each nylon fold symmetrical, with all the lines carefully stacked to unspool straight and clean, with no tangles. In theory, a perfectly designed and executed pack job should always result in a perfectly open, straight-flying parachute. Real life is never as tidy as that. But all jumpers agree that a good pack job is essential to stacking the odds in one's favor.

Jay patiently packed his canopy once, as a demonstration, while I followed him around the floor and took photos of each of the countless steps as he folded, clamped, and knelt on the parachute, forming it into a tight, compact package. Including the time it took for me to ask about the reason for every step, it took an hour for him to pack his parachute and neatly close the flaps around it, with the pilot chute carefully stowed into its pouch. It was a perfect pack job. I admired it for a moment, and then Jay pulled out the pilot chute, lifted the canopy out by the bridle, shook it all out into fluffy folds again, and coached me as I laboriously duplicated his pack job. By the end of the next hour, I was having a hard time remembering the steps from back in the beginning. There was so much nylon, with so many lines, so many folds, and so many steps. I wondered how I'd ever get it all straight and then be able to actually trust that I'd done it all right as I jumped into the air with my own pack job as the single safety net between me and impact.

A few days later, I stood in the hangar while I was waiting for a load, scrolling through the photos on my digital camera, trying to match the steps with the notes I'd taken. One thing was obvious. I would need to practice this a lot or I'd never learn it before Jimmy and Marta's jump course. Chris walked up behind me and gave me a hug. I spun around, startled. "Hey!"

"Those are some nice photos of Jay's canopy," he said, teasing.

"Well, I've already kind of forgotten the whole packing sequence. So I'm kind of worried."

"I'd be happy to teach you again. I pack a little different than Jay, and you can borrow my rig for a little while too if you want to practice packing it a bunch of times."

"Wow, that is really kind of you. Thanks!" I squeezed him back. Chris had been around a lot more in the last few weeks, joining me for some climbing sessions at the gym and even managing to get in a few tracking skydives with me between his camera jumps.

"Actually, I was going to ask you if you wanted a safety rigging job. And it would also be a good way for you to get exposed to some base jumping now that you're thinking of starting," he said.

"What? What kind of job?"

"Basically Triax—which is me, Damian, Kenyon, and Blake—has been hired to do a commercial shoot for Intel. They want some base-jumping footage to make a clip for a big sales meeting, and they're throwing a lot of money at it. They bought custom-logo base canopies, and we're going to the Little Colorado Canyon in Arizona to base jump and shoot. We'll have a helicopter to drop us at the top and pick us up from the bottom after each jump. So we need a climber to rig along the edge of the cliff, and to be there as a rescuer in case anyone gets hurt and needs to get pulled off the wall. I figure you're the most qualified person I know. They'll fly us all there, and it will be a three-day gig. It does pay pretty well. What do you think?"

"Are you kidding? That sounds amazing. And it would also be great to earn some money right now." That was the understatement of the century. "When do we go?"

"It'll be next week. Will you still be here?" Chris asked.

"I still want to do another climb or two up on the Diamond, and I'm close to a hundred jumps. I'm not leaving for a few more weeks."

"Jimmy and Marta's jump course is in October, right? So you could get plenty of packing practice by then, maybe a hundred pack jobs too," Chris said, smiling.

"But you probably wouldn't want to jump them." I laughed.

Chris got serious. "Sometimes I'm at an exit point and I remember that I was kind of in a hurry when I packed, and I sit down and review the whole process I did in my head."

"You can actually remember doing each step of the last pack job you did, every time?" I was amazed.

"Yeah. I've even repacked a rig without jumping it because I just got doubtful about the pack job. Everything needs to feel right," Chris said, his gray eyes intense. "You need to make sure you've done everything right that you can. When you're at the exit point, you want to feel warm and fuzzy about your gear. So I'll talk to you later about the Arizona trip. I'm on this load."

Chris took off toward the trailer, his small rig hanging off one shoulder, hopping up with his camera helmet in hand just as the truck started to roll off.

Everything seemed to be happening so fast now, one good thing after another, as though things were spiraling up as fast as they had spiraled down before. It made sense. What goes down must come up. But now I was liking the down as much as the up, and everything had changed completely. I picked up my rig just as Emily's melodic voice filled the hangar: "Otter load nine, this is your fifteen-minute call, fifteen minutes!"

Chapter Six

Base Simulator

Triax: Kenyon, Blake, Chris, and Damian

The Little Colorado Canyon is an enormous side spur of the Grand Canyon, controlled by the Navajo Nation, rather than by the National Park Service. Chris had heard of it through rumors from local Arizona jumpers, who were keeping the area on the down low. With enough money, permits could be obtained to fly a helicopter in and out of the canyon. The walls were fifteen hundred to eighteen hundred feet tall, some of the biggest jumpable cliffs in the States free from NPS restriction, though the Navajos were particular about use and flip-flopped between allowing base jumping and prohibiting it without any explanation. They especially didn't like people coming there and dying, because it was impossible to restore the good energy—they were permanently upset about a German hiker who had disappeared into the canyon some years back and had never been found. Travis Pastrana, a famous daredevil stuntman, had ridden a motorcycle off the edge somewhere out here, using a parachute to soften the crash of his landing while the motorcycle shattered to pieces in the rocks and sand below.

It was hard to imagine the sequence of events that had led this mega-company to essentially finance a Triax heli base trip to the Navajo lands of Arizona, but it was actually happening. Apparently Intel's budget for the short base jumping clip they wanted was nearly limitless. With this much money going into it, I'd assumed they were planning to make a global TV ad at the least. I was shocked to learn that they merely intended to use it for a minute or two at the opening of an internal sales meeting. It reminded me yet again of how out of touch with the "normal" world I was. Still, as always when confronted with the so-called normal world, I couldn't understand how spending money on this gargantuan scale for something so disposable was normal. They'd even commissioned brand-new, custom-logo base canopies, which I couldn't imagine having any use beyond this shoot, unless they were planning to use them as souvenir $10,000 car covers.

Damian and Kenyon stood at the Southwest Airlines counter with their IDs out. Brad and Chris stacked duffel bags into a mountain as I scrawled our names on paper luggage tags. Brad had been added to the crew as an additional cameraman, which I hoped was a little bit of payback for the month I'd squatted in his living room. As the safety rigger, my job would either be ridiculously easy or ridiculously hard and possibly traumatic, depending on whether any of the jumpers got hurt. Though I hadn't yet met Blake, I knew that all four were highly respected and experienced jumpers, all deeply immersed in the jumping world. Chris worked as a skydiving cameraman, Damian was a high-angle rigger and free flier, Kenyon was a tandem master, and Blake flew jump planes for the military. Between them, they'd done hundreds and probably even thousands of base jumps around the world, and none of them had ever been injured base jumping. I figured it was a pretty safe bet.

I had one enormous overweight bag filled with a thousand feet of static line, which I'd borrowed from Jay. It was part of his rescue and first-aid kit for the base trips he liked to organize, in case a jumper got hung up on the wall. I hoped a thousand feet of rope would be enough to get me down to anyone who might be hung up. I hoped even more that nobody would get hung up, especially since I liked them.

I pulled my other bag of climbing gear out of the pile and noticed another familiar-looking bag next to it. I pulled the zipper down a few inches and saw the telltale red and purple. Somehow in the unloading at the parking lot this morning, my skydiving rig had gotten mixed into the big pile of bags. I couldn't believe it. That was the last thing I'd need on this trip as a climbing rigger at a base-jumping site. Since my skydiving gear was worth about as much as my vehicle, I didn't want to cart it around unnecessarily, but I couldn't leave it here now that we were a shuttle ride away from the parking lot and a half hour away from boarding. It was ridiculous to carry it back and forth to Arizona, but I had no choice, and anyway, Intel was paying for all the travel costs, including the overweight baggage. A little unsettled, I put two extra ID tags on it and handed it over with the rest.

In Phoenix, we loaded everything into two SUVs. We were headed to Flagstaff to meet Blake, and we'd join the rest of the crew in Cameron, Arizona, a tiny outpost near the canyon. Suddenly it felt like a road trip as we drove north, talking and listening to music. Strip malls and palm trees gave way to steep hillsides legioned with saguaros, as we drove higher into the thick pine forests near Flagstaff.

Blake, gruff and good-natured, met us at a small café in Flagstaff. We continued north, with the mountains behind us, dropping back to desert. As we lost elevation, descending toward the Grand Canyon, the hills became dotted with dry grass and green juniper bushes. Creased, skirted mesas spread out in the distance on each side of the straight, flat, two-lane highway. Small round hogans appeared, scattered among broken-down trailer houses with old tires on the roofs. Sheep, horses, and dogs wandered on the strip between the road shoulder and the fence lines, and more horses grazed inside. Sand stretched along the roadway, changing tone with the miles—tan, gray, brown, beige, and pink—the only vegetation scrubby, squat bushes, dry mounds of grass, and tumbleweeds caught in slanted wire fences.

Hawks soared. The sky intensified from nearly white above the mesas to deep azure straight overhead. The sand was heaped in mounds of muted gray and mauve and yellow, changing to dark piles scattered with crusts of rough rock, and then sudden jumbles of smooth sandstone boulders leaned up against short cliff bands.

We passed the main turnoff to the Grand Canyon and drove farther, along clusters of identical new houses, Quonset huts, and structures in various stages of disintegration.

A tall, historic suspension bridge stretched high over a short rock canyon beside the newer, much less impressive roadway bridge. Below, scrubby tamarisks clustered next to the riverbed, flat sand braided with muddy water and hemmed in by hunks of dark sandstone.

The Cameron Trading Post was a surprisingly full-blown concession operating here in the middle of nowhere beside the two bridges and a historic stone post office. It boasted several stone-faced two-story motel wings, a restaurant, and a labyrinthine gift shop. The hotel rooms looked out over the canyon riverbed, surrounded by miles of open desert. It seemed random and isolated, but this was a turnoff to the Grand Canyon itself, which fed into the Little Colorado less than an hour's drive ahead.

We turned at the trading post and drove west on a flat dirt road, leaving Cameron behind. Everything looked the same, just miles of open desert as far as I could see. If I didn't know where we were, I would swear the earth was solid and flat everywhere around us. We pulled into a dirt turnaround to find a group of cars, trucks, and E-Z UP shade shelters. A local ambulance team sat in the shade, drinking water and snacking on chips. A small helicopter waited near a fuel truck. Various Intel executives wandered around in shorts and sandals at a cautious distance from the edge of the canyon.

The illusion of flat, sealed earth stopped right there. The earth cracked open into enormous gashes that stretched out and around for endless miles in dark corridors. Towers of stone formed ominous-looking walls and twisted around corners and islands of looming cliffs. The canyon was startling, breath-stopping, like an M. C. Escher drawing painted by Picasso.

The rim was capped with a layer of unusually pale, sharp rock, as pocketed and rough as coral or limestone. It would shred clothing, skin, or rope without much trouble. I wandered around the edge, looking across at the steep sandstone walls. They were richly colored, with horizontal striped bands, and they were impressively high, maybe taller than fifteen hundred feet. There was definitely no climbing here, from what I was seeing. The rock was steep and loose and looked adventurous at best, from a climber's perspective. From a jumper's perspective, it looked awesome.

The rimrock was sharp but solid, perfect for building climbing anchors, with cracks that would accept my climbing gear and boulders I could wrap with rope. I could see with just a glance that I would have plenty of ways to rig ropes for the cameramen at the rim, and in the event I had to drop down a wall to reach someone, which was good. The guys were talking and pointing at the island directly across from us, intently discussing wind directions and camera angles.

Way down below I saw patches of flat sand in the canyon bottom among jumbled boulders, rock ledges, and pools of water. I wanted to go down there. It was a base jumping dream site, miles of jumpable walls. But because there was no way to climb back out of the canyon or to get across to the islands that rose like fantastic cityscapes inside the widest parts of the gash, the addition of the helicopter to the equation turned it into a base jumper's fantasy come true.

I turned to see two dark-haired guys approaching, clearly not Intel executives.

"Hi, please be careful near the edge," I said. "I can rig up a safety leash for you if you want to scramble around close here."

"We just wanted to take a look. I'm Jeff, I'm the helicopter mechanic, and Dave is the pilot," said the taller, lankier of the two.

Dave had a more compact build and looked remarkably like a soap-opera star. This impression struck me as bizarrely random, since I'd never even owned a TV, until I learned later that Dave's brother actually was a soap star.

"Nice to meet you," I said. "I'm sure you guys will be fine here, and it's pretty flat at the edge. But let me know if you want a rope to get closer and check it out." From my perspective it seemed truly impossible for someone to be standing at the edge of a canyon and just spontaneously fall in. But I always had to remind myself that not everyone was as comfortable at the edges of cliffs as my climber and jumper friends.

"Well, I'd like to get closer to the edge, and I wouldn't mind having a rope," Jeff said comfortably. I helped him step into a climbing harness and buckle it. Safely rigged to a fifteen-foot leash of rope tied off to a boulder, Jeff carefully climbed down a short step and walked to the very edge.

"This is amazing," he said, gazing over the deep space of rock and chasm.

"It is. From the road I couldn't even tell it was here. I bet it's going to be unbelievable flying a helicopter down in there," I said.

Dave had followed us over to the edge, without a rope. "Oh, yeah, this is some fun flying," he said. "It's a cool site. It's going to be wild to watch these guys jumping in here."

We scrambled back from the edge and Jeff unbuckled the harness and handed it back to me. "Thanks a lot," he said, "that was great."

"No problem!" I smiled. "See you guys later. I hope I get to ride in the helicopter."

"Really?" Dave asked.

"Are you kidding? I'm dying to fly down in that canyon!"

"That's funny, most people are scared to get in the chopper. Especially this small one."

"Huh. I think I really need to see the walls up close and the landing areas for, um, you know, rigging. Safety reasons," I said with a smile.

"Well, if you really want to go, there will be times when I drop them across or pick them up from the bottom and there will be an extra space you could take," Dave said. "They're talking about going over to jump off that island across from us, and they'd need you over there to set ropes for the camera guys at the top."

"Awesome, thanks!"

Dave and Jeff walked back to the helicopter, and the air filled with the loud beat of the blades. Damian, Chris, and Kenyon scurried in, bending low and wedging their base rigs in with their legs. The blades beat louder and the chopper lifted straight off the hard-packed dirt, raising a cloud of dust as they turned over the gaping canyon. I watched them cross the air, enthralled by the flight of the chopper, straight as an arrow, growing smaller and quieter across the canyon. The helicopter settled down on the island mesa like a bird on a nest, directly across from me, then levitated back into the air, becoming louder again as it drew close.

Flying that chopper had to be the coolest thing ever. I was totally captivated by its absolute efficiency, the ability to carry people and equipment up and across thousands of feet in mere seconds.

Blake, Brad, and the other cameraman ran over for the next ferry. I was waiting, with my pack and the heavy duffel bag full of rescue line, when Dave touched down again on our side. Jeff helped me load the gear into the back, and I climbed into the front seat next to Dave. He handed me a headset. I cupped the soft muffs over my ears into sudden silence.

"Buckle that seat belt, please." Dave's voice entered directly into my ear canals through the absolute quiet, like thoughts in my brain.

"Wow, this is amazing!" I couldn't help but be carried away by my enthusiasm. The helicopter was small, with space for only three passengers, one up front and two in the back. Dave and I sat in a clear sphere of windshield, side doors, and a glass floor. As he maneuvered the foot pedals, the helicopter rocked up from the ground like a soap bubble. The ground fell away below our feet. Jeff watched us from the ground. I waved at him as he grew rapidly smaller. Dave steered out over the canyon rim and the walls dropped away below us. "This is so cool! I love this!"

"So you're a climber. Are you a jumper too?" Dave asked.

"I just started skydiving, and I climb a lot. I want to start base jumping soon, though."

Flying around the Little Colorado Canyon

"Yeah, I really like these guys. Blake's a pilot over at Eloy, and I'm thinking about learning to skydive there. My brother jumps."

"Mine too!"

We hovered over the mesa, whipping the small clumps of dry glass below us.

"Okay, I'm going to set it down," Dave said. I stayed quiet as he worked the pedals, expertly sashaying the chopper into a flat spot dotted with cactus patches and small, sharp rocks. "Watch the blades when you get your stuff out."

"Thanks!" I took the headset off and laid it on the seat, and my ears instantly filled with noise. The quiet space with only our voices inside it seemed like another world. I gave Dave a quick smile, jumped down, and hauled my bags out, turning my head from the blast as he spooled up and away.

The guys were already gearing up, putting on their rigs and checking one another's helmet camera sights from behind to make sure they were aligned.

I knew Damian from the drop zone, but I'd heard his name

mentioned long before that among climbers and then base jumpers. His stepfather was a legendary climber who'd gone into high-angle rigging, and Damian had followed in his footsteps. Unlike many base jumpers, Damian was as committed to skydiving as base jumping and spent every weekend jumping with the crowd of good free fliers at Mile-Hi. He was simultaneously reserved and disarmingly candid, and gave off an air of almost catlike competence even when he was just walking around.

Blake on the other hand was amiable and solid. He seemed to notice everything but generally kept his opinions to himself. Though I'd just met him, I noticed that, as with Damian, his mere presence was confidence-inspiring.

Among the four, Kenyon struck me as the foil for Damian's and Blake's more self-contained style. I occasionally saw him at the drop zone too, working as a tandem master. He was easy to talk to and unfailingly enthusiastic, making each jump fun and memorable for his customers. Like several base jumpers I'd met, Kenyon seemed to get a kick out of taking on a dubious attitude instead of the stereotypically stoic approach to jumping. It wasn't something I would have expected, having believed in the image of macho adrenaline junkies before I actually got to know real jumpers, almost none of whom turned out to be like that at all. I liked that unpretentious style of acknowledging the nerves in undeniably scary moments and had to laugh as I heard Kenyon joke about giving himself a pep talk before the first jump into the canyon.

I could sense Chris's elation that his work was coming to fruition since he had done most of the organization for this project, and I could see him mentally switching gears into jump mode as he made adjustments to his camera helmet and stepped into his rig.

I spotted the two tripods near the rim and picked my way over to them. It took only a few minutes to rig up some anchors and ropes so the cameramen could safely perch at the very edge of the canyon or even rappel down into it if they wanted. With my rigging done, I picked a good vantage point nearby so I could take in all the action and shoot some pictures with my little camera.

Chris tracking in the Little Colorado Canyon

The guys gathered at the top of the rim, at a point where the wall was sharply undercut below them. Damian backed up from the cliff and set off in a smooth run, launching into the air with his arms back by his sides, head tucked down, and legs straight back in a perfect tracking position. His execution looked as masterful as that of an Olympic dive or ski jump. I watched in sheer amazement as he flew through the air at a steep angle away from the wall. I knew exactly what the air felt like as his body dropped lower and lower down the canyon, reaching terminal speed. But I had no idea what it would be like to run off the edge of a cliff.

Way down below, Damian's canopy bloomed into the air, and I watched him fly safely down to a small, sandy patch deep in the canyon. I heard the static of a radio, and then Blake ran to the edge and projected himself into the air. Next was Chris, and then Kenyon. In just a few minutes, they were all small specks far below, their canopies puddled in the sand around them. I felt chills, even in the hot midday sun. It was funny, even strange now, to think that I'd been scared by seeing people base jump before. There was no question in my mind. I wanted to be doing this too, more than anything else.

The chopper dropped into the canyon and rose out. I stood at a safe distance from the loud blades as Blake and Chris hopped out, and I saw Dave beckoning me through the windshield. I ran over and jumped into the seat, putting on the headset.

"I need to go back for Kenyon and Damian, so there's space for you if you want to come for the ride."

"Thanks, Dave! I want to ride as much as I'm let."

"I think they want to have two of them jump off the chopper next, to get air-to-air footage of the other guys jumping off the cliff."

"They're loving this, it's like a dream trip for them." I smiled. "It really makes me want to start base jumping. Like right now."

"Yeah, I'm definitely going to start AFF at Eloy. My brother has been trying to talk me into it for years. I just never made the time."

The chopper swayed into the soft air, the blades stirring up rowdy, wild wind. At the rim, Dave dropped into the canyon, curving right beside the wall as we descended through the turns of the corridor. Ahead, I could see it branching off endlessly into others, creating complicated passageways. Rock towers rose near the walls like lunar cities. It was so big, but within just seconds the chopper was on sand, Damian and Kenyon had jumped into the back, and we were rising up again. This helicopter was the coolest thing ever. I wondered what it would be like to be a chopper pilot.

As the day went on, everyone seemed to be everywhere at once, three-dimensionally, unlimited by gravity. I loved watching the chopper beating up in and out of the canyons, shuttling the jumpers up from below. I could see the guys becoming more comfortable with the site and starting to get looser and more relaxed with each jump. They decided to try for some different camera angles, and the show became even more interesting to watch. Dave hovered in the air just in front of the cliff, while Chris hung straight off the skid with his legs dangling, helmet camera pointed straight toward Kenyon as he ran off. As soon as Kenyon's feet left the edge, Chris dropped off the chopper and followed him down through the air. Blake and Damian jumped off the cliff together, both their cameras rolling on each other as they tracked.

By late afternoon, the winds had come up and the guys deemed the conditions unsuitable for any more base jumps. Dave ferried us from the island mesa back to the other side, and the ambulance team drove off. Everyone was buzzing from the jumps and the excitement. The Intel execs all looked relaxed and happy. Clearly, enough good footage was in the bag to fulfill the project, even without getting any more. The guys could spend the second day shooting without the pressure of needing to get enough done to have something.

I walked over to Chris and smiled at his glowing expression. "That was such a good day. It makes me want to start base jumping right now."

"Dave seems like a really good guy," Chris said. "He says he wants to do his AFF."

"Yeah, we were talking about that. I think Blake wants to help him out at Eloy and get him connected with people there."

"Maybe you should ask him if you can do a heli jump."

"Whoa. I hadn't thought of that," I said, startled. "At all. But you're right—I even have my skydiving rig here. Do you think he would? I'm kind of afraid to ask."

"You're a pretty girl. I think you should ask him. All he can say is no. I'll go up with you and help you pick the spot if he says yes. If you want to start base jumping, you really need to do a heli jump to experience an exit into dead air. This is a perfect opportunity," Chris said.

I liked the idea. A lot. "I get the feeling Dave is kind of a maverick. Who knows, he might be into it, he definitely likes jumping."

"Just get your rig and be totally ready, and we'll go over there and talk to him."

The winds had made base jumping too risky beside the cliffs, but the conditions for skydiving couldn't be better. I could make a soft upwind landing on an open dirt road.

Dave and Jeff stood near the chopper talking, a few hundred yards away from the group. I casually pulled my skydiving rig from the back of the car and headed over.

"So, Dave, they're done for the day, and I was wondering if I could maybe come do a jump out of the helicopter on your way back to Cameron."

Dave gave me a level gaze, and I held his eyes, not saying any more. He slowly started to smile, fine lines fanning from his movie-star eyes. "You're not kidding, are you? You really want to jump."

I was a little puzzled. Didn't I say I wanted to jump?

"I have my skydiving rig, if you'd let me." I was almost sure he'd say no. It wasn't illegal for me to jump from a helicopter with a skydiving rig into the open desert, but it wasn't part of the project being done here. It was a long shot, asking Dave for a free heli ride to make a somewhat bandit jump. But I had to ask. I turned slightly so he could see the red-and-purple rig on my back and looked over my shoulder at him hopefully.

Dave's bemused smile broadened to a grin. "Where do girls like you come from?"

"Um, Utah."

"I have to fly the chopper back to Cameron whether you come or not, so it won't make a difference either way on fuel. Come on, get in. I can get you up to three thousand feet, but that's it."

I looked at Chris in disbelieving delight, quickly stepped into my leg loops and cinched the straps, and ducked into the back of the chopper as the blades cycled up. Chris followed me in, and Dave swept off the ground.

Everything felt different as I looked out the window, trying to figure out visually how high we were above the ground as we gained altitude. Instead of being a passenger carelessly enjoying the ride, my brain was running through all the things I had to do and remember. I'd never jumped without an altimeter before. Three thousand feet was my normal pull altitude, but I'd be leaving the helicopter at three thousand feet. I figured if I deployed around two thousand feet, it would still be safe enough, so I'd probably track for about ten seconds before opening my parachute. It would happen fast, especially compared with what I knew. I wondered how you could really tell when to pull when you were base jumping, with no altimeter to tell you how low you'd gotten. Since I didn't have my altimeter or my helmet with me, I was about to find out.

I scanned the desert, trying to pick out the safest landing spot. I couldn't make out any contours, but from the drive in I knew that most of the terrain was as purely flat as it looked from above. Dirt roads crossed the open desert, so I just needed to pick a good-looking spot, where I could be sure to land on a straight stretch of road.

I wondered what it would feel like, falling into dead air, instead of being held by the firm rush of airspeed. I wondered if I'd actually have the falling sensation, and if it would be scary. I didn't have anything to compare it to. Watching base jumps all day long was really no preparation for this moment of being here right now, about to drop off the helicopter myself. Everything changes when you're doing instead of watching. I looked over at Chris, knowing he wouldn't let me do anything too stupid, and he nodded at me with a warm smile.

Dave looked back and shouted over the noise, "Three thousand feet, this is the most I can give you."

The noise of the helicopter made things feel urgent and rushed. I reminded myself to think and slow down. I looked down and picked a straight stretch of dirt road to aim for. There was no wind flag, no giant green football field like at the drop zone, no procession of other canopies pointing the way in. The wind had been coming from the west, so I decided to land in that direction and hope it had stayed the same.

Dave was hovering, the helicopter swaying slightly. I spun my legs around and scooted down, reaching for the skid with my feet. The air was windy and noisy from the blades as I balanced on the skid, clutching the doorframe behind me for balance. Looking down at the miles of empty desert below the beating helicopter, I had a lot of second thoughts. I had some third and fourth ones too. It was loud and rowdy and kind of intimidating, especially without anyone else to watch going first. I was glad Chris was behind me, but I kind of wished he were jumping too. I could sense Dave wanting me to get going so he didn't waste fuel.

I took a deep breath and reminded myself to just do what I always do, make it be the same. I arched my back, threw my arms forward, and dropped off the metal bar. Everything went quiet as I fell below the helicopter and brought my arms back by my sides in the familiar tracking position. I counted in my head, ". . . one thousand eight, one thousand nine, one thousand ten," reached back, and grabbed the pilot chute, throwing it into the air.

I knew it was much lower than I normally opened my canopy, but I was still high above the desert. Usually when the altimeter read a thousand feet, I started my landing pattern, joining the other canopies flying in a three-sided box pattern to land in the field. Here I had no idea how high I was or if the wind had switched direction. I relied on my eyes, watching the ground take shape below me as the junipers started to look like bushes instead of dots. And in this moment I realized the difference. Even an altimeter was a rule, telling me when to pull, when to turn my canopy. Here, in the middle of the desert, there were no rules, none at all. Every decision, even the decision to be jumping out of the helicopter, was my own. That's what base jumping meant, and that's why it was so irresistible and yet also so terrifying. It was absolute freedom, and absolute freedom is scary.

My heart was beating hard as I lined up over the dirt road and flared the canopy for a landing. I came in fast in a cloud of dirt as the parachute wafted down in front of me. I looked around at all the emptiness around me, Dave and Chris dropping down toward me from above. I'd done my first helicopter jump, off-site in the desert without instruments. I couldn't ask for a better base-jumping simulator. I almost couldn't believe it had all just happened. The whole sequence of events, from Chris's offer to my skydiving rig's mysteriously ending up in the baggage pile, seemed clearly meant to be.

I tried to catch my breath as I coiled the lines and gathered up my parachute. The chopper set down and Chris hopped out to help me bundle up the nylon.

"You've got to be really careful with this. We don't have anything to stow it in, and you can't let the wind pull it out of the chopper or it could wrap the blades," he shouted.

That was a pretty terrifying thought, the entire helicopter falling out of the sky with my canopy tangled in the blades. Still shaky from the jump, I anxiously bundled up the nylon and sat on it firmly in the chopper, clutching it hard with my legs and arms while Chris grabbed it from the sides with an iron grip.

Dave looked back and gave us a thumbs-up. Chris and I grinned at each other gleefully as we shot back up into the air. It struck me how much things can change in five minutes. I needed to remember that. Things change so fast. This was who I really was, this person open to any opportunity, living in the knowledge that adventures were there for the taking as long I was there to take them. It was the me I'd always been before life had started to push down on my shoulders and stitch me to the earth.

The stitches were stretching and getting thinner. It wouldn't be long before they snapped completely, releasing me to shoot free into the sky. I would fly from these cliffs. The knowledge rose inside me like happiness, like a plane lifting off.

Chapter Seven

Emptiness

Pervertical Sanctuary, Longs Peak Diamond *Brian Kimball*

I sat on the cabin floor with my back propped against the worn green armchair, sifting my hands through the fur on Fletcher's neck. It was so fabulously thick and voluminous that I could gather the folds of skin in a big white ball over my fists to surprise people. Fletch breathed deeply in her sleep. She smelled warm and comfortable, the clean scent of outdoors in her coat. For the billionth time, I admired the rich brown and black markings on her forehead and ears. She was the most beautiful dog ever.

After the high energy of the Arizona trip, it felt good to sit quietly and watch the afternoon light stretch in squares on the floor. The room was sparsely furnished now with things that were mine: a metal lamp, a purple cushion with iron legs, some shirts, shorts, and jeans folded on the open shelf in the wall, all scored from the Boulder thrift stores.

There was a lot I liked about this temporary life. I especially liked the feeling of simple contentment here, living without most things I'd considered essential just a few months ago. For years I'd been reading Sufi poems and Tibetan Buddhist teachings and aspiring toward non-attachment. But I found it hard to actually live that belief. When push came to shove, I was attached to a lot of things, and had tenaciously fought to keep them.

Until now, I'd unquestioningly believed in marriage forever. I'd believed that relationships would endure like granite, and that absolute loyalty would naturally be returned in kind. Now I understood that the only one I should rely on so completely was myself. And Fletch. Everything and everyone else was temporary at best, not to be relied upon. And, all things considered, to expect eternal commitment or reliability from others was perhaps unfair, or at least unrealistic. People change. Business changes. Feelings change. Life changes. Everything changes. Change itself is the only sure thing.

It seemed logical that if I never relied or depended on anyone else, I would never risk being as weak or hopeless as I had been in those awful months of spring and early summer when everything turned upside down. Looking back at my thoughts during that time, I could see that my life might depend on it. It was up to me to eliminate that risk.

Though I'd always been independent in most ways, this sense of absolute unattachment and self-reliance was a new distinction. It gave me a powerful feeling of peace and strength. It made things so clean, so easy. Liberation was as simple as just letting go. Over the past few months I'd slipped into a stripped-down existence without making any real decision to do so. I'd let go of many things I'd most valued, both material and emotional, and I was finding that I didn't need those things.

The small room turned gold. The squares of light lengthened and lit Fletcher's white fur with a rich glow. It was a strange summer, in every way, but my unplanned escape here began to take on meaning. For a while, I felt as if I'd lost all control over my life. I'd started to believe that everything I touched would turn to disaster, seemingly inevitably, no matter how hard I tried to make things go right. Now it was the opposite. Plunging into the world of flight as a complete beginner, I was doing something that went against all my instincts but was still relatively safe. In my other world, the world of climbing, I was pushing the envelope and upping the ante of risk each time I emerged unscathed from the wall. And I was unable to deny that things didn't always go wrong; in fact, it was starting to seem as if they tended to go right. Every time I took a chance, I came out not just alive, but happier and stronger. My path seemed to be rolling out in front of me. With each jump and each climb, I found a little bit of belief, the confidence to take another step.

I'd been working to overcome fear for years in climbing. It looked to me as if my inability to manage fear in real life was precisely what had caused the fabric to unravel with such snowballing momentum once the first thread had been pulled. In the aftermath, blocking my emotions had been a simple survival strategy, a tool I knew how to use. It had also given me the powerful taste of freedom from fear. But burying all emotions wasn't a true solution. I couldn't live like a machine forever. If I wanted real freedom, I needed to understand fear more deeply and learn to control it, or how not to be controlled by it. My current single-minded desire to skydive and to free solo seemed like a logical course. I was coming at the problem the way I knew, taking apart my weakness and working at it relentlessly, like the complicated parts of a Bach fugue. I wanted to fix it. And I knew from years spent on a piano bench that through sheer discipline and focus, I could.

Free soloing the Casual Route was a major breakthrough. It was a good start. The Diamond had other, harder routes, and one in particular kept coming into my mind, Pervertical Sanctuary. Pervertical had always been a somewhat notorious climb, a soaring line of splitter cracks on the far left side of the vertical wall. While the Casual Route had just one section of greater difficulty, the sustained physical nature of Pervertical throughout the thousand feet of vertical rock was much more demanding, especially at the high altitude of Longs Peak. The route was strenuous, with steep terrain that widened from a small crack to a body-size one, demanding the full range of crack technique.

Crack climbing and moving in alpine environments were my strengths as a climber. In a way, this route seemed made for someone like me. To solo it would be taking my exploration of fear and control to another level of difficulty and risk. So that's what I would do.

It was early September, and the summer alpine season would soon be over on the Diamond. Contemplation and reflection were over. My mind locked down obsessively, the way it always did when I got pulled into a climbing project. All of my thoughts and decisions now revolved around Pervertical Sanctuary. I needed to climb it with a deep physical urge that was impossible to ignore. I felt a sharpening passion for the Diamond, even more than ever, a desire so strong that I didn't even question it. I knew exactly how things were going to be now. This new, almost presumptuous dream would be the only thing that would matter in life until I did it.

The cycle of obsession was one I knew well. It was part of being a climber, and it felt good to be in that simple reality again. Somewhat irrationally, I'd felt betrayed by the climbing community and climbing itself, on top of all the other betrayals I'd felt when I'd been thrown out with the bathwater of the arch debacle. I had walked away from the climbing media after the surprising venom that had spilled onto me in the wake of the farcical controversy, leaving me free even from the external pressure of being a sponsored athlete. No one knew or cared what I climbed now but me. That was good. But my feelings about the simple act of climbing had become complicated. I climbed solely because I needed to, but the pure joy had been bruised. I had wondered if I would ever again feel that clean, passionate drive, a fire that had fueled every major climb I'd done. Now my world revolved around this dream, as it had so many times before, and the path was straight and clear. Everything I thought and did was for Pervertical. I wanted it more than anything else, the way it should be, the way it had to be. The flames had leaped up, blazing.

Jacob agreed immediately to go back up to the Diamond with me for a recon climb, just as we'd done before on the Casual Route. I had climbed

Pervertical Sanctuary years ago, but couldn't remember much about it except the universal consensus that it was steep, strenuous, and excellent. I'd heard many climbers telling tales about their epic struggles on that crux pitch, fighting up the thin, steep crack, struggling to stay in the wide section and wishing they had more gear to use, and I remembered finding it tough and intimidating too. But that was a long time ago.

Jacob and I slept in the rock bivy and started the climb at first light. The rock was rough and textured, cold in the early sun. My body flowed up the cracked granite wall, almost as naturally as walking. I'd brought only four pieces of gear, rather than the standard selection of fifteen or more, purposely withholding gear throughout the most difficult sections. On the few disorientingly loose sections of the route, I noted hidden holds and memorized them, making sure I never touched anything crumbly or broken. When free soloing, I couldn't just climb casually, knowing that a rope would catch me if I fell. I had to make sure I felt beyond solid on every single move I made, that I never took a chance on grabbing a loose flake. That lockdown style changed the feeling of the climbing completely. With no second chances if I failed, I needed to be 100 percent sure of the route, the rock, and myself.

Fourteen hundred feet above the glacier, the air was even thinner. The hardest section of Pervertical did live up to its reputation. The crack started off steep and thin, but just a little too large to catch securely on my knuckles. I resisted the urge to set a piece of gear in the thin crack, intentionally exposing myself to a long fall if I couldn't do the moves, to heighten my commitment. I paused on each foothold and worked my fingers deeper into the crack than I needed to, searching around for the tight constrictions that would securely lock on my joints.

At the steep angle, it was challenging to keep my body weight squarely over my feet, and my muscles worked hard as I locked my fingers deep into the crack. Still, I was an endurance crack climber above all, and this alpine environment was a familiar home. My arms felt a little tired from pulling most of my weight up the rock at this angle, but the exposure, cold rock, and thin air actually energized me. From years of experience, I knew I could jam my fingers and feet into the crack and hold myself there for as long as I needed to. I knew that even at maximum fatigue, my muscles could always do a little more.

I stopped to shake the weariness out of my arms, one after the other, and slow my breathing. Finally the difficulty eased slightly as the crack became wide enough to slot my whole hand inside and the steep angle relented back to vertical. My feet slid comfortably all the way in and twisted snugly into the crack. I was safe. I allowed myself to place a piece of gear, knowing I would never fall here, ever. But I wondered how it would feel to climb that thinner stretch of crack with no rope, with absolutely nothing between me and a death fall except my fingers, feet, and mind. And I wondered again about fear. I felt completely unbothered climbing with a rope on, even though I was creating risks of dangerous falls for myself by choosing to limit the gear I placed. I knew from experience that everything felt different when the rope was gone. Everything became starkly exposed with nowhere to hide and no way to find safety. I'd have to be 100 percent sure I could climb this route without falling to come up here alone. Right now I was about 90 percent sure.

I locked into the crack, climbing as slowly as possible, stopping after every move to look down at the rope flapping below my feet and then past it to the glacier hundreds of feet lower. I soaked in the exposure intellectually, noting how safe and how solid I felt with my hands and feet fully jammed into the widening crack. "Remember this," I told myself.

At the notorious wide section, I wiggled in, quickly wedging my whole leg inside the crack. Though many climbers dreaded wide cracks and the unfamiliar technique they required, I'd been wriggling up them for years in Yosemite and in the mountains. I welcomed the chance to get my shoulder and thigh shoved deep inside the rock as I shimmied up the large gash. I felt absolutely secure, knowing there was no way I could fall out.

Almost as soon as Jacob and I returned to Boulder, I went back up to climb Pervertical again with a rope and another partner—another bivy in the granite cave and another day on the glorious, lofty face of the Diamond. By the end of the week, I was 100 percent sure of the climb. I knew the shape and texture of every handhold I grabbed, and I also knew the width and the feel of every crack I put my hands and feet into, from the base of the North Chimney to the top of Table Ledge, seventeen hundred feet of vertical terrain. My legs and my lungs were strong from running up, down, and around the Diamond. The air didn't seem thin at all anymore, and the three hour hike uphill to the base felt like an easy stroll. I was ready.

Back in Eldorado, I tidied up the cabin, making sure each small thing was in its place. My clothes were neatly folded, the sheets turned down on the mattress in the loft, the coffee things all washed up and placed neatly in line. It was peaceful and clean. I looked inside one last time as I pulled the door shut.

I had one stop to make in Boulder. Fletch grinned at Jacob, but wagged a little halfheartedly as I handed him her bed, food bag, and bowls. Jacob's house had a big yard, and he was a dog lover. He'd watched Fletch for a few overnights, and I knew she was safe with him.

"You be a good girl. I'll be back soon." I buried my face in her fur. "She loves you, Jacob. Thanks for taking care of her again."

Jacob smiled and scratched Fletch's ears. "No problem. I'll see you tomorrow." He gave me a fast hug and took her things.

I got in the truck quickly before I got all emotional, and drove toward Estes Park, winding up the familiar curves. Fletch was in good hands. I'd left everything clean and tight, in perfect order. I wouldn't be going up there if I thought I wouldn't come back. But I also wouldn't be going up

The trail to the Diamond

there if I didn't have a clear-eyed understanding of all possibilities. When setting off alone up a sheer wall of granite, it would be foolish to deny that not making it to the top is one possible outcome.

It was well before noon when I pulled into the wooded parking lot and hiked quickly up the trail, enjoying the warm pine smell of the forest. Above the tree line, the smooth, jewel-shaped face of the Diamond jolted me hard, its muted hues blending across the lofty face. I couldn't wait for tomorrow, to be climbing among those shimmering colors in the cold, bright sun. It was the same Christmas-morning excitement I had felt before I started up to free climb El Capitan in a day, one of the most memorable experiences of my life. I felt the desire rising inside me. I stood, just gazing at the Diamond, then felt the sudden chill of the higher elevation as I cooled down fast. My hands went numb. I pulled on my windbreaker and thin gloves and got moving, over and down the small pass that led to the stream-braided meadow below Chasm Lake. Columbines bobbed beside the high trail in thick blue and white patches. I skirted the jumbled boulder field around the clear turquoise water and watched the Diamond grow larger and darker above me as I followed the final narrow foot trail to the bivy cave. I was relieved to see empty dirt inside the rock shelter instead of another party's backpacks or sleeping bags. It was just me up here in this cirque of granite walls, snow, and boulders. I sat down on the soft peat and unzipped my pack to get another layer on before I cooled off again.

It had taken me just a few hours to get there. I had plenty of daylight in which to organize and get rested. There wasn't much to do, just the normal, simple tasks of preparing to sleep and climb. I laid out my thin pad and small sleeping bag and screwed a fuel cartridge to the ultralight stove. I used my empty pack as a clean surface on the flat dirt for my spoon, titanium pot, tiny espresso maker, lighter, and food—a few tea bags, coffee, powdered soy milk, lentil soup and nutritional yeast, six Clif bars, and some dried fruit and nuts. The food all fit into a single Ziploc bag, fuel for dinner, breakfast, and a climb up an alpine wall. I set out my climbing gear: rock shoes and a chalk bag. I liked having the barest minimum of equipment and food, only what I needed and nothing more to exist in the rock shelter and climb up the granite face of Longs. I checked my watch to be sure the alarm was still set for three thirty. Without fail, I'd always woken up one minute before my watch rang for an alpine start. But I always set it.

It was still early afternoon. Going to bed at seven would give me more than eight hours of sleep, the minimum I needed. To fill my water bottle and the tiny pot, I walked down a few hundred feet to the open spot in the boulder field where water ran out from the glacier. Back at the bivy, I heated water for the lentil soup and stared out at the rocky ridge-line across from me as I ate.

This too was part of my plan, this time alone below the Diamond to think. I needed to be sure I belonged up there on the wall tomorrow. A considered, honest meditation of this question had to be made before setting off on a long free solo climb. I didn't want to be thinking about any of this tomorrow. I needed to ponder it now, get my answer, and then I wouldn't have to think about it again, freeing all of my focus for climbing. If I decided to go. I had confidence in myself, and I knew I was fully capable of safely climbing the route. I had the ability, and I'd done all of the mental and physical groundwork I'd deemed necessary. I also knew it was extremely possible for me to fall, for any number of reasons, and I had to decide if that was an acceptable outcome for me. If it wasn't, I had no business being up there without a rope.

The light had moved behind the Diamond, and the cirque was in shadow. I looked at the texture of the gray granite boulder above me, the stacked stones that climbers had built into a small wall around the sides. Three months ago, climbing without a rope had almost no meaning for me. The stakes weren't high because I didn't want to be here anymore. Now I felt positive and hopeful, and I was looking forward to the future. I wasn't looking for an escape. But something had shifted inside. Although I didn't want to leave the world, the idea didn't unsettle me. I felt at peace with the possibility of falling from the Diamond at this positive moment in my life. The thought of death had become tangible to me for the first time, and I'd realized it was the one thing I could be sure of in life. Death was the only certainty in an uncertain existence, in some ways a comfort to know. The only questions were how and when.

Thinking over the last six months, I realized that it would have been sad for my life to end when I was desolate and hopeless, rooted in misery. The idea of stopping things right here and right now, when life was positive, seemed like a much better way. I knew how easy it was for things to go spiraling down, for life to turn in a minute. I felt oddly ambivalent as I considered the chance that I might fall and die tomorrow. Life might spin upside down again in the future; it seemed that it would almost have to. To stop at a good time seemed better. Looking up at the darkening face, I believed I could be content with either outcome. Though I accepted the reality that I could die on the Diamond in the morning, I believed I wouldn't. For that reason, and that reason alone, I felt I belonged up there tomorrow.

I needed to think more thoroughly on fear. I knew that I could become intensely gripped by it. I still felt unusually free from emotions, but I had seen that the shell could crack. I knew all too well that engulfing fear is the ultimate performance destroyer. On my second solo of the Casual Route, I had no problem with the climbing itself, even when the rock was wet. If I had fallen the first time I'd climbed it ropeless, it would only have been because I'd been taken over by fear. While I felt able to accept death, I wasn't here looking for it. I especially didn't want to die because I'd lost to fear. That was exactly what I was trying to extinguish. To climb this harder route safely tomorrow, I would need to be so in control of my mind that fear would be unable to seize me without warning and cause me to falter. Climbing without a rope wasn't dangerous if I didn't fall. Quite simply, the fear was the danger.

I'd started to believe the theory that whatever you imagine yourself doing is what you will do. I'd lain in my sleeping bag countless times picturing myself doing each move of a rock climb that I had rehearsed, preparing for the next day's attempt. And if I managed to stay awake and focused throughout the entire visualization, it always worked. The problem with free soloing is that the vision of falling is always floating around, ready to be thought about. To do a long free solo, I needed to focus all the way on my mental state. I needed to believe in myself completely, and to picture everything being perfect. I resolved to take complete control of my thoughts tomorrow. I would not allow the idea of falling to enter my brain, at all. I would not even tell myself "not to fall." I would picture myself only climbing, moving up the rock. Above all, I resolved to be relaxed and have good feelings. I would repeat those five words in my head from the moment I left the ground until I reached the top, like a track on an endless loop: "Be relaxed. Have good feelings." I knew it could be hard to anchor my mind for such a long time, for two or more hours. The sheer mental endurance was part of the difficulty. The only images I would hold in my mind would be of my body confidently moving upward, climbing perfectly. I wanted to be calm and focused, totally unattached yet also fully present, consciously impenetrable by fear. My goal was not so much to do the climb and survive as to maintain that mind state. Tomorrow I would find out if I could.

I crawled into the cave, zipped myself into my sleeping bag, and looked at the rough granite above my face. I thought of all the other times I'd followed those crystals and contours with my eyes. I'd spent a lot of nights in this cave. It felt good, like home. I was safe and comfortable here, alone in this high cirque at the foot of a mountain wall, surrounded by clean stone. I watched the granite turn from light gray to dark, and then it was night.

I woke in the dark and reached for my headlamp and watch: 3:29. I sat up, propping my back against the flat rock behind me, and lit the stove. I'd set everything beside me the night before, so I just had to reach for the prepacked espresso maker and the titanium pot already filled with water. The stove roared softly with bright heat. Almost immediately, the coffee started to bubble up. I boiled water for the ginger tea I always drank after my coffee to offset its diuretic qualities and added a little hot water to the espresso shot in my plastic cup, the nicely rounded cap of a thermos I'd had once in Argentina. I sipped the strong, hot coffee and watched the stars in the dark sky, still in my sleeping bag. I didn't intend to start for another hour or two, so I could leave the cave without a headlamp. I wanted plenty of time to drink coffee and then tea and to focus my thoughts. I wanted to feel slow and calm every step of the way. As soon as it turned light enough to see, I'd start up the snow tongue toward the North Chimney.

Suddenly voices floated through the darkness. I froze, listening, like a small animal in its burrow. As they walked past the bivy, I caught a snatch of conversation. It was two climbers. Naturally, of all the different lines up the Diamond, they were headed for Pervertical Sanctuary, the same route I wanted to climb. I didn't want anyone above me in the North Chimney, since I'd nearly been hit in the head many times by parties kicking off loose rocks above me. And I didn't want to negotiate around anyone on Pervertical while starting up it. That would be both distracting and possibly dangerous. I needed to go.

I downed the pot of tea in one gulp, grabbed my shoes and chalk bag, and moved fast up the snow and talus to the North Chimney. As I changed into rock shoes at the base, I looked back to see the two head-lamps far below me in a boulder field. I scampered up the apron of granite into the familiar terrain and climbed up the wall without stopping. I reached Broadway Ledge in cold darkness. I looked down again and realized my foolishness when I saw the two headlamp beams still bobbing in the boulders, not even at the base of the chimney yet, eight hundred feet below me. I should have stayed in my warm sleeping bag for another hour, as I'd planned, and I would still have been well ahead of the other party. More vexingly, it had taken me only one second to abandon my plan of starting slowly and leisurely. I had charged up the North Chimney like I'd been shot out of a cannon, and now I would have to wait for dawn in my single layer of clothing, trying not to get chilled. I lifted the hood of my thin windbreaker and cinched it tight, and popped the heels off my climbing shoes so they wouldn't squeeze my feet and make them colder. In the dark, at this elevation, the air was piercingly cold once I stopped moving.

I roamed around and found shelter in a small circle of stones by a small cave, enough to keep the slight breeze off me. In the back, a set of plastic-coated rain pants and a jacket sat folded neatly under a helmet. It was unbelievable. I put on the rain gear and perched on the helmet to in-sulate my legs from the rock. I knew if I got chilled to the core, it would make the climbing harder, unsafe. I wondered who had stashed this gear here, in the middle of a massive granite wall, just what I needed to stay warm. The darkness went on and on. I was getting cold. I paced back and forth on the ledge, staring out to the east, willing the sun to come. I could see the first traces, the dark orange glow on the horizon, the changing tones of black to gray in the sky. I concentrated on feeling warm and open, accepting the cold instead of tensing against it. The sun would come. It always did.

Finally the bright rays broke from the east. I folded the clothes back under the helmet, sending fervent thanks to whoever had left them there for whatever reason, and climbed over the final broken rock bands to the start of Pervertical Sanctuary. I stood on a small ledge of granite. Steeply angled terrain dropped below me to the glacier; the vertical wall shot off a thousand feet above. I stared into the clean line cracking the wall in front of my face. There was nothing left to do but climb.

So many times in the mountains, I've locked my brain onto one thought or phrase, twining it into a soothing circle to ward off exhaustion, fear, and despair, even just the simple mechanics of counting sets of ten while kicking up snow in the dark. Right now, I felt my entire reality could be reduced into one simplistic mantra—"Be relaxed. Have good feelings." If I could force my brain to stay in that loop for as long as it took to climb this wall, everything would go right. I looked up at the crack and smiled. "Be relaxed. Have good feelings," I said out loud. I breathed deep, all the way into my stomach, and breathed out all the way. I reached out, took the sharp granite edges, and stepped onto the rock. Time dropped away.

The granite felt coarse under my hands and feet. The chilled air surrounded me without penetrating. It was the coldest day I'd had so far this season, but I seemed to be generating heat from the center, keeping my fingers and feet warm against the cold stone. "Be relaxed. Have good feelings" looped over and over in my mind. I smiled, savoring each edge I grabbed, pressing the shoe rubber onto the cold granite. Every movement felt precise and secure, my limbs loose yet fully engaged. I focused my emotions completely on the positive granite, the confidence in my shoe rubber, and the joy of climbing light, with nothing to carry.

Pervertical Sanctuary, Longs Peak Diamond *Brian Kimball*

From nowhere, a Velvet Underground song I hadn't heard in years started playing in my head, in a duet beside the repeating words of my own voice. I smiled. It was good. I let it stay there and play on, accompanying me up the wall. I reached the first belay ledge, with loops of faded nylon slings tied around a rock flake. I stepped past them and kept going, savoring my freedom. I had no rope, no gear, no partner to wait for. All I had to do was climb. It was the simplest thing in the world. I climbed gently through the loose-rock section, making myself light and delicate, never pulling or pushing too hard. I was at thirteen thousand feet now. I breathed deeply and rhythmically. The cold air felt clean in my lungs, giving me energy. It seemed like no time had passed since I'd stepped off Broadway.

Fifteen hundred feet above the glacier, I reached a tiny ledge below the steep finger crack, the crux of the route. I balanced over my feet, resting, making sure my arms weren't tired. I gazed up at the crack. I knew beyond a doubt I could climb it without falling. There was nothing to fear. I closed my eyes and felt my breaths cycling up and down through my body. I envisioned the moves I would make to climb the next thirty feet. I watched myself climbing perfectly, easily. I smiled. It was time. I raised my hands and twisted my fingers into the rough granite and stepped high with my feet against the wall.

Every lock felt solid, every foot perfectly frictioned. My arms felt nothing, no trace of fatigue, the air flowing in and out more intensely. Lou Reed's voice and my own words played on through my head, my vision filled with the granite before me and all around me. The crack

Pervertical Sanctuary, Longs Peak Diamond *Brian Kimball*

widened, the angle eased. Hands and feet buried in the crack, I stood in relaxed tension and waited until my breathing slowed again. I was safe. I looked down at the exposure. Empty space dropped down for over a thousand feet, snow, boulders, and granite walls spreading all around the floor beneath me. I observed it dispassionately. I looked up at the deep gash above, the final difficulty of the route, and wriggled up into it gladly. Granite pressed around me, holding me safe.

I still had another two hundred feet of climbing. But the real difficulty was now behind me. I kept my mind smooth as I moved up. It was before nine when I reached up to grab the flat edge at the top of the wall and pulled myself onto Table Ledge. I'd been on the vertical face for almost two hours.

I sat on top of the Diamond, watching the gleaming blue-green colors of Chasm Lake surrounded by gray talus and snowfields way down below. I could make out my little rock cave, the dark dot of my food sack hanging from the top, out of reach of marmots and pikas. I felt washed clean, stripped to an elemental state, hanging between tears and bliss, raw and vulnerable, but bursting with life. I let go, letting the powerful feelings wash through me with full intensity like rushing water, surrendering to them. I had done it. I was alive.

I found the hiking shoes and socks I'd hidden in a crevice and hung my rock shoes off the belt of my chalk bag. Carrying essentially nothing, I scrambled around the south shoulder of the mountain, up the stony ledges to the top of the Diamond and across the shifting boulders to the North Face. The extra-early start turned out to be a blessing, as clouds had been building and darkening all morning. A few big raindrops hit me as I scrambled down the granite slabs.

I reached the lookout notch at Chasm View and looked across the sheer face of the Diamond. The two climbers I'd passed in the dark were up on the face, partway up Pervertical. The Diamond looked big and exposed. I shivered with delight and started down the boulders toward the long gully above my bivy cave, climbing shoes and chalk bag bobbing gently around my hip. Everything looked so beautiful—the knobby granite boulders, the dainty flower patches hidden in the springy peat, the sweep of the cirque spreading out below me. I felt kind of shell-shocked, almost high, supernaturally vital. I felt light. I felt new.

A week later, I went back and free soloed Pervertical Sanctuary again, absolutely in control, even more than the first time. It was like the spell had been broken, and I could do it whenever I wanted to. I trusted myself completely. I would never let myself down.

September was the end of the climbing season on the Diamond. I was ready to leave it. Maybe even for another ten years. The relentless drive that had been burning in me for weeks was calmed. I felt smoothed

The top of the Diamond

down inside, cleansed. And climbing felt right again. I'd taken it back. I knew from experience that nothing was ever finished. The way I felt now would definitely not last. It wasn't as simple as reaching an enlightened state and moving ever higher. Another time would definitely come when I became attached or lost, when the tendrils would begin to emerge and wrap around me, blooming with the possibility of loss and fear. But I had walked this path, and I might know how to find it again.

Chapter Eight

Home

Flying into the sunset with Chris and Alan *Alan Martinez*

On September 24, I'd been skydiving for exactly three months and I'd made exactly 113 jumps, which I knew because I'd filled out all the boxes marked Date, Jump Number, Place, Aircraft, Gear, Altitude, and Freefall Time in my logbook. I found it unnatural and even a little distasteful to turn wild moments of flying through the sky into cramped numbers in an account book. But the numbers clearly meant a lot here, and I would even be prevented from doing things I wanted to do if I didn't have enough jumps logged in my book. And my friends Jimmy and Marta had told me I had to do at least a hundred skydives before they would teach me to base jump.

To be allowed to skydive at all, I now held a membership card from the USPA, the United States Parachute Association. A beginning jumper like me could get an A license after twenty-five skydives. It took fifty skydives to get a B license, two hundred for a C, and five hundred for a D. Then a jumper might want to get lots of other qualifications for all the other licenses or ratings. For insurance reasons drop zones had to comply with USPA guidelines, and some recreational jumpers themselves were noticeably eager to help apply the guidelines to their fellow skydivers, perhaps out of the desire to keep things safe for everyone.

As a climber, accustomed to complete independence and self-direction, all the tallying and licensing wrapped into jumping was hard to get my head around. There's no governing body issuing climbing licenses. You don't need a minimum number of climbs or a United States Climbing Association license to go up Everest—in fact, there's no such thing as a United States Climbing Association. If you want to climb, you find a rock and go up. I couldn't see why I would ever bother to get all these different jumping licenses. My A license seemed like plenty to me, allowing me to show up at any drop zone and board a jump plane.

But I noticed that most skydivers seemed to take the licenses and logging more seriously. Many conversations at the drop zone started off with how many jumps one "had." Always overly literal and sensitive to semantics, I was bothered by the concept of *having* skydives. As far as I could see, a skydive was an event or an action, something that happened in a moment of time, not an object. It was an experience to be lived, fleeting and finite. As a climber, it would never occur to me to count each climb I did, or even the number of days I'd climbed. It would be like counting up sunsets or kisses—a sweet idea perhaps, but not something I'd actually do or bring up in daily conversation. When a jump was finished, it was gone, and the idea of notching it on my bedpost or considering it a possession was somehow disquieting. Certain elements of the jumping world would most likely always mystify me.

Having spent most of my adult life climbing and critically gauging my ability versus risk, I also found it slightly ridiculous to have outsiders judging my readiness to handle new experiences. I wasn't sure how to feel about regulations that seemed designed to save me from myself. The rules I was used to obeying were those set by the mountains and by my own intelligence and skill.

As I sat on the trailer at Mile-Hi, waiting for the Otter, I eyed the wingsuiters enviously. They wore gown-length, brightly colored suits, their arms unzipped and the wings draping behind. Few wingsuit fliers were ever at the drop zone, and when there was more than one, they wanted to fly together. The wingsuiters could turn, float up, dive down, do barrel rolls, get side by side and fly in formation, essentially maneuvering like tiny jet fighters in the sky as they raced forward at ninety miles per hour. With a wingsuit, a jumper could fly through the air for more than two minutes. With the most advanced big suits and refined body position, wingsuit pilots could decrease their fall rate into the 30 miles per hour range. When I landed and gathered up my parachute, the wingsuiters were just beginning to come down from the sky like colorful angels floating under their canopies.

Though I now had at least a rudimentary knowledge of all the different types of skydiving, all I wanted to do was track, speeding through the air like Superman, staying airborne as long as possible. But with a wingsuit, I would actually be able to fly. It had got so I couldn't see the point of skydiving without a wingsuit, except to learn to fly one.

My mounting desire to start jumping a wingsuit had been met with varying degrees of temperature by my friends at the DZ. I had been skydiving for only three months, virtually the blink of an eye, and I was a complete beginner. But about a hundred of my skydives were tracking jumps. I seriously doubted that many other jumpers had become so single-mindedly focused on tracking in their first few months of skydiving, mainly because everyone else at the drop zone found it a little weird. While I didn't think my climbing expertise made me somehow inherently special or better than other new jumpers, I was objective enough to see that my years of extreme climbing had given me an above-average ability to deal with risk, pressure, body awareness, and gear. I couldn't see how the wingsuit could be that much different from simple tracking, aside from the obvious complications of being zipped into arm and leg wings and not having freedom of movement to grab the steering toggles or to deal with any potential parachute malfunctions until my arms were unzipped from the wings. Of course, I'd been warned many times that new wingsuit pilots were at higher risk of getting unstable in the air and tumbling into an accelerating, uncontrolled spin.

A few roadblocks were between me and a wingsuit. The USPA recommended a minimum of two hundred skydives before learning to fly one. More of a problem, though, was not actually having a suit to fly. Wingsuits were made to order by a few different companies, mostly Phoenix Fly from Slovenia, Birdman from Croatia, S-Fly from France, and Tony Suits from the United States. A wingsuit was pricey, usually costing from $1,000 to $2,000. Even more prohibitive than the expense was the wait to get one—a wingsuit could take up to six months to be sewn and shipped. With luck, a used suit might be found in the classified section of Dropzone.com or Basejumper.com, if the seller and buyer were of similar size.

I was much smaller than most of the guys at the drop zone, and so far I hadn't seen any women flying wingsuits there. Brendan had an old Birdman Classic suit of Jay's that would be the perfect beginner suit for me, and we were close to the same size. But they were both significantly quiet on whether I should start flying a wingsuit, and Brendan had uncharacteristically made no offer to lend me the Classic. I couldn't fly a wingsuit without a wingsuit, a situation that was all too clear.

My friend Alan was one of the few jumpers who flew a wingsuit at Mile-Hi, though he did just about everything else too, including AFF instruction. Another of the climbing enthusiasts I kept discovering at the DZ, Alan was young, easygoing, and quick to smile, with dark eyebrows and a slight gap in his front teeth. Only his cropped hair and excellent manners gave a clue to his military job at the Air Force Academy, where he'd taken an administrative position after graduation. The first load of the morning had just gone up when Alan walked into the hangar with his gleaming Phoenix Fly Phantom wingsuit draped over his arm in black and blue folds.

"Here, see if this fits you," he said.

"What?"

"I think we should do wingsuit training today. I mean, if you want to," Alan said teasingly. "You know I'm a wingsuit instructor, right?"

"No, I had no idea," I said, startled.

"Well, I am, and that means I can give you wingsuit training. We just have to see if my suit will fit you."

"Wow. Let me see!"

Alan was several inches taller than me and a little heavier. I put my feet into the booties and zipped up the two long zippers from knee to neck up the front of the suit, feeling like a kid in footee pajamas.

"It's really supposed to be tight from your shoulders to your feet. But as long as the feet stay on, you can probably wear it to learn on," Alan said, examining me.

"It does seem pretty big," I said, looking down at the loose material, "but I can wear my mountain boots to make myself taller too."

"Okay, take it off, and I'll show you how to hook it up to your rig and go through the basics with you, and then you can go do a jump."

I was speechless. This had become the thing I wanted more than anything. I had started to lose faith that it would happen in the week or two I had left in Colorado, and now suddenly I was about to get in a wingsuit and fly. Skydiving was so interesting; I always found myself doing something for the first time, with all the anticipation and uncertainty of the unknown. It seemed like life training for doing new things, and that alone explained the passion and energy that so many people devoted to this rather impractical sport.

I followed Alan to the side of the packing carpet and watched him lay his wingsuit over my skydiving rig. He fed my leg straps into the body of the suit and passed the detached wings through my shoulder straps, using a long, yellow plastic cable to connect the rows of small sewn tabs between the arm wings and the body like a piano hinge. When he held it up, the rig was attached to the back of the wingsuit like a backpack affixed to a prom dress.

"Okay, there are just a few things you need to know. You've been tracking a lot, so you know the body position, and you're used to looking at your wrist altimeter with your arms back by your sides and reaching for the pilot chute from that position. But it's really important to be stable and closed up when you exit the plane, and also after you throw the pilot chute."

"What do you mean 'closed up'?" I asked.

"Well, as soon as the wings catch air, they're going to inflate. So you need to close the wings down when you leave the plane, because otherwise you could pop up and hit the tail. And if you don't keep your wings and your body symmetrical, you'll tumble and get into a spin right away. The best thing is to keep them completely closed, exit like you would for a track with your head up, and then slowly open up once you're in the air."

Alan showed me how to waddle over to the door of the plane, face the wing with my arms pressed into my sides. and hop out with my legs together and my head high.

"So when you're in the air, open your arms and legs. If you start to spin, cross your arms over your chest and arch, so you're like a badminton birdie. That should get you out of it. Don't try to fly out of the spin. Just close up and give it a little time. If you're spinning when you deploy, your canopy lines will twist up completely and you might have to cut away. That's not really ideal."

That didn't sound good. I resolved to stay symmetrical and not make any sudden moves. I wondered how easy it was to get out of control and go into a spin.

"You should do some practice touches to make sure you can reach your pilot chute and the wing fabric doesn't get in the way," Alan went on. "And watch your altitude. Pull high, around five thousand feet. As soon as you pull, cross your arms over your chest and pull your legs up so you don't get into twists as the canopy opens. Then you can unzip your arms and legs. Where you can really get into trouble is if you have a canopy malfunction and you can't get unzipped fast enough to get your arms free. If that happens, pull these handles on your hips. That will yank out the cables and the wings will come free. So make sure you do a lot of practice touches on these cutaways too so you can get to them fast if you need to. You have to pull them pretty hard to get them free. You may even want to use the cutaways instead of the zippers to free your arms at some point after you're under canopy, just to see what it feels like. But probably not on the first jump—you have enough to think about."

"Okay," I said, imitating Alan's movements.

"And the other thing to know is that you need to do a flight pattern so you can avoid the jump run where everyone else is opening their canopies below you. You'll get out last since you'll be higher than everyone else when you pull. But you don't want to follow the jump run of the plane where everyone else is. So you'll need to fly either a left-hand pattern or a right-hand pattern. It's kind of like your landing pattern with your canopy, because you will be covering a lot more distance than you're used to. So get out, turn left, fly a little, turn left again, fly a little, and then turn left again toward the DZ. And the most important thing is, you'll be pulling high anyway, but make sure you know where you are so you don't end up flying away from the drop zone and landing out somewhere. That's a big no-no for the wingsuits. You need to stay aware of where you are, because you can get pretty far away in the suit, way more than tracking. If you just get out and fly straight, you could end up a couple miles away from the drop zone, and you definitely won't be able to make it back under canopy. So be careful and remember to try to fly a box pattern—stay off jump run and near the DZ. And that's about it. So just remember your exit position, the practice touches, and what to do if you get unstable."

It was a lot to digest. "It's a bummer you can't go with me since I'm wearing your suit," I said.

"I know, but you'll be pretty busy with everything anyway. It's almost better to do the first jumps without any distractions."

"Alan, thank you so much. I can't believe this is really happening!"

"Well, I think you're more than ready. And I know how much you want to start flying a suit. I'm psyched to see you start to fly, Steph. I think you're going to do fine. Go to manifest and tell them it's a wingsuit jump so they can mark it on the pilot's flight sheet. And remember, you need to get on the plane first since you exit last."

"Thanks, Alan, really!"

I walked over to the manifest counter and looked at the screen on the wall. The next load was in fifteen minutes. "Can I get on the next load?"

"Sure, what's your number?" the girl asked. Emily wasn't working today, since she was at her law firm on weekdays.

"Oops, let me go check, I always forget. And it's a wingsuit jump."

"Okay, you'll be on Otter four in fifteen minutes."

Alan helped me get into the suit, a somewhat awkward endeavor with the weight of the rig on the back. I straightened the fabric under my shoulder straps and tightened my leg straps. I pulled up the two long zippers along the body and left my arms and legs unzipped, as I'd seen the other wingsuiters do until they got in the plane. I felt dressed up and costumed, like something between a superhero, a prom queen, and a football mascot.

I strapped my altimeter to my wrist and went back toward manifest to check the time on the computer screen, passing a long-haired guy in a worn baseball cap. He worked at the drop zone doing various odd jobs, though I'd never actually seen him jumping, and he never talked much. Generally awkward at starting conversations myself, I always made a point of saying hi, because I thought maybe he was shy.

"How many jumps do you have?" he asked bluntly.

"One hundred and thirteen," I answered, thinking about how I'd be learning to base jump pretty soon.

"You can't get on that load."

"What do you mean?" I said, startled. "There's still slots."

"There's no wingsuit jumps with less than two hundred jumps. You can't fly that."

I looked around for Alan, confused and kind of angry. I wasn't sure what was going on. This was the first I'd heard of such a rule at Mile-Hi.

I knew several guys who'd started jumping a wingsuit there in the last month with less than a hundred skydives. A lot less. Alan and the long-haired guy stepped off to the side of the hangar and got into a heated discussion, the first time I'd ever seen Alan in a disagreement with anyone. A few minutes later he walked over to me, his darkly tanned skin flushed red with suppressed anger.

"I'm really sorry, Steph. Apparently the owner of the DZ is on vacation and left this guy somewhat in charge while he's gone. So he's digging in his heels on the USPA recommendation about wingsuit jumps, which is ridiculous. First of all, it's a recommendation, not a regulation, and it doesn't matter anyway, because I'm a certified wingsuit instructor. So I can give you wingsuit training with less than two hundred jumps if I feel you're qualified, which I do. But he refuses to let you go unless we can get a direct okay from the drop-zone owner. Which is completely absurd, because I have the authority to give you the jump training. I'm totally frustrated right now."

"Okay," I said. "So let's call the owner."

"He's in Spain."

"Seriously?" Disappointment was starting to sink in. I was still wearing the black-and-blue Phantom, feeling a little sweaty in the nylon fabric. I heard the speaker come on from manifest: "Otter load four, this is your five-minute call."

"I need to get off the load," I said.

"I don't know if we're going to be able to reach him or what the time change is," Alan said, visibly irate. "It might not be today. This really burns me up. At least you know what to do, since we went through the training."

"Yeah," I said, slowly unzipping the front zippers of Alan's wingsuit. After all the excitement, I felt deflated. "This is one thing I really dislike about jumping, all these people getting carried away with all their rules. I just don't get it."

"Well, not to mention this is completely within the rules and that doesn't seem to matter at the moment." Alan frowned darkly.

"I think I'm going to go climbing or something. I'm really sorry for all the hassle, Alan, it's really nice of you to go through all this." I was embarrassingly close to tears.

"Like I said, Steph, you're totally ready to fly a wingsuit. We'll work it out."

"Okay. Thanks again, Alan, and I'll see you later."

I gathered up my gear and walked out of the hangar, feeling more dejected as it all sank in. What really got to me was being stopped from doing what I wanted to do for basically no good reason, by someone who didn't know anything about me. I loved climbing because it was an escape from artificial restrictions. When climbing up the side of a mountain, the restraints were natural and clear, not arbitrary. Storms, darkness, strength, fatigue—those were real limitations I could accept and knew how to yield to. Contrived, human-created limitations made me crazy. They always had.

I seethed as I loaded my skydiving gear into the truck and tossed out the remaining water from Fletcher's bowl. I felt aimless for the first time in a long time, catapulted straight back to the empty place I'd thought I'd left behind. It scared me to see how much I needed to jump right now, and how fragile a solace it was. As usual, I was dependent on the whims of others.

Normally I wanted to skydive all day, and now I didn't even want to be at the drop zone. I watched the trailer rattle past, with all the jumpers smiling and laughing around the sides, the load I was supposed to be on. Fletch and I got in the truck and started to back out of the parking area.

Alan came rushing across the gravel to my open window. "Steph! We got the owner on the phone, and he gave the go-ahead for you to jump the suit. Let's go!"

What an emotional roller coaster. I could have done without all the drama. Even worse was the helpless frustration I felt at being singled out and stopped from making my own decisions. After being hit by a wave of negative emotions, I found it hard to shrug them off and get back to the headspace of simple excitement and all the things I needed to do right on my jump. I decided to just forget about those feelings, let them go, force myself back to the moment of newness and good feelings. I also decided that in the future I wouldn't answer casual queries about how many jumps I'd done. This counting business had gone from petty and annoying to downright unbearable. As soon as I had whatever USPA licenses I needed to jump without ever being hassled for anything, I wasn't even going to count my skydives anymore. That wasn't what I was looking for in the sky.

I pulled my bag back out of the truck, refilled Fletch's water dish, and walked back into the hangar. This time I hooked the wingsuit up to my rig myself while Alan supervised. I rehearsed all the procedures again and got on the trailer. As the jumpers and the tandem passengers lined up on the wooden planks around me, a grizzled, older tandem master slid in across from me and glanced at my wingsuit.

"So, how many jumps do you have?" he asked offhandedly.

I no longer saw this question as a common, somewhat annoying conversation starter. I saw it as a metal-toothed coyote trap. "Oh, I don't know," I said, with steely nonchalance. "Enough. How about you?"

He dropped his gaze and turned to his customer. I looked toward the open fields ahead, feeling my unzipped wings flutter behind my elbows as the trailer picked up speed.

I wondered what it was going to feel like. I did have a tiny bit of doubt after all the fuss that had been made. Would I burst into flames the minute I left the plane? I knew that Alan would never hear the end of it if I did mess up somehow. I hopped off the trailer and shuffled over to the plane, the long leg wing swishing between my legs like a heavy skirt. I felt a little clumsy climbing up the four-step ladder into the Otter's open door, treading on the leg wing and getting slapped as the arm wings flapped wildly in the propeller blast. I bent my head and walked all the way to the front of the plane and took my seat on the bench just behind the pilot. Having a climber's lean build had the unfortunate result of making me chilled as soon as a plane climbed up a few thousand feet, while everyone else was hot and yelling for the door to be opened. The wingsuit felt comfortingly protective, like a one-piece Gore-Tex suit or a bivouac sack. I was comfortably warm, and it made me feel more relaxed than usual. I leaned over to close the leg zips down to the foot booties and touched both of the cutaway handles on my rig, the right handle to release a malfunctioning main parachute, the left handle to deploy the reserve. I reached back and felt the hacky sack on my pilot chute, pushing back the fabric of my arm wing to get to it. I hoped I wouldn't have a problem reaching for the pilot chute while I was flying. But if I did, I could always go for my reserve handle.

The Otter climbed. I watched the needle of my altimeter move like a clock hand on fast forward, half aware of everyone else in the plane jostling and talking. The most important thing was to leave the plane in good, stable flight and to remain stable and controlled. My limited experience had shown me that the exit from the plane often set the tone for the rest of the jump, for better or for worse. Above all, I did not want to tumble or get thrown into a spin as I exited.

My altimeter needle climbed past nine thousand feet. The tandem masters started to turn on the bench and pull their passengers onto their laps to clip their harnesses securely to the rigs.

The needle moved toward eleven thousand, and the fun jumpers began fastening their goggles, helmets, and video cameras, leaning down the aisle to hand-slap and fist-bump as many people as they could reach.

I zipped my arm wings shut and reached back again to touch the hacky-sack handle. I heard the familiar sound of the Otter slowing, the loud roar changing frequency to a lower sound. The red light over the back of the plane changed to yellow, then to green. Someone threw open the door and the cold wind rushed into the plane. Alan's wingsuit was like a full-body wind jacket, protecting me from the sudden chill at thirteen thousand feet. The fun jumpers dropped out in groups of two and three, and the tandems slid down the benches to the open door. I watched the emotions tear across the tandem passengers' faces as they crouched in the door for a few loud, hectic seconds, then tumbled into the air, the tandem masters and camera fliers nodding and shouting to one another. Within a minute, the plane was empty except for the pilot up front. I stood in the door with my hands together at my waist, keeping my arms firmly closed in.

I looked up at the rivets on the airplane wing to make sure my head was high. I took a quick breath and hopped out left into the sky, watching the plane get smaller above me.

Leaving the Otter and not bursting into flames

I was stable, moving forward, and I didn't seem to be spiraling into a spin or bursting into flames. Instinctively, I opened my arms and legs. With a jolt of delight, I felt my wings inflate and catch air for the first time in my life. I felt the sudden lift under my body as my fall rate slowed. The air rushed past my face with forward speed, as it would on a motorcycle or on skis, making my eyes tear a little behind my goggles. I was flying!

I reached back to touch my pilot-chute handle, doing it with both arms to stay symmetrical. It was right there, where it should be. I touched it again, to make sure, as I'd been coached. My altimeter seemed to be working in slow motion as I flew. The normal fall rate of a human body is about 120 miles per hour. Even with no skill in the wingsuit, the extra surface area had decreased my fall rate to about half, turning the speed to forward motion. I kept checking the dial, expecting to be a thousand feet lower than I actually was. Still, there was so much to think about. I had only a minute or two to take it all in, trying to be aware of the sensations of flight at the same time that my brain kept track of all the things I needed to do. The time was elongated but at the same time so fleeting.

The altimeter said five thousand feet, and Alan had instructed me to pull high so I would have time to deal with any problems. I reached back, pulled out the pilot chute, and balled up quickly, hoping I was doing it right. I felt the parachute snivel behind my shoulders, and it popped out into a clean square above me, ending my fast flight through the sky. Now I was floating sedately through the air under my canopy, unzipping my arm wings. I noticed I was breathing fast, maybe from excitement, or maybe I'd just forgotten to breathe for the entire minute of speeding flight with the wind tearing across my face. I watched the other parachutes come in to land below me and started my own landing pattern at the edge of the field.

On the grass, I stood for a moment and looked up at the sky. With the same certainty I'd had sixteen years before, when I'd taken my first step onto a vertical wall, I knew I wanted to fly for the rest of my life.

I walked into the hangar with my canopy bundled up over my shoulder and the long blue tail wing swishing around my legs and gave Alan a rib-cracking hug. "I love it. I mean, I *love it*. Thank you, Alan, really."

His smile lit up his face. "So it went well? I knew it would. Do a few more—you've got all day."

I made jump after jump with Alan's suit. I made my turns carefully, like a kid on a bike with the training wheels just off, not wanting to lose control or get into a spin. With each jump, I was able to take in a little more, get some awareness that I was actually flying through the sky, as close to being a bird as I could get in this body. I couldn't imagine ever skydiving without a wingsuit again.

The next day, Brendan walked in with his Birdman Classic suit. "I think this will fit you better than Alan's. You can just keep it for a while; I have another one now."

The suit was dark gray, with small black wings. It had a white Bird-man patch on the arm and large-toothed metal zippers up the front. A handful of companies sold wingsuits now, but Birdman had been the first to produce suits for commercial sale in 1998. The gray Birdman Classic was an early model, vintage and tiny now in the accelerating pace of wingsuit innovation.

"Brendan! Thank you!" I stepped into the booties and zipped it up. It fit me much better than Alan's Phantom, and the small wings meant it would be easier to fly and safer to manage, a perfect beginner suit. "It's the gray sparrow," I said without thinking. I had a fleeting mental flash of the silvery blur I'd seen in the sky on Half Dome when the wingsuit jumper had flown past me. He must have been flying a gray suit.

"It fits you well. Have fun," said Brendan.

Flying changed everything. I thought I loved skydiving before, but it was nothing compared with soaring across the sky as the air streamed along my body. People who really knew how to fly wingsuits could pop barrel rolls, fly side by side or stacked on top of each other, float up or dive down, change their speed and loft. For a few minutes at a time, a human could feel like a bird. My free-fall time had just doubled with the suit on. I amused myself by calculating that my skydives had just become half as expensive. Being up in the air twice as long suited my climber's sense of speed, which was innately so much slower than a skydiver's. I relished the time to look around, think, and refine my body position. Each time I slipped out of the plane, I flew straight toward the Diamond, watching it float on the horizon ahead of me until I turned around to fly back to the drop zone. With every flight, I became more confident, understanding how to move my body more efficiently. Now I continued the flight down to three thousand feet before throwing out my pilot chute.

As soon as I landed, I wanted nothing more than to get back in the air. Each flight was almost a cruel tease, as the altimeter read pull-time just as I was becoming most aware of the sensation of flight. As soon as the parachute opened and let me down from the sky, I had an almost addictive yearning to get back there as soon as I could. I jumped and packed and jumped and packed at a frantic rate. The next few days went by in a blur of flight and credit slips.

Only three months ago I was learning how to do my first skydive. So much had happened in that time. All summer I'd lived only six hours away from Moab with just the single bag of clothes and climbing gear I'd thrown into my truck last June. But I felt strongly that it was time to stop being a runaway, time to think about real life. September was almost over. I knew the time was coming for me to go home. Then, quite suddenly, with no warning, it was my last day in Colorado.

Fletch was starting to falter every time she climbed up the steep cabin walkway. She didn't appear to be in pain, but her back legs consistently seemed strange, unstable. I knew acupuncture worked wonders on humans, and alternative medicine was rife in Boulder. Maybe it would fix Fletch right up, as good as ever. I'd never had acupuncture, but people swore by it. I was willing to try anything to make sure she was healthy and happy.

I took Fletch to a homeopathic vet, and he put some tiny needles into her while she patiently lay still. I waited anxiously for his opinion of the problem. He diagnosed arthritis and prescribed Rimadyl, the same non-homeopathic anti-inflammatory that I'd started giving her last year when her front shoulder had caused her to limp after long days. That was not enough information to ease my worries or to make a game plan to fix her. Why would arthritis make her back legs unsteady? She didn't limp, she wobbled. I was starting to think this was serious. We needed to go back home to our real vet, Dr. Sorensen, a kindly, practical doctor who treated horses and cows as often as cats and dogs. He would know what was wrong and what I should do. I felt a deep unease. I called Dr. Sorensen's office as we left the acupuncturist and made an appointment for the next afternoon, in Moab. We were going home.

That evening in the cabin, I packed my few possessions and sat quietly on the floor with a glass of red wine, stroking Fletcher's head. I'd had no idea I would live here in Boulder for three months when I spontaneously showed up for my AFF course. I thought about the summer, all the things that had happened—free soloing the Diamond, learning to skydive, flying a wingsuit, learning to pack a base rig. In two weeks, I would be in Idaho at the Perrine Bridge with Jimmy and Marta, learning to base jump at one of their first-jump courses. I reflected on all of those amazing experiences with satisfaction and was excited to have more to look forward to.

But I felt surprisingly melancholy about leaving. I had loved living in this little cabin in Eldorado Canyon, in never-never land. It was strange to think of all the unknown moments to come, stepping out onto a truly unfamiliar road again, just when things seemed on a good track. Unexpectedly, the thought of death crossed my mind as I rubbed the soft fur on Fletcher's pointed ears, and I wondered how it would be if everything just stopped right now, at this moment of contentment and anticipation. Okay, maybe. It could be okay. Somehow the thought of death wasn't a scary thought, as it had been in the past. It didn't seem fraught with a painful fascination as it had been more recently. It just seemed natural, a part of life like anything else that would happen, as simple as getting hungry. I wondered where life was going to take me, what was going to happen next. Whether the road stretched out long or stopped at the next curve seemed equally possible, equally fine. The road would be the road no matter how I felt about it. I no longer felt held back from going down it by a fear that it would end or split.

It was dark. My truck sat outside, packed and pointing forward. I was taking the purple ottoman and the white coffee cups. I lay in the loft,

Driving away from Just Rite

OBJECTS IN MIRROR ARE CLOSER THAN THEY APPEAR

looking at the stars above me until I drifted off to sleep. The next morning, I stood in the doorway with my sleeping bag and Fletch's bed and pillow in my arms, feeling a pang as I scanned the empty space. I'd been happy here. Things were so different now from how they'd been when I rolled into Colorado three months before, bereft and directionless. It was hard to leave my new life. But it was a new life, this life I'd found. I could go home, and things would still be different, better. I was different now.

I helped Fletch up into the passenger seat and started the truck, looking back in the rearview mirror at the cabin and the small wooden sign with the crescent moon as we rolled forward down the steep dirt driveway. We crossed the bridge over the creek and drove away from Eldorado, the smooth iron slabs receding behind us, going west, to Utah.

Chapter Nine

Learning to Fall

Marta instructing a base student at the
Perrine Bridge, Twin Falls, Idaho

The drive to Moab wasn't long, about six hours with a couple of stops for gas. I passed the turnoff to Rifle just after the halfway mark, and then I was on the familiar stretch of I-70, less than three hours from home. I wondered how the grass was doing and if any houseplants had survived.

It was possible; most of them were cacti I'd found in the desert and put into pots. A few months of neglect and dehydration probably did them good. In that time, I'd become thoroughly settled in Boulder, as though I could just live there forever. Home had been hazy, almost an idea or a memory. Now the entire summer began to lose solidity as the highway spooled behind me and the vision of home became more and more real.

When I was twenty-eight, I had decided I needed a base. It was getting too hard to live out of a vehicle and a storage unit. Paying rent seemed like a waste; going into debt would be unthinkable, a chain around my neck. Though I longed for some security, I would not take it at the expense of my freedom. Living in my car and spending as little as possible had allowed me to save a small nest egg. So with major trepidation, I bought a run-down, 1968 doublewide in a quiet little neighborhood near the Moab town park, just off Main Street.

The only thing I liked about it was the price, which allowed me to get a mostly solid roof over my head without being strapped to a mortgage. Everything else was depressing at best, from the sinking porches to the fake-wood-paneling interior and mismatched carpet remnants that covered the floor even in the kitchen and bathrooms. The yard consisted of brown grass, two trees, and a battered chain-link fence providing a waist-high separation from the other neglected yards on all three sides. I could wave at all the neighbors just a few feet away in their own yards. Always private about my living space, I was perfectly content in a truck or tent surrounded by miles of empty space, but I felt deeply uncomfortable living at such close quarters to other humans. After years of dirtbagging it in tents, snow caves, and portaledges, I also discovered that I couldn't tolerate ugliness, dirtiness, or disrepair in my official living space. Something had to be done. A lot had to be done—there was no question of that. And the budget had been busted in acquiring the place, so it was all going to have to be done creatively.

The carpet clearly had to go, and the walls and ceilings needed to be white. I started painting on the first morning. I refused to take any "before" photos because I didn't want to waste a single second taking them when I could be using those seconds at the hardware store buying discounted paint or applying it to siding, walls, doors, cabinets, window casings, heat registers, and the insides of closets. Also, the before was so dismal and so overwhelming, I didn't want to be reminded.

Because of my overall lack of experience with living in a structure with solid walls, I had no idea at first how to fix things, or how a house or a garden actually functioned. The kitchen stove and the refrigerator were daunting machines, with pilots that needed to be lit and filters that had to be cleaned. For the first few years, my decision to move out of my truck into the cheapest possible fixer-upper structure was a nightmare of trial-by-error, shoestring-budget home repair. Between climbing trips, I was tearing out carpet and eternally painting, nervously replacing light switches and electrical outlets, or digging holes and hauling flat rocks from the desert for flagstone paths. Over time, I learned how to lay tile, install sprinklers, sew Roman blinds, fix the roof, change light fixtures, and trim windows, because I had to.

The doublewide transformed

Gradually, and at some unnoticed moment, the place changed from a decrepit, depressing trailer to a beautiful, peaceful home with wood porches and fences, tiled floors and counters, and a climbing wall in the backyard surrounded by flagstone walkways, flower beds, cactus gardens, and shade trees. Six years later, my house was not just pleasant and comfortable to live in; it was completely without burden, since I had no debt and the taxes and the bills were nominal. It was also conveniently located a few blocks from downtown Moab, one hour from splitter sandstone cracks at Indian Creek, three hours from steep limestone cliffs at Rifle, and twelve hours from the huge granite walls of Yosemite Valley.

That was important, because my husband was not only less enthusiastic about home improvement than I was but also less enraptured with Moab. He liked the desert, but for him the sun rose and set around the big walls of Yosemite Valley. Moab was a place to migrate to for the winter, when the snow was too deep and the rock was too wet in the valley. He wanted to be in Yosemite as much as possible—in an ideal world without snow, all the time. His departure to Yosemite took place as soon as possible after the winter, usually around April or March, while I stayed in Moab with Fletch through the blooming, mild days of May, trying to soak every delicious moment from the desert spring with its perfect climbing temperatures.

Moab and Yosemite are perhaps two of the greatest climbing destinations in the world, yet they could hardly be more different. Moab is the land of the eccentric, a little outpost that grew out of a uranium boom in the 1950s to reach its current population of five thousand. Being somewhat in the middle of nowhere, surrounded by miles of desolate desert canyons and a few strings of mountains, Moab seems to have natural protection against the real world. Which, being surrounded by the rest of Utah, it doesn't have that much exposure to anyway.

In Moab you can do pretty much whatever you want, and as long as you're not hurting anybody, no one's going to bother you either. Jeepers and ATV folk trundle along trails next to mountain bikers and runners, dogs are free to be dogs, ranch families live beside hippie artists and river rafters, and everyone simply coexists. It seems normal enough, until you step into the outside world, with all its feuds and people outlawing one another from things. About the only thing you'll never see in Moab is pretension.

When I first rolled into town in 1995, I walked into a restaurant and got a waitressing job just like that, parked along the Colorado River at night, and camped for free. Before too long, I had roots in Moab. I had a library card, a bank account, and a storage unit just off Main Street where I could keep all my extra climbing and camping gear so it wasn't all cluttered in my car, where I was sleeping. I worked my restaurant shifts and went climbing and running in the mornings. I met Fletcher, and she moved in too. My boyfriend/future husband popped in and out to work a few restaurant jobs here and there, but mostly to climb the perfectly parallel-sided cracks that slice up through sandstone walls everywhere you look. When he was around, we tended to live in his big, old Ford Econoline van since it was roomier.

Like any climber who's serious, I made pilgrimages to Yosemite Valley, home of giant granite walls and the legendary Camp 4, where all the climbers live together among tents and picnic tables between climbing adventures. All those tips I got, in crumpled $1 and $5 bills, added up to road trips, when I could spend weeks or months living the simple life of traveling, eating, sleeping, and climbing without running around a restaurant all night. But Yosemite never felt comfortable to me, no matter how much time I spent there. After a few weeks, being there became a big headache of lots of people, lots of cars, lots of regulations, and lots of rangers enforcing them. Simple things like filling a water jug or washing clothes somehow always turned into multihour projects, with drives around and around the one-way loop road that circled the Valley floor, seemingly designed to multiply the amount of emissions put into the air.

All the standard outdoorsy stuff I did in Moab, like picnicking or walking with Fletch, was apparently borderline illegal in the Valley. Like all the other climbers, I developed a habit of skulking around a lot and turning my face to the side whenever I saw a ranger car creep by. It made me edgy, defensive, paranoid. It also made me resentful that I was slinking around like a criminal in America's showpiece national park out of simple necessity. I considered myself a pretty upstanding member

The climbing life with Fletch,
Hueco Tanks, Texas

Freeing the Tombstone,
Moab, Utah *Jimmy Chin*

Outer Limits free solo, Yosemite,
California *Dean Fidelman*

El Capitan free in a day, Free Rider *Heinz Zak*

FACING PAGE CLOCKWISE:

Salathe Wall free, El Capitan *Jimmy Chin*

The Salathe headwall, El Capitan *Jimmy Chin*

Tracking with Jay above Mile-Hi *Jay Epstein*

At Skydive Moab

The gray sparrow wingsuit

Riding up beside Mario in the Cessna at Skydive Moab

Hanging on to
the strut with
Brendan in Moab
Mario Richard

Taking a dock with Mario
Mario Richard

Learning to
base jump at the
Perrine Bridge

"Span," Twin Falls, Idaho

Pervertical Sanctuary free solo,
Longs Peak Diamond
Brian Kimball

First wingsuit base jump, Monte Brento, Italy

Monte Brento, Italy

Running off the
Tombstone, Moab, Utah

LEFT TO RIGHT:

Exiting at Myles of Earl, Utah *Keith Ladzinski*

Freeing Concepción, Moab, Utah *Jim Hurst*

The North Face Route
free solo,
Castleton Tower
Damon Johnston

Jumping off Castleton
Krystle Wright

Mario launching a gainer off the Tombstone *Keith Ladzinski*

Jumping from the Roan Plateau

Jumping an antenna with Brendan

The via ferrata jump in Lauterbrunnen, Switzerland

Mario exiting the Eiger

Mario at Monte Brento

Two-way with Mario in Lauterbrunnen, Switzerland

Flying in Lauterbrunnen Valley, Switzerland *Mario Richard*

Flying from the High Nose,
Lauterbrunnen *Mario Richard*

Skydiving with Mario in Eloy, Arizona

INSET: Jimmy, Steph, Mario, and Marta

Wedding day on Parriott Mesa, Castle Valley, Utah *Chris Hunter*

Steph and Mario flying off Parriott, past Castleton Tower *Chris Hunter*

Wedding jump, Parriott Mesa

Fletcher, queen of the desert, Fisher Towers, Utah

of society. I had a master's degree, I waited tables and guided to support myself, I paid my taxes and health insurance and the park entrance fees, and I was a dedicated athlete. I was offended at being treated like a second-class citizen in Yosemite, but decades of tradition seemed to be ingrained in the culture of the place. Dodging rangers was as much a part of climbing in Yosemite as hanging out in El Cap meadow or lying on a portaledge two thousand feet up on El Cap. The park rangers seemed hardwired to harass climbers, much the way dogs are mindlessly compelled to chase squirrels. I guess they just couldn't help themselves.

The hard-core Yosemite climbers, my husband among them, didn't seem to mind the oddly symbiotic relationship with the rangers, disdainfully referred to as "the tool" in climbing circles. The climbers complained but seemed oddly comfortable with hiding out and being covert all the time. Sometimes I got the impression they liked it, in some perverse way, as if they didn't get enough adrenaline from scaling vertical

Freeing the Salathe Wall, El Capitan, Yosemite *Jimmy Chin*

granite walls every day. Certainly, it didn't stop them from enjoying every last shred of the legendary climbing that Yosemite has to offer.

I just wanted to be free, in every sense of the word—for me, that was the whole point of being a climber and disappearing into the itinerant life-style. I wanted to mind my own business and climb rocks. Eat some soup in the back of my truck at night with my dog and wake up when the sun rose again. Such is the addictive power of good rock on climbers that, even before my marriage, I always seemed to find myself driving to Yosemite yet again, at least once a year, climbing as much as I could before I needed to escape and drive away, as El Capitan, Half Dome, and the whole strange social scene faded into an alternate reality that was impossible to explain to anyone who hadn't experienced it. But in the Valley I was always looking over my shoulder and subtly becoming a social deviant through the power of suggestion, and I didn't even like being there after a while.

So I always felt conflicted in the Valley. It was like a climber's rock fantasy with big granite walls all over the place, full of amazing routes to climb of all difficulties and lengths, a place you could climb forever and never finish climbing everything. Yet the atmosphere had the bizarre feel of living in the wrong part of LA.

And after getting married, in what was frankly a last-ditch effort to smooth the tempestuous relationship, I realized with dread that I would have to try to live in Yosemite, at least for part of the year. Because that was my husband's dream, never mind my painstakingly fixed-up home in the climber's paradise of Moab. So I needed to make it happen.

I always lingered in Moab as long as I could, in the achingly perfect early-spring climbing weather. Climbing is a demanding obsession, and good climbing conditions can be unbelievably elusive. You can almost always go climbing, especially if you don't mind being too hot or too cold or too wet. But if you want to climb at your limit, things start to get more particular. Spring and fall are the prime climbing time almost everywhere, when the air is crisp but not too cold, your hands don't sweat on the rock, and your feet don't swell up in your climbing shoes. Winter can be frigid in the Utah desert if clouds cover the sun, but spring is invariably perfect. Flowers bloom here and there among the cacti, and moisture holds the red sand firm underfoot.

When I was a kid, being half-Greek and kind of a bookworm, I read a lot of Greek myths. One story was about a young goddess named Persephone (pronounced like Stephanie). One day she was out picking some flowers with her friends when Hades, the god of the underworld, swooped up from hell and snatched her away. She was quite beautiful, being the goddess of fruitfulness or something like that, and Hades was carried away by lust and decided that was a good basis for marriage. Persephone apparently didn't feel in a position to protest, and Hades carried her down to the underworld to be his bride.

Meanwhile, her mother, Demeter, the goddess of the earth and growing things, fell into a depression, which caused barrenness and winter over the whole planet. This became enough of a problem that Zeus sent someone down to hell to fetch Persephone back so Demeter would cheer up, and people could have some crops again and stop freezing to death. Unfortunately, Persephone had eaten three pomegranate seeds during this time, which seems as if it must have been months. I guess she got really hungry.

However, to eat anything in the underworld meant you were stuck. Zeus tried to find some loophole and finally decided that Persephone could return to earth (so Demeter would snap out of it, and there would be some crops again), but she would need to return to her husband down in the underworld for three months of each year. Which explains how we got winter, because Demeter perpetually falls into a funk every time Persephone goes back to hell to see her husband. Who knows what Persephone does down there the whole time. Maybe climbs big walls.

I tried. I really did. For six years I migrated to Yosemite each spring, setting off on that twelve-hour drive between Moab and California on Highway 50 across Nevada, "the Loneliest Road in America," to climb those huge granite walls until it was too hot or too cold. Highway 50 wasn't as lonely as advertised, with Fletch curled up in the passenger seat of my Ford Ranger pickup and music playing as the pale mountains of Nevada slipped past, but it was a pretty long drive.

I spent days on the sides of El Capitan and Mount Watkins and ran up and down the trail to Half Dome. I free climbed El Capitan, then freed it in a day, then freed a harder route on it. I walked the trails and climbed the walls in the dark and in the light and knew all the tricks for avoiding rangers and spiriting Fletch out of sight quicker than a flash, since she stubbornly insisted on being a dog and thus inherently illegal. I got a PO box in Yosemite, and a library card, and told people when they asked where I was from that I lived in Moab and Yosemite. But to me Yosemite was a place of strange conflict—tantalizing beauty sullied by maddening restriction, consumerism, and the dark legacy of iniquity that was quietly remembered by the Native Americans' annual gatherings in the park. The place felt deeply wrong, as much as I tried to immerse myself in the granite and forests and make it my home.

The end of my marriage also meant the end of my penance in Yosemite. For me, Moab would always be home, heaven on earth.

Freeing El Cap in a day, Yosemite
Heinz Zak

I turned from I-70 onto the final stretch toward Moab, feeling emotional as the landscape turned red and orange, with the pointed tops of the La Sal Mountains above it. I crossed the Colorado River and turned off Main Street past the park. Fletch stood up expectantly as I pulled into the driveway, where the creeping William vines were spilling over the wood front fence, the rosebushes blooming furiously in the front garden. The sprinkler timer had done its job, and the yard was lush and green, almost junglelike. Inside, everything was just as I had left it, quiet and clean. During my marriage, my husband's refusal to dig, plant, build, renovate, or repair with me had been a constant source of disappointment and occasional conflict. Walking down the hall as Fletch nosed around, I realized for the first time there was almost no trace of him in this house. Being home felt simply good.

That afternoon, Dr. Sorensen took X-rays of Fletch's back legs and shoulders. He showed me the spurs that were growing from her bones, the gradually increasing arthritis in all of her legs and also her spine. The spinal arthritis explained the strange floppiness in her back legs. He said she didn't seem to be in too much pain and to take her on easy walks if she wanted to go. But why would she limp if she didn't hurt? The only thing I could do was give her Rimadyl and glucosamine and make sure she had lots of soft places to be comfortable. I bought the biggest bottle of Rimadyl, the one with one hundred tablets for half a pill each morning and night. I hated the idea of my happy, stoic little dog hurting with no way to stop it. She smiled at me in the truck as we left the small office, an extension of the doctor's house with a barn and horse pastures beside it. Was I just being paranoid, or was her grin a little less wide than it used to be? We would definitely never be running anymore, but I'd lost all my interest in running anyway without Fletch careening ahead of me on the trail. It was time to do different things, and mostly I wanted to do things that Fletch could do too. If I climbed at Rifle, where the longest hike to a climb took about two minutes, she could poke around the bottom of the cliff during the day and survey things in camp at night. She was happy nesting under the truck when I went skydiving. In a week, we would drive up to Idaho and she could lie in soft grass next to the Perrine Bridge while I learned how to jump off it with Jimmy and Marta.

Marta and Jimmy were icons in the small world of base jumping. They had based in Moab for years, but the circles of base jumpers and climbers took a long time to overlap. When I'd finally met them, well before I ever entertained the thought of jumping myself, Marta turned my preconceptions about macho, adrenaline-junkie base jumpers upside down.

Marta was a slender, gracious Brazilian who had been base jumping since the beginning in the 1980s. A keen businesswoman, she had channeled her interest in sewing and testing the quickly evolving base equipment into a gear-manufacturing company called Vertigo BASE Outfitters, which eventually grew into Apex BASE. When she married Jimmy, an equally avid jumper, they began organizing special events for base jumpers to pool the costs of permits and helicopters, and first base jump courses for people who wanted to learn in a structured setting. Jimmy and Marta were revered almost like parents by the many jumpers they'd taught, and it would be nearly impossible to find a base jumper who didn't know them. Living in Moab, they were the quintessential locals in one of the world's base jumping meccas, and they'd been in the forefront of Moab's expansion into a world destination for base jumping.

A former pro free flier, Jimmy had curly, sandy hair, relentless energy, and a penchant for practical jokes. Both he and Marta had done plenty of stunts that might appear reckless to an uneducated observer. But Marta emphasized the "conservative approach" to base jumping. I'd seen a few YouTube videos of guys riding bikes off cliffs and yelling *"Woohoo!"* as they executed sloppy backflips from a bridge after swilling cheap beer. Jumping off objects looked like a crazy, gonzo free-for-all, an adrenaline-junkie pursuit for people who weren't athletic enough to do real sports. Getting to know Marta made me see that my ideas about base jumping were based on stereotypes. Respected throughout the base-jumping world, she had never been injured in her twenty years in the sport. Her style was graceful and deliberate, like a dance with gravity. Listening to Marta talk about intelligent decision-making and procedures for dealing with gear problems made me consider that perhaps those off-putting videos were merely portraying a loud minority.

I got some insight into the mental differences between climbing and base jumping through my friendship with Marta, well before I'd ever thought of starting to jump myself. Marta had become interested in climbing after being so completely immersed in base jumping for so long. She had the perfect build for a climber, small-framed and naturally lean. Like many Moab climbers, she occasionally came over to use my backyard climbing wall, and she was eager to learn about techniques and body positioning. Like me, she wanted to know specifically how things work and how to do things better, asking tons of questions and analyzing her efforts.

As a climber, I was used to seeing quivering muscles, to hearing grunting, heavy breathing, kung fu screams, and near–mortal combat in the effort to slap at one final hold before falling off. Sometimes that's what it takes. Most climbers throw themselves at things that are beyond their reach and progress in the sport by persistently trying climbs that are too difficult for them. Watching Marta climb on the wall, following the routes I'd marked with pieces of colored tape, I was puzzled by seeing her let go of holds and step off before she even got tired. She often held herself back from making moves that were well within her ability. My wall was no taller than ten feet and was surrounded by a bed of deep pea gravel that was covered with thick foam pads. Falling off it was about as dangerous as bouncing on a mattress. Surely this woman who made a career of leaping off tall objects and flying a nylon wing into boulder-strewn landing areas wasn't afraid of dropping a few inches onto a padded surface? With her natural physique and her years of experience in a technical adventure sport, I couldn't figure out why Marta wasn't climbing better on the wall, and I could see it bothered her to let go before finishing a climb. One day I flat out told her that she was capable of much more than she was doing, and that she just needed to try harder.

Marta sighed. "I know, Steph. I get very frustrated climbing sometimes."

"I see that," I said, "but it makes no sense because you have the strength to do a lot more than what you are doing. You're so light, and you have the perfect build. You just need to push yourself more."

"It's a hard mental change," Marta said in her light Brazilian accent. "With jumping, I am very conservative. So I always make the effort to hold myself back, below what I know I can do. That's the way to jump safely, for a long time, and to be ready for the unexpected things."

That made sense. It was the same as my approach to climbing without a rope. When free soloing, I would never consider trying to push the limits of my climbing ability. Rather, I wanted to know those limits and operate below them, exactly as Marta had described. And Marta knew what she was doing. She was one of the best; she'd been base jumping for decades and had never been hurt.

But climbing was not a high-risk activity when using ropes or crash pads to cushion falls. Falling off climbs was just a side effect of pushing oneself. A person could climb for a lifetime without ever being at serious physical risk, and my backyard wall was all about training with no concern for safety.

"I think that for rock climbing, it's kind of the opposite mind-set," I said. "If you're not pushing to the point of falling, you're not trying hard enough. So I think it's a mental shift from your approach to base jumping. When I'm free soloing or climbing in the mountains, I can't fall. Sometimes it's really hard for me to make the switch from that to normal rock climbing with a rope, where if you don't fall, you're not trying hard enough—my brain is still sure that getting out of control equals death. It can be really frustrating for a while during the transition time, freezing up, and being unable to commit to hard moves in a situation where it's completely safe. I've just seen that it's two different brains, for two different times, and you have to learn to make the switch."

That difference was so simple yet so hard. It was like non-attachment, or never getting angry—easy to believe in, but hard to put into practice. Much later, I would live firsthand the conflict between the base jumping brain and the rock climbing brain. It wasn't the same as the difference between climbing without a rope and climbing with a rope. When climbing, whether roped or not, my instincts told me to hold on, and that's exactly what I wanted to do. When jumping off the edge, my deepest instincts were telling me not to do it, but I forced past them with my mind. The trick was understanding which to listen to, and when. That's what a veteran jumper like Marta knew, and what a new jumper usually couldn't hear above all the other voices shouting in the brain.

Jimmy and Marta's base jump courses were held at the Perrine Bridge in Twin Falls, Idaho, three hours north of Salt Lake City. The Perrine, sometimes referred to as "the potato bridge," is famous among jumpers because of its comparative safety and extreme accessibility. The bridge supports a four-lane road, Highway 93, atop a strut-work metal arch that spans 486 feet above the Snake River. It's the entrance to Twin Falls, and the town's main link to the outside world, and it was built to its current design in 1976 as a replacement for the original bridge. Nice grassy meadows are at both the top and the bottom, and jumpers spend the whole day there jumping, hiking out, repacking their parachutes, and chatting with spectators. The railings and the iron park benches around the viewpoints all echo the arch design of the bridge, clearly the town's pride and joy.

The Perrine Bridge is a major tourist attraction, and the people of Twin Falls love base jumpers. Instead of outlawing jumping from the bridge, they quickly decided to encourage it as a boon to the economy. The Perrine Bridge is the town's emblem, and the residents proudly

The Perrine Bridge, Twin Falls, Idaho

commemorate with a monument and a plaque Evel Knievel's attempt to jump his motorcycle across the canyon in 1974. Base jumping just adds to the show, drawing even more tourists to visit the bridge and spend time watching the jumpers. The jumpers themselves pour money into Twin Falls, staying in hotels and eating out, especially on windy days when they can't jump. Twin Falls was savvy enough to embrace base jumping and its revenues rather than to waste resources and time by trying to outlaw it. Though this sort of attitude is inherent in Europe, it's almost an anomaly in the United States. No other bridge in America permits, let alone encourages, base jumping. It takes a visitor only five minutes at the park beside the end of the bridge to see that everyone is happy: the base jumpers, the town, the visitors, the dogs, the kids.

When jumping off cliffs or buildings, it's possible to either fall or fly into the wall, which is at the top of the long list of bad things that can happen to you. The Perrine is considered a safe object to jump since the bridge is an open arch and you won't hit it if you find yourself facing the wrong way. The Perrine also spans a river, so if you find yourself in serious trouble you can aim for the water, which is a lot softer than the ground. Still, a handful of jumpers have died or become permanently injured there, maybe because most everyone goes there to learn to base jump or to try out crazy tricks.

Base jumping was not really to blame for some of the deaths, though—most notably that of a man who jumped alone and landed safely on a winter afternoon, but found himself unable to make his way twenty minutes up the rocky hillside at the base of the bridge to the lights of town. Somehow he didn't come up with the idea of wrapping himself in his massive nylon parachute or simply walking back and forth until dawn, and he froze to death.

Jimmy and Marta vetted all applicants to the courses, and their absolute minimum requirement for skydives was a hundred. They also asked that students arrive at the course prepared to pack their own gear with supervision. Because we were friends and my transformation from a whuffo to a jumper was exciting for them, Jimmy and Marta had offered to let me tag along on one of the courses, as long as I had my packing down and enough skydives. Jay had sent me off with two of his identical base rigs, so I would be able to be more efficient by doing two jumps in a row before having to stop to repack.

The hotel that Jimmy and Marta preferred, less than a mile from the top of the Perrine Bridge, even offered a discount to base jumpers and welcomed dogs. So we all gathered there the night before the course, a group of six men and two women, everyone excited and nervous.

The first day of the course was spent inside a hotel room as Marta took everyone through ground school. Her English was softly accented, with each syllable equally emphasized in the Brazilian style. We all sat and listened as she went through a hit list of the main problems that can happen—facing the wall when the canopy opens, having all the lines wrap into twists above you, losing a steering toggle, coming in too fast on landing, landing in water—and the procedures for dealing with them. She gave explanations of wind conditions, body position, equipment, and, most important, decision-making. Marta told us about a few of the accidents she'd seen in jumping, to illustrate each potential problem and how not to deal with it. She offhandedly mentioned that all the carnage she'd seen in the sport had reinforced her belief in conservative decision-making. She told stories of jumps she had chosen to walk down from, even while the rest of the group jumped with no problems, and some stories of scary malfunctions she had corrected by using the right procedures. She told stories of choosing to drop and roll when coming in too fast on landing, while jumpers next to her tried to stand it up and broke their ankles. Having fast reflexes, a lot of experience, and a lack of ego seemed the key to staying uninjured in the sport.

I didn't envy Jimmy and Marta their job, though they had created it. Every single jumper in the room was dying to start base jumping and, despite Marta's sound explanations and practical advice, most would assuredly not make any intelligent decisions if those decisions involved deciding not to jump. New jumpers were desperate to jump and couldn't see much past that. All new base jumpers were also sure nothing would ever happen to them. I knew this because I too was desperate to jump, and I was secretly convinced that I would never mess up or do any of the careless things that had clearly led to all those other accidents. I'd taken all the steps required to be prepared to learn to base jump, and now I was learning from the best teachers. I would just keep doing everything by the book. What could possibly go wrong?

Late that afternoon we followed Jimmy and Marta to the bridge like ducklings, all of us dressed for battle in our base rigs, heavy boots, moto-cross kneepads and helmets. We walked through the small, lush park just beside the bridge, passing the manicured green grass and small rows of young trees. Jumpers packed on the lawn, while families walked by with dogs and toddlers, asking questions about parachutes and jumping. The bridge stretched across the canyon, a huge arch of hollow-framed iron scaffolding below the flat top of highway, each end built into the iron-colored rock bands of the canyon.

Base students beside
the bridge

We walked along the bike path right under the edge of the bridge, hearing the sound of cars through the metal just a few feet overhead.

On the other side, we all leaned against the stone wall overlooking the canyon. The wall, made of the same bumpy, pocketed rock as the canyon, was mortared together with cement, as thick as it was tall and obviously built to last. I looked down at the olive-green expanse of the Snake River, flowing smoothly along the waterway. Green, bushy trees waved at the water's edge, giving way to slopes of dry, yellowed grass, sagebrush, and dark gray talus that had fallen down from the blocky cliff bands. The rock was bullet hard, obviously some kind of igneous stone, coated in spots by iridescent yellow lichen. The valley stretched out in the distance like an oil landscape, in muted pastoral tones of green, gold, tan, and gray, rising from water to earth to sky. The bridge vibrated above us with the thundering echo of cars rushing steadily back and forth. Marta leaned over the edge of the stone wall and pointed out the small meadow with an American flag posted in it, way down beside the river.

"This is our landing area. You can see the flag, and you can also see the trees by the water," Marta said, smiling. "Those trees are very soft and flexible, so they are going to move a lot in the wind. You can always look at trees to check wind conditions if you did not plant a flag. If the trees are rocking and rolling, we are not going to jump. You can also check water. If there are whitecaps, the wind is about twenty miles per hour, which is much too strong. So if you have no flag or no trees, no smokestack to look at, and you see whitecaps on water, that is another wind indicator you can use. So here we look good, the trees are not rocking and rolling, the flag is blowing slightly away from the object. When you open up, fly to the landing area and turn back to land toward the bridge, so you are landing into the wind. If anything is wrong at all, go to the very edge of the water and land in the water. If you land right next to the shore, you will have no problem getting out, but be prepared to cut away. So remember, if you have any malfunction, take the water. If you're coming in too fast, drop and roll. Don't try for a stand-up landing, just roll it out. It's better to get wet or to drop and roll than to break your ankle."

The bridge cast a thick, dark shadow across the deep green water. The meadow looked small. This bridge was 486 feet tall, so my parachute wouldn't even be open until I was only 450 feet above the ground. Sky-divers think that opening at two thousand feet is sucking it down close to the ground. Jay's rig felt so small and light on my back compared with my heavy skydiving gear with its second, reserve parachute. It was really happening.

Geared up in Jay's rig

We left the overlook and walked up to a small landing between the walkway and the bridge.

"So we're going to practice our exit here," Jimmy said. He climbed over the metal railing, holding it behind him with his arms as his toes stuck over the edge, his rig pushing against the railing and forcing his body farther out into the air, a grassy patch two feet below him. "You'll climb over the railing; make sure not to let your pilot chute scrape against it. Get turned around and reach back to the railing. It might feel strenuous because your rig is pushing you off a little. So hold on. Look up at the horizon line and push off hard," he said, launching forward into the grass. "So everyone practice climbing over. And practice the launch too if you want, into the grass."

We all climbed back and forth over the railing, some people hopping out into the grass as Jimmy had done. After a few minutes of circling up and around like lemmings, we continued up to the sidewalk along the side of the bridge. The walkway was hemmed in by a cement guardrail on the traffic side, and by the vertical posts of the metal railing on the side that faced air. The huge bridge shuddered under my feet as big trucks thundered past. It was a strange contrast, walking on pavement beside speeding vehicles, surrounded by metal, noise, and vibration, with the pastoral river valley curving off into the distance just below. If I turned my head in one direction, I saw the Magic Valley Mall, T.J.Maxx, Old Navy, Famous Footwear, IHOP, and the Outback Steakhouse. In the other direction, I saw angular rock bluffs above a soothing expanse of water, a fall palette of greens, yellows, and browns. It was like being between two completely different worlds, separated by only five hundred vertical feet. We straggled out in a line, taking glances over the edge as we walked farther from the earth, toward the middle of the bridge. Jimmy and Marta stopped when we were standing just above the river.

"We'll jump here so we are over the water, but we are also still close to the landing area. Who's first?" Marta asked, looking around.

I didn't want to be first. When trying a new climb, the more climbers I watched trying it first, the more information I got about how to move up the rock. If everyone fell in the same place, I knew it was difficult there. By watching which edges other climbers touched or moved from, I could tell which were good handholds and which were more difficult to pull on. Being the first to try a climb with no information was more challenging and exciting. Being the last to try it after watching everyone else was more conducive to success. On my first base jump, success was much higher on my priority list than excitement. I wanted to jump last after observing and analyzing what everyone else did. This didn't seem like it would be a problem, since most of the group were eager to get over the railing. In a way it was harder to wait, with the anticipation of the jump jangling up inside, but I felt sure that taking the opportunity to watch was worth it.

486 feet above the Snake River

Several of the guys stepped forward, and a thin guy in a black helmet climbed over the railing. Everyone stood at the railing, watching him intently. Behind him, Marta stood petite and blond, with his pilot chute in her hand to give him a "pilot chute assist," or PCA. This way he didn't even have to reach back to grab his pilot chute and throw it into the air in the three seconds of time he had to free-fall. As his body fell forward, the fifteen-foot bridle of flat webbing would stretch straight from his rig and rip the pilot chute from Marta's hand. The resistance would be enough to pull the curved pins out of the small loops, open his container, and tug his canopy out into the air. A lot was going on in a first base jump, to the point that a person could get completely overwhelmed. So Jimmy and Marta insisted on a PCA jump for the first one to ensure that all jumpers would have a canopy over their head, no matter what they did when they left the bridge.

The jumper crouched forward slightly, his hands gripping the metal bars behind him, and shouted, "Three, two, one . . . *see ya*," as he pushed as hard as he could away from the bridge. His body shot forward into the air, his arms flying straight up overhead and his body arching up in the AFF student position. He dropped down fast. Jimmy bent over the railing with a small video camera, following his trajectory. In a flash, I watched the bridle yank straight up to Marta's hand, tearing the pilot chute from her grasp just as his parachute banged open. We all leaned over the railing, watching the blue-and-gray square fly straight over the water, turn toward the flag, and then billow down as he touched down, with a loud whoop of elation. Everyone broke into smiles, looking over at one another. "Nice!" Jimmy shouted down. Then he turned back to us. "Who's next?"

I held back as each person stepped forward. It was engrossing to watch the different emotions and styles as they left the bridge, one by one. Some shouted with excitement, some were quiet; one guy yelled the punch line of an inside joke as he dropped from the side, making the small group at the railing burst out into surprised laughter. After watching the sixth jump, I felt I knew the sequence pretty well. The next to go was the other woman in the course. I watched her more carefully as she clambered over the rail, leaned forward, then quietly dropped off into the air. Her parachute opened and she flew over the water and then into the meadow, just as everyone else had. I looked at Marta and said, "I guess it's my turn now."

"You got it, Steph," Jimmy said enthusiastically. "We'll see you down there."

I buckled my helmet and climbed over the metal railing, happy to start with something that felt easy. Climbing around in high places was second nature for me, but the familiarity stopped abruptly when I rotated around with my back to the railing to lean out face-first above the open air. I was surprised by how shaky I felt. Though my arms were strong enough to hold me on a rock face, I felt them getting tired on the railing behind me with the rig pushing me forward. I turned my head to look at Marta, holding my pilot chute. It was strange to know that I wouldn't be totally responsible for deploying my canopy, but if I trusted anyone to do it, it was Marta.

"Is it okay?" I asked.

"Yes, all perfect. Have a good jump, Steph," Marta said encouragingly.

I looked down at the green river below and at the meadow surrounded by rocks and trees. As soon as I let go of the solid metal, I'd drop into soft air. It was a strange moment, at once exhilarating and intimidating. In these seconds, I'd make a choice that couldn't be unmade. Once I left the edge, there would be no way to go back. I might reach the ground safely, I might not. It was like the old saying "You pays your money and you takes your chances." In this moment, it became totally clear. The future was entirely unknown.

I looked up at the horizon line between earth and sky, out in the distance. I took a deep breath and felt my heart race as I decided to go. I counted for myself as most of the others had—"Three, two, one!"—and threw my arms up into the air. Almost as soon as I felt myself falling, the parachute billowed open above me, and then I was flying out over the water. Quickly I reached up for the steering toggles and yanked them free. I held them tightly in my hands. The steering lines ran straight from my hands to the back of the canopy, without going through small keeper rings above my shoulders as on my skydiving parachute. If I dropped a toggle, I wouldn't be able to get it back and would have to crash-land the parachute without being able to flare it properly. The unattached lines made the steering feel different, somehow kind of clumsy and loose with my arms moving all around instead of within a narrow pivot range. I tried to adjust to the difference while turning the parachute to get set up over the meadow for my final landing. It was all happening so quickly, and it was somewhat disorienting to be making all of my decisions without the help of an altimeter. I had no idea how high I was, but the ground was getting closer. I could see the dry, grassy stretch becoming bigger ahead of me. At the last moment, I pulled the steering toggles down to my knees and came down with a hard thump, knees bent. My toes hit the front of my boots. The parachute billowed down in front of me. It had all happened so fast.

Automatically, I reattached the steering toggles to their stow points and daisy-chained the parachute lines as I always did after landing, my hands shaking. I looked up at the bridge, at the small figures at the railing. I'd been up there and now I was down here. I'd thought about this moment so much, and now it was done, just like that. I felt strangely unsure of how to feel.

I unbuckled the chest strap, loosened the leg buckles and stepped out of the rig, pulled out the large stash bag, and stuffed everything inside. Suddenly I realized I was still wearing my helmet, and I unclipped the buckle under my chin. The trees were now tree-size, the bridge impossibly high above, its arch stretching from one side of the canyon to the other like an iron rainbow. It was quiet, this span of meadow surrounded by rock slopes to the left and the smooth river to the right, belying the world of bustling commerce and rushing cars just five hundred feet above. I looked around almost in wonder, at this place I'd never been to until I dropped out of the sky. It was calm here, natural. There was no going back.

I looked up again just in time to see Jimmy and Marta drop into the air together with an exuberant whoop, their canopies bursting open almost simultaneously. I could hear Marta laughing delightedly. I smiled, watching them fly together.

Chapter Ten

Jumping the Gun

Running off the Tombstone, Moab, Utah

I made the seven-hour drive back to the Perrine twice more for bridge jumps. On the last few jumps, I intentionally crossed the risers inside my pack job as Jimmy had told me to do, so the canopy would open in a 180—an off-heading opening in which the parachute comes out backward, flying toward the open arch of the bridge. A 180 is one of the worst things that can happen, especially when jumping from short cliffs like the ones in Moab. On a cliff jump, if the canopy opened facing the wrong way, I would need to turn it around in a split second to avoid flying into the wall. By packing to have a 180 on purpose at the bridge, where there was nothing to hit, I could safely practice the maneuver to correct it and see if I did it fast enough to keep myself from a wall strike.

Jumping from the bridge into the air knowing that my canopy was packed to open wrong gave me an eerie feeling. Though it didn't have the true element of surprise, I was still a little unnerved to find myself facing the metal arch instead of the empty air as the canopy opened. As I'd been drilled, I instantly pulled on the rear riser, the shoulder strap that rose from my right shoulder to the back of the canopy, to turn away from the bridge instantly, without even taking an extra second to pull down and release the main steering toggles like I would normally do after opening. This was an important reflex, and I wanted to have the muscle memory drilled into my body. Using the rear risers to turn could save a fraction of a second, which could be the difference between flying away unscathed or scraping down the wall with a collapsed canopy and crashing to the ground. The need for this lightning-fast reflex was a major reason the Moab cliffs were not considered appropriate for inexperienced jumpers.

After learning the basics in the safe Perrine environment, the recommended progression would be to do many more jumps there at the bridge, then to go to a three-thousand-foot "terminal" cliff for the first jumps from a solid object. I was all in favor of that plan, but there was one problem. In America, all the tall, "safe" cliffs are in national parks, which prohibit base jumping under an old wartime regulation against "aerial delivery," which has been stretched and massaged to include aerial delivery of "oneself," mainly because the Park Service admittedly holds a grudge against base jumpers and base jumping. The cliffs in Moab are just tall enough for base jumping and miraculously free of NPS boundaries, but their low height makes them more risky to jump.

This creates something of a conundrum for a beginning base jumper in the States, trying to gain experience safely—and has also created decades of bitterness and animosity against the NPS from the base-jumping community, which is exponentially returned, creating a vicious cycle of conflict and legal aggression from both sides. America's tall cliffs are the right height to be safe enough for a new jumper to gain experience, but the added complication of having to jump in the dark or run from park rangers detracts from that safety. In Europe, however, huge cliffs are about as common as trees, and base jumping is lumped in with all the other typical mountain sports, like paragliding or skiing. If I wanted to keep following Jimmy and Marta's direction and continue on the approved path of base jumping, I needed to ignore the low cliffs all around me and travel to Europe for my first cliff jumps, which did not exactly fit in with my notion of conserving money by switching to base.

It seemed much too good to be true when I received an e-mail invitation to come and speak at a mountain film festival in Poland, which would pay for all my expenses to Europe. I could appear at the festival and then go to Italy to make some jumps at Monte Brento, a mountain with a three-thousand-foot wall above a long expanse of forested hillside. After that, it wouldn't be completely unreasonable to come home and start cautiously jumping in Moab. I felt lucky that things were falling into place so well, even if this apprentice phase required me to travel across the world to get the skills to simply jump my cliffs right here at home.

I couldn't deny that I was on an extremely accelerated path, one that any jumper would agree was not the smartest way to get into base. I was trying to do things right, but I was charging full speed ahead into jumping, the way I'd always done things since the day I'd first climbed up a rock face in Maryland. The full-speed-ahead method had taken me up some of the biggest walls in the world. As a climber, it had always been the right approach.

A packed base rig is kind of like a loaded gun. In two months I'd leave for Europe. From every window in my house, the sandstone cliffs glowed red at sunrise and sunset. Only three miles from my front door, the Tombstone waited, a four-hundred-foot-tall cliff with a perfectly sheer face, split by a single thin crack from bottom to top. I'd walked the narrow path that wound up the back of the Tombstone, past petroglyphs and sandstone arches, countless times. The Tombstone was one of the best-known and tallest jumps in Moab, and I'd seen plenty of jumpers run off the top or fall past me on the wall.

The more I thought about it, the more it seemed ridiculous to drive back to Idaho again to jump off the bridge. The Tombstone was right there. I knew it bottom to top, back to front. It seemed destined to be my first cliff jump despite what I'd been advised. I'd spent so much time on that rock, it almost felt like a member of my family. But I understood that the Moab cliffs are not for beginner jumpers because they are low, four hundred feet or less. Altitude equals safety in jumping, since that gives more time for reaction and to get away from the wall during free fall. On a tall cliff, you might have up to fifteen seconds to fall through the air before you have to deploy your parachute. On a short Moab cliff, you often have one second, maybe two, to free fall. When the parachute opens, you are still close to the cliff, maybe just twenty feet away from it, so you are much more likely to hit the wall if anything goes wrong or if your parachute comes out in the wrong direction. This is the big danger in base jumping, or at least one of the biggest.

A lot of things that made sense at that time don't look so clear from the now. What mattered most, I think, was to feel that I had direction. Jumping gave me that, was what kept me moving forward. Everything else was confused, at best. I'd felt a lot of doubt when I'd first left school to be a climber half a lifetime ago, but things had been simpler somehow. My passion for climbing and for adventure had been clear, simple to follow. I'd made it in that life, succeeding to the point of being able to support myself through climbing, but now it looked like there wasn't a place for me anymore. I'd lost my job and my self-esteem, and I felt that I had nothing to offer. I wondered if it might be time to let go of the climbing life and look for a job doing something else. Take a new direction. I agonized over this idea for months, along with everything else. But somehow, just as I'd been driven to leave academia and become a climbing bum, I knew inside that I needed to hold on, though I didn't know quite how to do it. The climbing life might be finished with me, but I wasn't finished with it. Not yet. This feeling was based partly on instinct, partly on the same deep passion that had led me out of grad school and into my truck, and partly on the unexpected support I was getting from the climbing community of people I didn't even know.

In the aftermath of the arch debacle, and the virtual drubbing that had come from the climbing chat boards, I'd asked myself why there wasn't more positive energy in the online climbing world. It was the early days of the Internet, before people even used the term *social media*. Friends who were more up on trends had encouraged me for some time to start a website and a blog, and to join this new thing called Facebook, which I didn't fully understand, though I was becoming addicted to the convenience of instant communication through e-mail. I did know plenty of climbers, and they all loved climbing and being part of the global family of climbers, being able to show up at any campground in the world and sit around a fire with people who would become new friends and climbing partners. It just didn't match up with the snarky nastiness that seemed to appoint itself as the voice of the climbing community on the Internet, if only by default.

I found it disturbing to see climbing devolve into negativity and malice, and having experienced the shock of having some of it directed at me and my life almost made me want to quit being a climber at all, much less a professional one. I wasn't sure if I wanted to coexist in a world like that. For me, climbing had always been something pure and aspirational, a path to become better in every way. Why share my deepest love and passion with people who wanted to hurl meanness at it? But the negative energy and pettiness that infected the climbing chat boards just didn't add up. These weren't the climbers I knew. Something was not right, and though that loud, malicious voice proclaimed itself to be the voice of the climbing community, to the point that sponsors reacted by trying to disassociate themselves from anything it chose to tear apart, I didn't think it was.

The arch debacle was like a crash course on the power of the Internet. Though the experience was deeply negative, it left me strangely compelled to find the positive side that had to be out there, the hundreds and thousands of people I'd personally met who were enthusiastic, positive, and caring—climbers who just loved climbing.

I started a blog, without even knowing what it was or how to do it, writing the way I wrote in my own journal, and asking people to write me back. I discovered the liberating joy of having my own forum for storytelling, photos, and connection. Suddenly I didn't need someone else's magazine or catalog to reach out to the climbing community. I could create my own world. It was life changing. I discovered that I could help people, and they helped me immeasurably.

I started to receive beautiful, heartfelt letters from climbers and out-doorspeople, telling me I'd inspired or helped them in some way through my book or my stories. Several people told me they were grateful to have found a place on the Internet where they could find other people who shared the simple love of climbing. Many people wrote to me from the depths of turmoil, looking for some guidance or help in trying to recon-cile their passion for climbing with the pressures of a more mainstream society, thinking I might have some insight on the struggle because of the things I'd written. Many people wrote to me simply to say hello, often from other continents, and to tell me they liked knowing I was out there, living the climbing life of simplicity and adventure. Getting these letters meant everything to me. I was feeling deeply vulnerable about climbing, my path, and about life itself. But this community was telling me that I still had a place and I was contributing something. I wasn't worthless, though I'd felt that way after being unceremoniously dumped by both of my main sponsors and losing my spouse, and that strong, positive com-munity was there, even more than I'd imagined. They were a lot more numerous, though a lot less loud, than the few unhappy people writing on chat-board forums under fake names, and they made me feel like a part of something pure again. Though things were unclear and not easy, as usual, I wasn't going to stop doing what I loved. Things would work out somehow.

Harder to resolve were my feelings toward my estranged husband, Dean. With no warning, he had concluded that we should reunite and make things work, and he had suddenly appeared in Moab, with the idea that he would move back in and everything could be fine from now on. I felt that it was almost another life since I'd driven out of Yosemite, though it had been only four months. The life-altering experiences I'd had through the summer, on the Diamond, in the air, and in my mind had transformed me even more than many of the extreme experiences we'd had together on walls and mountains. He wanted to "try again," as though things were the same as they'd always been—which was perhaps not unreasonable, since we'd been in a regular pattern of breaking up and getting back together since we were twenty-three years old. But nothing was the same anymore, although Fletch was clearly delighted to have both her humans together with her.

He'd been jumping for several years already. Now that I'd suddenly started to skydive and learn to base jump, and he'd suddenly decided he wanted to be married again, he saw it all as an ideal opportunity to reunite and start over. He wanted to help me learn, and to act as my mentor, in the long-standing tradition of base jumpers. He hoped to show me that things really were different, that we could start something new together, with him helping me. It sounded nice, more than nice, and I wanted to believe in the promise of a happy future together. But I'd heard it before. I wasn't sure I wanted to mix the complications of our relationship with starting to base jump, but realistically, it was all hopelessly mixed together and had been since the first day I'd jumped from the Otter.

Seeing him made me feel torn in half. I couldn't believe he'd decided to show up now, just when I'd pulled my life back together on my own. I knew for sure I didn't want to go back, ever, to where I was that day in El Cap meadow four months ago. That was a risk I would not take. And rationally, I didn't see how I could try again this time. After living through the experience of being left on my own when my life fell apart, I knew that when I most needed support, I could expect to be abandoned. It's strange to love someone who's let you down so dramatically. I wanted to trust again; I just didn't know how. Still, I couldn't seem to tell him to leave, though I knew I should. I suggested that he rent a different place, and we take it from there, but he found that impractical. I took what I knew was the easy way out and told myself I would just let things unfold, despite my better judgment. I was done with trying to take things in hand and manage them, and to a certain point, the simple reality was that he would do what he wanted to anyway, as he always had. What I had recently learned was that taking action felt better than agonizing over emotional distress. This new development was almost too much for me to deal with. It was easiest to ignore my concerns about the murky situation and pour my energy into the new project of base jumping, which he was eager to join. I just wanted to start jumping, for things to stay simple and good as they'd been all summer when Fletch and I were in Boulder. I was tired of the emotional roller coaster.

We walked together to the top of the Tombstone, on the trail we'd walked together so many times before. Together, we'd made the first free ascent of the crack line up the center of the face, so we'd spent many hours on this rock, working out the difficult moves. I dropped my stash bag and sat on the top, looking around at the familiar view, the brown cliffs and canyons stretching out for miles around, the Colorado River smoothly flowing, the ravens circling in the blue sky. I felt a lot of doubt. Why exactly did I want to do this again? I remembered how shocking it was to watch people jump off the top of this cliff, to see their bodies falling. I wanted to do this jump, but I also wondered why I wanted to do it. I put on my base rig, knee pads, and helmet. I felt comfortable here, as much as being in my own yard. It was nothing like the bridge. As I walked toward the edge to look down, I realized I had no idea how to jump off without holding on to a railing behind me. The cliff felt empty and exposed. I had imagined that I would feel totally confident because of all the jumps I'd done at the Perrine. I thought I would just take a few steps and jump off, but as I looked over the edge, I felt a sharp stab of panic. I knew I couldn't do it. I hadn't been this deeply afraid maybe ever. I was surprised by the level of fear I felt, making me unable to do anything. I'd never been totally stopped by fear before, but that's what was happening. I simply couldn't run off the cliff.

"I don't know how to exit without the railing," I said. "I didn't realize how different it would feel. I wish I'd been able to jump off the bridge without having the railing there, to learn that feeling of going off the edge with nothing. I don't think I can do it." I looked down, feeling hopeless.

"I can PCA you," Dean said. He would be standing right behind me, holding my pilot chute. All I'd have to do is step off the edge, just the same as my first bridge jump.

"Okay." I turned my head to watch as he pulled the pilot chute and the bridle out of the spandex pouch at the bottom of my rig. He folded the bridle and held on to the top of the pilot chute, and we stepped to the very edge of the Tombstone. Trust is a strange thing. Though I didn't trust him with my heart, I had an unwavering trust in his ability here on this cliff. He'd been my partner in mountains and storms, roped and unroped, and in those life-and-death physical and psychological situations he had never let me down. In all the years we'd climbed together, I'd known that I could count on him more than anyone else to keep it together in high-risk moments in the mountains. Together, we'd never been hurt and never had an accident, though we'd pushed the limits of risk regularly and had many arduous and frightening experiences on rock walls and glaciers. In the wild, natural environment, he was the best, most reliable partner I'd ever known. He stood close behind me, holding my pilot chute. Though in two seconds I'd be in the air on my own, I no longer felt quite as exposed. It was the extra hand I needed to get through this moment of go or don't go.

"Are you ready?"

"Yes, okay, on three," I said. I took a shaky breath.

"Eyes on the horizon and arch," he said mechanically. "Try to give a good push and get away from the wall."

I looked out where the sky touched the distant canyon rims and cleared my brain of everything. It was strangely hard to function. All I had to do was step off the edge. I took another breath.

"Okay." I would need to start the base jumper's countdown to get my feet to move. "Three. Two. One. *See ya!*" I shouted, and stepped straight off the edge, without giving anything like a good push. Almost immediately, my body twisted as the parachute started to come off my back. The lines stretched tight and straight, and the canopy flew forward while I rotated around under it. For a moment I saw the wall, and then I twisted back around to the front, flying straight ahead, and the panic disappeared. I grabbed the steering toggles and pulled them free. The large boulders at the base of the Tombstone were getting closer as I flew over them. I turned left and lined up with the dirt road that stretched out ahead of me like a perfect runway, pulling the brake lines down hard as the road started to rush up toward me fast. I landed hard, gasping for breath, the parachute puddling over the hard-packed dirt. I heard the pounding of feet behind me as Dean landed.

"Wow" was all I could manage. I stood there for a solid minute before I could start picking up my parachute. "Wow. I want to do it again!"

"Maybe tomorrow." Dean looked drained of energy.

At home, I looked at the calendar. October 24, exactly four months to the day since my first skydive. It was getting almost eerie, the way these completely unplanned events continued to fall on successive calendar dates, insistently reminding me of when and how it all began, the string of events that had brought me to now. I might be trying to forget or just

Tombstone free fall

to let it go and move ahead, but every twenty-fourth seemed to be shaking me by the shoulders and trying to snap my attention back to June 24, to El Cap meadow and the door of the Otter.

Having survived the first cliff jump, it seemed all right to do a few more, since the slope is always slippery. The hardest thing for me with jumping was the inability to practice new things before doing them. There was no way to rehearse jumping off the edge of a cliff for the first time. I'd just had to do it and hope for the best, literally jumping into the unknown. My natural confidence and strength were rooted in discipline and practice. I found it difficult to do dangerous new things knowing I didn't have any practice or experience to rely on. But continuously pushing myself to break through and enter this new style was teaching me how to go into the unknown and manage things as they happened. It gave me a new type of confidence, seeing that I could handle the unexpected.

On the next two jumps, the extreme fear of leaving the edge had subsided, at least enough for me to execute a decent base jump, giving a good push off the edge and pulling out my own pilot chute in the air.

As I packed and folded my canopy on the living room floor, Dean looked at the clock. It was just before noon.

"Maybe we should do Castleton," he said offhandedly.

Castleton Tower is perhaps the most iconic rock in the Utah desert, at least for climbers. It's a square-sided column of sandstone that rises straight from the pointed top of an enormous pile of sand, rock, and dirt. It takes about an hour to walk up the steep, thousand-foot trail to the base of Castleton, and then anywhere from one to five hours to climb up the four hundred feet of sheer vertical rock to the summit. The only way up is to rock climb, and the only way down is to rappel with ropes—or jump. Castleton was first scaled in 1961 with pitons and hemp ropes by my climbing hero, Layton Kor, with Huntley Ingalls. Now it's climbed regularly by one of several routes of varying difficulties on the four different sides. Many people arrive at the summit, exhausted and exhilarated, with an enormous rack of gear. I had taken to free soloing one of the standard routes, the North Chimney, carrying a shoestring-like four-millimeter rope on my back for the rappels back down. I'd also climbed it a few times with my husband in the past years since he'd become a jumper, watching him go off and then rappelling back down alone. As a base jump, Castleton is about the same vertical height as the Tombstone, but with a much longer distance to fly under canopy because of the long hillside under it. But unlike the Tombstone, no two-lane dirt road stretches out in front.

"Where do you land for Castleton?" I asked. I couldn't picture any large, open space in that landscape, but maybe I hadn't been paying attention in that way before.

"On that dirt trail we cross in the beginning of the hike. It's a long runway, it's just narrower than the road at the Tombstone. It's fine," he answered.

It was impossible for me to judge what was fine and what wasn't fine. This was my fourth base jump from a cliff. I trusted his judgment.

"Don't you think it's kind of late? We'd still have to organize, drive out there, and walk up and climb and haul the rigs."

"There's plenty of time. We'll just free solo together and it won't take any time to get up there. It's a better jump for you than Tombstone."

"Okay." I finished closing the pins of my container and folded my pilot chute into the pocket. "I need to get my shoes and chalk bag, and we can go."

We drove out to Castleton Tower, feeling almost furtive, as if we were doing something wrong. We both knew I should be jumping taller, safer objects for these first jumps, and we knew Jimmy and Marta would disapprove. In the car, we agreed that after this I would stop jumping in Moab until it was time to go to Europe and jump the bigger cliffs. We wound through the sandstone canyon to the large trail that had once been a dirt road. I looked down it. It was narrow, no more than three feet wide in some places, though it had sections that were closer to five feet wide. Although generally a long, straight stretch, the trail sloped up and down and made small bends. Stout, scrubby juniper trees and boulders hemmed the sides in between the wider parts. It looked much different from the wide-open dirt road at the Tombstone.

Castleton Tower, Moab, Utah

"We land here?" I asked doubtfully.

"It's a huge runway," Dean said authoritatively. "You just line it up straight. It's one of the easiest landing areas around."

I turned toward Castleton Tower, the familiar square spike rising out of the talus cone. We hiked at our customary brisk pace up the steep trail, carrying only our base rigs, climbing shoes, and one thin rope. The North Chimney was perhaps my favorite route on the tower, and one that I'd guided countless times in the past. Many cracks ran up the straight wall, leading into a giant chimney that split the side of the tower. Like all sandstone, some blocks and edges were loose, but the cracks themselves were straight-edged and completely positive. It was four hundred feet of vertical climbing to the top of the tower, with three small ledges along the way where you could stop. For most base jumpers, Castleton falls into the category of dream jumps. The top can be reached only through technical climbing, which is prohibitive for those who don't climb much. My climbing skills made it extremely easy for me to get to the top of pretty much anything I wanted, and to feel comfortable there. For a new base jumper, this seemed like a big asset.

We free soloed together, as we'd done so many times before in Yosemite and Patagonia, stopping at the small ledges to pull the rigs up with the thin rope. It was a bit hard to remember that it was now, when everything was different, in every way.

It was early when we climbed over the top of Castleton, onto the large, flat summit. I looked around in all directions, at the other sandstone towers lining the ridge and the faraway mud castles of Fisher Towers to the east. The La Sal Mountains were delicately pointed and coated in snow, in contrast to the red rim below them. Grayish sage and deep green junipers dotted the rusty ground below us. It was hard to discern the contours of the landscape from above. Everything looked kind of flat, and having just walked up a hill for an hour, I knew it was anything but flat. But I felt more excited than nervous. The jumps from the Tombstone had revived my feelings of confidence. This would be very much the same, followed by a skydive-length canopy ride, and I had plenty of experience with that.

I stepped into my rig, cinched the leg straps and buckled the chest strap, then zipped my climbing shoes and chalk bag into the front of my windbreaker. Dean coiled the thin tagline into long loops and fed it into his pants before stepping into his rig. I was glad I didn't have to jump with the extra bulk of the rope running down inside my pant legs.

We hadn't brought helmets or knee pads, wanting the bag to be as light as possible when we hauled it. I felt unusually light and exposed as I walked toward the pointed edge of the tower. A lot of gravel and dirt sloped toward the clean edge of rock, where there was just enough room to stand.

"Take your heading toward that big round mesa out ahead," Dean said. "It's a two-second delay, just like Tombstone. Just fly out and line it up over the runway. Eyes on the horizon and arch."

I reached back and touched my pilot chute for about the fiftieth time. I looked at the islandlike mesa to the southwest, then lifted my gaze higher to the rim that ran beyond it. I bent my knees slightly, preparing to push off hard from the edge. I needed to hear a voice counting to get me moving. "Three, two, *one!*" I yelled, and pushed forward, throwing my arms up overhead as I shoved off the edge.

I counted out the seconds for myself out loud in free fall so there would be no mistake—"One thousand one, one thousand two"—then reached back with my right hand and yanked the pilot chute out of my container. Time slowed as it inflated and pulled the canopy into the air. I watched the big boulders at the base growing larger, then my legs rag-dolled up in front of me as the canopy opened with a bang and I was floating high over the talus slope.

I headed straight out, toward the dirt road, and the air became bumpy. My canopy bounced around, and I pulled on the brake lines, trying to quiet it. Since we'd started climbing in midday, the change in tempera-ture between the sunbaked, south facing hillside and the air was creating turbulence, which happens regularly at Castleton, a basic behavior of air that I wouldn't learn about for some time. Right now, I knew only that my parachute was bouncing around and refusing to stay in a smooth line of flight as I got closer to the dirt trail perpendicular to my flight path.

I turned right and let the parachute fly as I descended closer to the earth. The wind pushed me from right to left, and I felt alarmed as the ground started to rush up. In skydiving, it had been drilled into me never to make any turns low to the ground, which in the world of skydiving means less than a couple of hundred feet. As I started to flare the canopy, about ten feet above the ground, a strong puff of wind pushed me a few feet to the left. I was already bringing both of my hands down to make my flare and didn't know what to do. A juniper tree appeared right in front of me, with gnarled, iron-hard broken branches sticking up like spikes among the scrubby evergreen clumps of growth. Marta had gone over tree landings in the first jump course. I squeezed my legs together as hard as I could and finished the flare, just as I drove straight into the ju-niper branches. A spearlike limb hit my right hip and then drove into my inner thigh. My feet were just touching the ground, the canopy draped over the small tree with the lines tangled in the tough, spiky branches. I felt the numb, emotionless dread you feel when you've been hit hard and aren't sure if you're actually injured, when it's too soon to feel pain. I looked down and saw my pants completely torn apart at the crotch, dark blood soaking the light fabric and dripping onto the red dirt. I stepped up on my tiptoes and lifted myself off the jagged spear of the broken juniper branch. The blood flowed faster. I didn't know exactly where it was coming from, but it was making me nervous. I wasn't feeling sharp pain, just a sense of hollow dismay. I'd messed up. I lay down on the ground and pressed my hands hard into my crotch. There was so much blood.

Dean walked up the road with his parachute over his shoulder, then saw me on the ground with my canopy tangled in the juniper.

"Are you hurt?"

"I think I'm okay. I got blown left. I landed on the juniper. I think I'm okay. I just need to lie down for a minute."

He stepped forward fast. His eyes widened when he saw the torn fabric of my pants, the blood staining my legs and the ground.

"Can you walk?"

"I think so. I just need a minute. It's a lot of blood."

He untangled my lines from the tree and stuffed my gear into the stash bag. I sat up, feeling light-headed, and reached up for his arm to climb to my feet. As I stood, I felt a sharp pain in my left groin muscle and another sharp pain in the front of my hip. I looked down at the bloody shreds of my pants. It looked bad. The descent through the small canyon normally took only five or ten minutes, scrambling down rock gullies and small ledges to reach the parking lot. I needed to get out to the car and get home quickly before the adrenaline wore off and the pain really kicked in. I took a step and sucked in my breath hard at the sharp pain. It was going to be a long way. Holding myself up on Dean's arm, I hobbled slowly to the top of the canyon. I started to feel more pain as we made our way out, step by slow step. I was past the numbness window, and the blood wouldn't stop flowing down my right leg. As the nerve endings started to go off, I could tell that the blood wasn't coming from my femoral artery, which was good. I'd literally impaled myself on the branch I'd landed on, high up inside my inner thigh. It didn't seem to have hit anything major, though it certainly could have with just an inch of difference in any direction, but there was a lot of blood. All the other pain was probably just from slamming the juniper so hard. Like all desert plants, junipers are deceptively compact and incredibly tough. I knew someone who'd driven too close to a dried juniper limb and had to replace the entire front panel of his car. The jagged, dead branches are stronger than metal.

I collapsed into the front seat of his car, on a folded fleece blanket to keep from soaking the upholstery.

"I should probably go the hospital," I said reluctantly. Since my insurance policy was mostly for catastrophes, I assumed the costs would be staggering if I ever walked into a medical facility. I almost never went to the doctor for anything. I either got better eventually or asked my brother for advice or a prescription. "Just because of where it is." I didn't want to say it, but I was kind of afraid of how bad it might be.

"Do you want to go home first and take a shower?" Dean asked.

"I don't seem to stop bleeding. I think we should probably just go straight there," I said tonelessly.

I hobbled into the emergency room and stood in front of the admission desk.

"I fell and landed on a juniper branch. I'm bleeding, and I might be bruised," I said quietly to the receptionist. She placed a clipboard on the counter with several forms to fill out. I took the pen and leaned against the counter. It was hard to stand, and the blood started flowing, dripping onto the floor and making a small pool around my feet on the white floor. I saw her face turn from professionally polite to startled as I folded down to the floor, and two nurses rushed over to lift me into a wheelchair.

It would take seven stitches to close the wound, the nurse informed me as she sewed. A year later an X-ray in another hospital would reveal that I'd also fractured the front of my pelvis on the branch. But I didn't get X-rays because I was afraid it would cost too much. They gave me a prescription for ibuprofen and Vicodin and sent me home. By the next morning I was swollen downstairs to the point that I was afraid to look. Blood leaked continuously from the stitches, which were stretched almost to the point of tearing. I tried not to feel as horrified as I was and stayed in bed for two days, packed in ice and towels, keeping the Vicodin levels steady. Fletch stayed on the floor beside the bed, quietly waiting with me. I was scheduled to fly to Canada in six days to speak at a film festival before an audience of a thousand. Aside from my fundamental inability to bail on a commitment, my career felt so tenuous that I didn't even entertain the option of canceling my appearance and letting down the festival organizers who'd invited me. If I could walk with my legs close enough together to look normal, I'd be there.

Six days later, thoroughly dosed on both Percocet and Vicodin, I walked carefully across the stage of a large auditorium and leaned on the podium for the hour of my presentation. I have no idea what I said, but people clapped at the end. My flights got delayed on the way home, and I sat in an airport for several hours wondering if I should go directly to the ER when I got back to my car. A stitch seemed to have pulled, and I hadn't stopped bleeding since I'd left home. Back in Moab, I collapsed in bed for days with ice packs and towels, not entirely sure if the trip was real or a hallucination, getting up only to waddle to the kitchen for food and more ice. Dean seemed uncertain of how to handle my helplessness, which added to the shame I felt for getting hurt, for being incompetent. I couldn't tell Jimmy and Marta about my poor judgment and I didn't want anyone else to know. I blamed myself for my lack of skill and inability to keep myself from injury. I was afraid that Jimmy and Marta would see my bad decision-making as disrespectful of their generosity in teaching me to jump, and it made me even more ashamed.

Lying in bed, I willed myself to heal quickly. I believed I was lucky to have got hurt in a somewhat trivial way, just as I was starting to charge forward too fast. In the quiet days in my bedroom, I tried to step back a little, look at myself with some perspective. I could see I was obsessed and a little strung out, like any new base jumper. Maybe a little more than most. In only five weeks, I'd be leaving for Europe, where I could finally make legal jumps from a tall, "safe" cliff. Dean thought we should go together, so he could continue to mentor me. We both seemed to feel the crash was entirely my fault, but I did ask myself why he'd considered it a good beginner jump for me when it clearly took some skill to avoid obstacles there. This was just the kind of complication I'd been worried about, and it made me wonder yet again if it was too risky to be mixing a tangled personal dynamic with a start in such a judgment-dependent sport. Somehow I couldn't take a firm stand about this remnant of a relationship. I didn't have the energy to make a decision about it. I watched myself keep going forward without actually choosing a direction. I was trying to make intelligent decisions, but above all I believed that I had to let events unfold as they would. The one thing that had been pounded into me over the last year was the certainty that I could not force outcomes, at least not ones that involved other people. I was well cured of even trying. This time I was just letting the threads spool out, not running around trying to wind them up or crochet potentially useful things out of them. What I could control was myself, and never more than when I stood alone at the edge.

Chapter Eleven

Leaving the Nest

First wingsuit base jump, Monte Brento, Italy

Monte Brento is a grand wall of limestone, at least three thousand feet from top to bottom. A long expanse of sloping forest leads to the landing field, conveniently located across the road from the Zebrata espresso bar. Driving a few kilometers farther will take you to Arco, a village renowned for sunny limestone cliffs, and for the annual RockMaster's challenge, where top competition climbers gather to vie for the champion title on an artificial climbing wall in the town center.

I'd driven past Brento several times before, to climb in Arco when the weather was too stormy and cold for long routes in the Dolomites. Now I stood below the limestone massif, looking up at it as a jumper, not just as a climber. The pale-gray-and-beige headwall curved into slabs about halfway down like a petrified wave, meeting a talus slope at the base. The sheer size of the stone from left to right made it difficult for me to gauge the vertical rise, and the long stretch of trees made it seem far away. Just then, a canopy popped open in the air, and a tiny blue rectangle floated out. The wall was big, nothing like the small Moab cliffs I'd jumped, and I shivered as I thought of standing up on the top. I eyed the sweep of forest. There weren't any junipers. The spacious grass meadow I was standing in was as friendly as a landing area at a skydiving drop zone. The canopy floated forward, still high above the trees. I watched for a long time as the jumper grew from bug size to doll size to human size, seeming to pick up speed as he flew in from the edge of the forest for a landing. He ran a few steps while the parachute delicately wafted down to the grass and stood still with the thin lines stretched out in front of him, unbuckling the chin strap of his helmet, his face glowing. It was beautiful.

The Zebrata bar bustled with locals at opening time. Drivers and workmen crowded around the small bar flirting with the two slim, dark-eyed baristas and knocking back cups of espresso and jam pastries. The café was also a destination and meeting point for base jumpers, the walls covered with framed photos of people leaping off the top of Monte Brento. A digital anemometer on the wall showed the current conditions, and the locals called to ask the girls how the wind looked before driving there. Outside on the patio, the Italian sun took the bite out of the late-December air. Parachutes were spread on tarps in the flat, grassy area across from the tables. A crew of Austrian, Slovenian, and Croatian jumpers wandered in and out with coffee, mineral water, beer, and panini, packing their rigs and counting heads. Twelve could fit into the local taxi van that would drive jumpers up the winding mountain road to the start of the trail.

Being here at Brento with Dean had a strange dynamic, though I had agreed to the plan. I was reluctant to accept him as a base mentor, especially given our unsettled situation. I didn't have the mental energy to figure out what our relationship now was, and I wasn't even sure we should be here together. I had started jumping on my own, seeking out knowledge and instruction from friends, and my deep instinct was that it should stay mine, free of the complication of our dynamic. After getting hurt on my last jump at Castleton, I also realized that even at this early stage I couldn't rely on the judgment of others, no matter who they might be. Just doing what someone else told me to do was not an option, even if I didn't know what I was doing. No one was going to keep me safe or help me once I stepped off the edge. Now I'd experienced opposing, and equally problematic, scenarios of being discouraged from progressions when I was more than ready, and being encouraged when I wasn't ready. Though as a beginner in this sport it would seem reasonable to listen to others with more experience, I realized that, as in climbing, all of my decisions needed to come from me—even if I was in most ways the least qualified person to make them right now. And I was starting to understand that this was all a lot more complicated than simply jumping off a cliff.

Terminal base jumping was an entirely different animal from the subterminal jumping I'd been introduced to at the bridge and on the Moab cliffs. Though I'd been told over and over that terminal jumps were more suitable for a beginner, they presented a lot more to deal with. Jumping from a height of four hundred feet, I could see everything from the top of the cliff. I could count out loud—"One thousand one, one thousand two"—and toss out my pilot chute. My body position had little time to go wrong in those two seconds, as long as I kept my eyes on the horizon and arched, which had been well drilled into me. When the parachute snapped open, the landing area was right in front of me. I just had to steer a little bit and get ready to land. In less than a minute, it was all over, and in sequence, it was exactly like the Perrine. On this high cliff, my body would continue falling until I reached terminal speed, 120 miles per hour. After I left the edge and started to accelerate, transitioning from dead air into the lift of airspeed, I'd need to get into a tracking position, fly forward, and decide when it was time to throw out my pilot chute. I didn't understand this part. Since I'd never done a terminal jump from a cliff before, how would I know when it was time to deploy?

When I was skydiving, I had an altimeter—two, actually, thanks to my brother—which told me exactly how high above the ground I was until the moment my feet touched it. Looking at trees and buildings on the ground, both riding up in the plane and riding down under canopy, I couldn't tell if I was one thousand or two thousand feet above them, much less eight hundred versus six hundred. This was definitely something you didn't want to mess up. Waiting a second too long could mean hitting the ground or a rock slab instead of opening in the air, or landing in the trees instead of the grassy meadow.

Just before leaving Moab, I'd talked to Marta about how I would know when it was time to deploy. She understood that I wasn't asking for a vague suggestion to just look at the wall and go by "visuals."

At Brento, Marta told me, the height of the wall allowed for a conservative free fall of ten seconds. With a good track, it could be all right to go for eleven or even twelve seconds, but if I threw my pilot chute out at ten seconds, I would run no risk of falling too low and impacting the slabby section of the wall, and my canopy would be open high enough that I could certainly make it all the way down to the landing area even if I had any kind of trouble on opening or an unexpected headwind. I hadn't yet encountered wind on a base jump because you don't jump off low objects if it is windy. There was a lot to know.

"How can you tell if it's ten seconds, or eleven or twelve?" I asked Marta.

"Just count, like you do at the bridge," she suggested. "Then after a while you will start to understand the visuals. But if you count during your entire track on the first jumps, you will know you are taking the exact delay you want."

Marta was the first person who'd answered this question with a concrete solution. I thought it was brilliant.

I'd had a long time to mull over my first terminal jump, from the days I'd spent in bed healing from my Castleton crash and the long travel from Utah to Poland to Italy. The final pieces of the jump blended into each other—piling into a van at the bar to ride up winding switchbacks, hiking over wet leaves through the forest on a gradually rising trail, sitting on a limestone step at the top of Monte Brento while people shrugged into rigs and adjusted shoelaces and helmet straps. My base rig felt much tighter than usual as I cinched down the straps because I was thoroughly bundled up, both against the cold and against any trees or sticks I might land on. I had a new pair of military cargo pants with a Kevlar-lined crotch, which after my recent impalement I'd decided was more relevant body armor for me than the motocross kneepads most everyone else wore. I had two fleece layers under a soft-shell alpine jacket, and a hat and gloves. Still, even in the late-morning sun, my hands were

At the exit point, Monte Brento, Italy

on the edge of numb up here, several thousand feet higher than the grassy meadow at the Zebrata bar.

I watched a few other jumpers launch off the smooth limestone edge, leaping out over some thin branches that poked up from below. Everyone had a different pre-jump style, with gear checks, hand slaps, fist bumps, or countdowns. Some shouted an exit count and rushed toward the edge aggressively; others were more still, visibly turning their focus inward as they pushed into the air. It became almost normal to see a solid, life-size shape push off the edge of the mountain and disappear, reappearing way down below as a small rectangle of floating nylon over the long expanse of forest. Everything was so big, from the lake glimmering out in the distance to the pale ridges and walls of Brento stretching out to each side. The meadow seemed miles away as the tiny canopies settled down into it.

I thought about counting, about the difference between counting too fast and counting too slow, about how it's hard to know if the seconds you count are the same as the seconds on a watch. Time had never been solid for me, and I'd never needed it to be. Now it mattered, a lot. I wanted to count real seconds—one thousand one, one thousand two, one thousand three—as close as possible to clock time. I checked my leg straps and chest strap again, reached back to touch my pilot chute for the millionth time, and looked around to make sure no one else was about to jump. Dean was standing back, waiting for me to feel ready. The last jump I'd done, off Castleton, had shown me without a doubt that no one would be with me on a jump. In that way, it was just like a free solo. Though other people might be there, talking and laughing in a group, as soon as I left the edge I was the only one who could save my life. That understanding put me into the place I knew so well, the place of unshakable calm where the only thing I needed to control was myself, the place where I felt good. I was the only person I needed to trust. I was all I needed. There was nothing else to know. It was simple, pure.

I stood at the edge with all the unknowns stretching out in front of me, waiting for me to cross the gate. When I left the solid rock, there was no way to return. I worried abstractly about fumbling the nylon pilot chute at pull time, then worried about my fingers being too numb to feel it. It was a tough decision on the gloves. They might save me from numb fingers, but they might also keep me from feeling the pilot or even make my hand slip off the fabric. Reluctantly, I pulled them off and stuffed them in a cargo pocket. My right hand had to stay warm enough just for ten seconds until I got the pilot chute out, then both hands could go numb all they wanted once they were in the big steering toggle loops. I looked out at the sky to the horizon, took a deep breath, then took the two steps forward to the edge and pushed out as hard as I could, throwing my arms up above my head as my legs drove straight out. My body dropped into the air, and my brain dutifully began to count: "One thousand one, one thousand two"—arms swept back to my sides—"one thousand three, one thousand four, one thousand five . . ." Then I felt the air start to hold me as I sliced forward, tracking out from the clean limestone all around. I kept counting, though the height I was seeing took shape from the slab below, the trees out in front. Visually, it all made sense somehow, just as people had said it would.

I watched the rock as I flew down it. There was so much time. I felt no urgency as I reached one thousand ten, grabbed the pilot chute with my right hand, and yanked it out into the air. The canopy fluttered open above me, the lines holding me at shoulders and hips like a marionette as it glided forward. The trees stretched out below in a dark green carpet. I tried to guess how high I was above them now that things were moving slower and was bothered that I had no idea. My hands were fully numb. The trees grew bigger as I approached the meadow, big enough, finally, to have some perspective for my eyes. I made a few turns above them to shed some altitude and then flew straight into the open grass, taking a few quick steps forward as my parachute came to a stop and dropped down before me. I dropped the toggles, leaned forward, and pressed my hands between my thighs, gritting my teeth as my fingers returned from numb to painful sensation. I hadn't felt that pain in a while, what ice climbers call "the screaming barfies." I should have worn the gloves. Or, at least, the left one.

Rubbing my aching hands together, I turned and looked back at the wall, seemingly miles away now. I'd just launched off a mountain, flown through the air, and floated to the earth. How could it even be possible that a person could do such a thing? How could I do such a thing? I smiled wildly, exhilaration rising up in my chest. A dark shape appeared in the sky, like the silhouette of a jet fighter. My husband, looking like a dark angel in his wingsuit, was straight overhead, growing closer and larger until his canopy burst out. I watched him touch down in the meadow, emotions tangling inside me. I didn't know what I thought about anything, except jumping off this wall. It felt better than I'd imagined it would. It felt better than anything. *Delicious* didn't even begin to describe how good it felt. I picked up my parachute lines and coiled them neatly in a daisy chain up to the canopy.

Monte Brento from the landing area

For the next few days, I rode in the van and walked up through the forest to the exit point with small groups of jumpers from different countries. Dean and I had drifted into our normal pattern of following our own paces and motivations, and as a result we often didn't even go up to the top of the cliff at the same time. I found myself jumping with people

I'd talked with on the hike. I liked seeing the European jumpers gear up at the top, and the different rigs and equipment they had. The most intriguing to me were the wingsuit fliers. Oddly enough, I felt a little strange reaching terminal speed in my regular clothing, though I'd done it so many times in my first months of skydiving. I'd quickly become accustomed to the good feeling of the extra, full-body layer of a wingsuit, and without it I felt exposed. Tracking also made me fall through the air much faster, which was a little disconcerting. Seeing the Slovenian and French jumpers shuffling around with their long leg wings and arm wings made me yearn to be wearing my wingsuit. Watching them lance forward into the air and then slice out over the trees as tiny, speeding dots was breathtaking. I had packed my small gray Birdman Classic wingsuit, unable to resist bringing it, though I didn't envision using it. Wingsuit base jumping is considered an advanced form of the sport, and it would be completely frowned upon to skip straight to it on the first trip to a high cliff, a bit like doing your first cliff jump in Moab.

Robi sending off a new wingsuit jumper

One of the Slovenian jumpers, wearing a large black-and-orange wingsuit with a matching base container, was clearly the leader of the group. He had a boyish twinkle in his eye and joked with his friends as they geared up, shifting back and forth from Slovenian to English with a strong Slavic accent. When he left the cliff, it was obvious that he'd done it hundreds or probably thousands of times, diving into flight as naturally as a falcon. Robert, known to his friends as Robi or Robibird, had been flying for decades, devoting his life to mastering human flight and to perfecting the suit he used to fly through the air. His company, Phoenix Fly, designed and built wingsuits to custom measure, and they were the tool of choice for base jumpers. All the best jumpers in the world seemed to be using the Phoenix Fly Vampire, the biggest, fastest suit on the market. I had ordered a Vampire almost as soon as I had got comfortable flying my small Birdman Classic and had just started to skydive with the new suit. Robi remembered sewing my gray-blue-and-purple wingsuit, a smaller size than average, and asked me how I liked it and why I wasn't jumping it here. I explained that I was a brand-new base jumper but I was obsessed with wingsuit flying and was skydiving it as much as I could. I wanted to base jump my wingsuit more than anything, but this was my first trip to a terminal cliff.

Though Robi was a legend in the base jumping world, he was extremely approachable, with the charming Eastern European manner of natural directness. I watched him instruct some new wingsuit fliers on their exit and watched them push into flight. I knew exactly what it felt like to be flying through the air, rushing forward with full wings. I also knew that Brento was a perfect place to learn to fly a wingsuit from a cliff, thanks to its extreme height and steepness, and it might be a long time before I could get back there. And I knew I'd been charging full speed ahead into a world that requires experience and time to live in safely. I hadn't heeded Jimmy and Marta's warnings, and I'd gotten hurt almost immediately. I was lucky that it hadn't been worse, and I didn't want to make that mistake again. Base jumping was so tricky for a climber turned jumper. Most things were so physically easy, but you could get seriously hurt in the space of a second. It was not like climbing, where you could and should always push yourself more, where if you don't have enough skill, you may not even get high enough to fall. In base, it seemed that I should work to hold myself back whenever I gained confidence. What confused things even more was the contradictory need of always having to push through doubt when I did something new, which was basically on every jump during the learning phase. I didn't know what was reasonable for me, and there didn't seem to be any consistent agreement among experienced jumpers, at least none that made sense to me. It occurred to me that Robi, who was perhaps the best wingsuit pilot in the world and had instructed countless new wingsuit jumpers, was a pretty good judge of whether someone might be ready to fly from a cliff. He'd seen me jump several times in the last few days. I knew enough about him to know that he would give me an honest, possibly brutally honest, answer if I asked him about jumping my wingsuit here, and to know also that I should listen to whatever he said. Based on the extremely protective, and generally discouraging, advice I'd received from most jumpers so far, I was sure he would tell me bluntly to forget about it. But I had to ask.

After I landed, I found Robi at the Zebrata bar and asked him what he thought about my jumping my old wingsuit here. I told him I'd been skydiving for six months, base jumping for two months, and flying a wingsuit for four. I had made several tracking jumps from Brento. I'd done about sixty skydives in my small wingsuit before switching to the Vampire.

Robi listened seriously, then offered a pragmatic and unadorned assessment. Though overall I was new, he said, I was extremely current because I'd jumped almost every day for the last six months. I had good general ability. Currency and proficiency were in my favor, and since I'd been jumping the Vampire, I would feel even more comfortable going back to the small suit. Therefore, he didn't see anything wrong with my taking the Classic off Brento, if I felt ready.

I was astonished to have someone tell me that it was okay for me to do what I wanted, with an analysis that was purely logical. It made me hesitate more than if Robi had been bluntly dismissive. I knew I was literally jumping into everything at a madly accelerated pace, and I understood why those with more experience wanted to slow me down for my own sake. But what Robi had said seemed completely reasonable, uncolored by the uniquely American urge to save people from themselves—a trait that had always grated on me.

I thought about my wingsuit constantly for the next few days, folded safely inside my gear bag while I jumped without it.

December 23 was our second-to-last day in Brento. It was dramatically cheaper to fly home on Christmas, and calendar dates had never meant much to either of us. I'd made two good tracking jumps that day, exiting now with my arms back instead of flung out overhead, the way they are when wearing a wingsuit. I had also intentionally landed in the smaller, gravel cliffside landing area, the "out" to use if you couldn't clear the forest.

At the end of the day, I sat in the grass next to the Zebrata bar, packing my parachute and thinking about my jumps. Then I opened my gear bag and took out the small gray wingsuit. I laid it out and started to thread the yellow cables through the small loops, attaching it to my base container.

Dean looked over from his pack job, watching me rig the wingsuit.

"I'm thinking about jumping my suit tomorrow," I said without fanfare.

I could tell he was mulling over how to say what he wanted to say, wondering how to make me decide not to jump it without telling me not to. We both abhorred being told not to do things, and he knew all too well that our being told not to do something nearly always resulted in our going straight off and doing it.

He thought for a little while and then brightened. "I think you should ask Robi what he thinks." He knew I would do whatever Robi advised me to and naturally assumed that would be to keep doing tracking jumps until I had more experience.

"Well, I did," I answered, "and he told me to go for it."

My cell phone, a cheap UK model that I'd bought for the trip, buzzed with a new text message. Curious, I leaned over to check it. It was from Robi, who had left for home with his crew.

If u feel confi with exit and height perception and pull go for it Steph. It is not difficult. Just be fresh and focus on exit, start of flight and pull time. U have good number of jumps w classic and good overall base performance and it will be ok :-). No worries. U can handle it.

I was deeply touched by the encouragement, and even more so that he'd taken the time to send it. The tick list was reasonable and gave me a sequence to concentrate on. It was exactly the way my brain worked, and it made sense. I felt my confidence grow.

I finished attaching my suit, and Dean suddenly said, "I forgot you'd done those helicopter jumps in Ogden with your wingsuit last fall. You're probably more ready than I was when I did my first wingsuit base jump. But just think carefully. You really are going too fast, and we know that's wrong in base."

I didn't sleep well that night, turning things over in my mind. A big part of me warned not to trust my own decisions because of my track record so far.

The last day of the trip, December 24, dawned sunny and calm, a perfect jumping day. I could easily make two jumps. I read Robi's text message again a few times and folded my rig into the stash bag, with the wingsuit attached.

We walked up to the top of Brento in the crisp morning air, the big group now gone home to their various countries, and I pulled out my rig. Putting it on felt good. I'd missed being in the gownlike wingsuit, feeling the swish of leg wing as I walked.

I used the short piece of rope tied to a tree to cross the sloping limestone on the top, less sure-footed now with leather booties covering my shoe rubber. I shuffled carefully to the edge and scooted down to a small point that jutted out from the top of the mountain, with nothing but clean air below it. Vertigo and nerves made me feel off balance, and I clutched the limestone behind me to steady myself. Standing at the very edge of the solid rock, I felt nervous, but somehow more at ease in my familiar wingsuit than I'd been without it. I took several deep breaths, looked up at the horizon, and pushed into the air. Almost immediately, I tipped head down, just as I had on my first helicopter wingsuit jump, diving straight down the wall for hundreds of feet, with the pale-gray-and-beige limestone rushing in front of me. On that heli jump, I remembered, I'd just stayed calm and stable, and I'd pulled out of the dive into forward flight. I waited for long seconds and forced myself to hold still in what I knew was flight position, watching the slabby ledges coming up toward me, and then suddenly I shot forward, away from the wall, out above the long, forested expanse. I flew for a little while but didn't want to push my luck, so I opened my parachute high above the trees and landed in the gravelly clearing near the wall. I landed safely, thrilled but a little shaken.

I looked straight up at Brento, the lower wall so close here that I could walk over and touch it. Life has a lot of firsts, and in the sport of jumping you can do a new thing many times a day. At drop zones, you learn not to come into the hangar saying it was your first anything, because then you have to buy beer for everyone. The experienced jumpers know to keep their firsts to themselves. As I grow older, some things that would have been exciting become less special than those kinds of moments used to be, like the disbelieving ecstasy of the first time riding a bike without training wheels. Maybe firsts lose some of their shine, or maybe they need to be more profoundly significant to catch your attention as more of life gets lived. Some firsts in my life I was happy to get out of the way, and others weren't that important to me, though I had the feeling they should be. Other firsts remain unforgettable, moments when the fabric of life shifted slightly and things would never again be the same. The first day I grabbed holds on rock and stepped up off the ground, my life changed forever. And when I felt the air lift my wings, and I shot forward over the trees, something unlocked. Nothing would ever again be the same.

Still reeling with the emotions of a life-changing moment, my mind continued on to the analytical mode. I'd flown off the cliff, nothing bad had happened, and I decided to count it a success. But I wasn't sure about making another jump. I was bothered by my bad exit and wished I'd done a better job. Right now, though, I felt drained and wiped out, my adrenal glands depleted.

I walked out to the Zebrata and packed my rig and sat at the bar with a small cup of espresso. I thought back on all the first things I'd done in jumping, especially the first cliff jump off the Tombstone. I was feeling worn out, and it would take at least another espresso to get me up the hill again. Pushing through usually turned out to be the right thing to do in climbing and the wrong thing to do in base jumping, as far as I could tell. But I had a strong instinct that I should do a second jump in the wingsuit, so I wouldn't be left with the mind and muscle memory of exiting incorrectly. I wanted to fix it.

The van ride up to the trail felt even longer than before, but I felt my energy return as I hiked up through the quiet forest. At the top I quickly stepped into the leg wings and leg straps and shimmied my shoulders into the arm wings and shoulder straps. Everything felt easier, more relaxed, because this time I knew what to expect. I shuffled down to the exit point, almost eager to get into the air. Balancing on the tip of the small point, with open air before me, I felt only a touch of fear, overridden by anticipation. I launched more consciously with my back arched hard, determined to get it right this time, and I felt the air lift me as I flattened out into real flight. Much later I would learn that to avoid falling head down, I should actually dive off the cliff into flight, rather than exiting head high, beginner style. But it worked. I shot forward, watching the trees pass below me as I flew straight toward the meadow. The forest rose slightly at the end of the slope, appearing to come up at me, and I pulled my parachute well before the rise, floating gently over the last stretch of trees and then down to the grass. I stood there alone, feeling almost tearful. I watched Dean drop out of the sky, and I thought about everything that had just happened. In the moment your feet leave the cliff, there's no going back. The past is simply finished. And it's you who must fly forward.

Never one to figure things out quickly, apparently I had to come all the way to Italy to understand the difference between forgiveness and trust. Trust, once lost, can't be found again easily, or maybe not even at all. I couldn't live without it, and I couldn't seem to get it back.

When Dean had first come back, I'd been paralyzed by indecision and tired of trying to control things. I'd given in to the simplicity of not making choices, trying diligently to let things flow. It was crazy to have him come back so abruptly, just when I'd gotten over his being gone. And it was hard to imagine life without him floating in and out of my orbit. We'd grown up together, shared more adventures than most people will ever dream of; we'd struggled with and then against each other. I loved him almost more than myself, so much it hurt even to think about not having him in my life. Our time together had been tempestuous and often divided, but had also felt enduring, inevitable, with a sense of unbreakable connection. I loved him elementally, without needing to know why, and without expecting it to ever end. That would never change, I understood. But I saw myself with clarity at last. The trust was broken and had been since the day I drove out of Yosemite with my world shredded around me. Marriage is trust, and in this one it had been lost. My whole life I'd been strong enough to handle anything. The first time I wasn't, I'd found myself alone. And I almost hadn't survived it. I might be incurably independent, but I would never be abandoned again. I wasn't willing to take that risk. As much as this trip had been a beginning for me, it was also an end of the journey I had shared with this incorrigible, untamable person who was lodged firmly into my soul and into my history. For once and for all, though it seemed impossible to imagine, it was over, though it would take months to figure out how to work it out on paper, how to become officially not married. Paperwork is one thing. Stopping love is actually not possible. I didn't expect that pain to ease ever, and as time went by, it proved to be an invisible thread that would never break. But I also saw the choice had been made long before I knew it. I didn't know what the future looked like, but I knew it looked nothing like the past.

I couldn't go back. I would go forward.

In the Munich airport, I texted Robi to thank him for all the encouragement, and to let him know everything had gone well. *Bravo! :)*, he answered back, right away.

Chapter Twelve

The Ceiling Lifts

Climbing is an exceedingly high-maintenance pursuit. If you're not climbing, you're coming back from climbing, getting ready to go climbing, training for climbing, stretching for climbing, eating for climbing, organizing for climbing, reading about climbing, writing about climbing, talking about climbing, thinking about climbing, or earning money for climbing. I'd found it hard to juggle the requirements of climbing even with my simple love for trail running with Fletch (though technically that could be categorized as training for climbing) and the basics of life. Now I'd added base jumping and skydiving into the mix, with all the attendant needs for gear maintenance, packing, hiking, airplane riding, and learning. New base jumpers are like drug addicts, and I was no different. But if I didn't climb constantly, I suffered racking climbing withdrawals and, even worse, loss of painfully earned climbing fitness. So every day was a desperate attempt to satisfy my vertical cravings. Fletch couldn't run anymore and was moving sedately, happiest with short walks. I tried running without Fletch or with borrowed dogs, but that proved to be depressing, and before long something I'd loved to no end became no fun and fizzled out. So that helped the schedule a little.

Winter in Moab is the quiet season, the best season. If I had someone else to jump with, we often went to spots I didn't know, but for the most part every morning I drove the three miles from my house to the Tombstone. It took less than a half hour to hike to the top, and the daily jump of the same cliff was the best possible way for someone like me to learn the nuances of body position and canopy control. With the wide dirt road below it, and a soft, sandy clearing below the road near the creek, I had two good landing areas to choose from. I felt all right jumping it alone, though I knew that wasn't the best policy for a new base jumper. Since mountain bikers or hikers were almost always in the parking lot, I figured I had somewhat of an unsuspecting ground crew in case I crashed or hit the wall.

I craved the feeling of the free fall, my body dropping through the air, and I woke up every morning and looked out the window to see if there was any wind. Going out to the Tombstone every day became almost a need rather than a habit, somewhat like climbing. Every jump was different, even from the same cliff. Registering everything that my eyes were seeing in those two seconds of free fall was strangely mercurial. Sometimes I had flashes later of the rocks growing larger, the road rising up, things I'd seen without being aware of them, like snippets of dreams. My brain couldn't seem to handle everything all at once and let the images come out later. As always, reality felt shifting, variable.

Fletch liked sitting in the dirt parking lot next to my truck, watching for my parachute. She got to her feet, her smile wide, as I landed and ran to greet her, and as we drove home along the river, she rested her head on my leg so I could stroke her ears. Our daily run was a thing of the past, but now we had our Tombstone mornings.

I began to feel aware of the smallest nuances of my exits. I had frequently seen that one could leap off a cliff with arms akimbo and legs flailing, yet still get a parachute out and down to a landing area. But I was discovering that with a perfect body position, the parachute could be almost guaranteed to come out flying straight and without a whiplash-inducing force. An interesting balance existed between the momentum needed to get as much distance as possible from the cliff and the control needed to hit the perfect body angle in the air.

Before each jump, I ran through the first few seconds in my mind, over and over and over, often even during random times when I was not jumping. I imagined standing back from the edge, arching my shoulders back and giving them a little shake, taking a deep breath. I imagined running the few steps to the edge, pushing off and out with my right foot, as I arched my back and threw my hands up in the air.

I counted in my mind, "One thousand one, one thousand two," then felt my right hand reaching back to my pilot chute, grabbing the nylon top and throwing it out in the air. Almost simultaneously, I pulled my legs back and reached back with both hands to my risers as they unfolded from my rig, the canopy exploding into the air.

It was as compelling as trying a climb over and over, looking for the right sequence and economy of movement to perfect the crux moves. I didn't want to just survive my base jumps; I wanted to do them perfectly.

The Tombstone in winter, Moab, Utah

Harder to nail down was the canopy flight. I knew how to work on perfecting the free fall—the same way I worked on climbing body positions—but once the parachute was out, things always changed and moved fast. The slightest fluctuations in wind, air temperature, and height made each canopy ride something new to be handled, literally on the fly. And unlike in climbing, you couldn't just stop, stand on your feet, and think about it for a while. It was all happening fast, and the ground was coming up with no escape from gravity. You had to do it right and deal with anything that happened, or you were going to pound in or land in an injurious place. And unlike in climbing, with every jump you were guaranteed to meet the ground—it was up to you as to how soft the impact would be. Practice was the only way to gain experience, and I was determined to get it. Every day I did one and usually two jumps from the red cliffs. The numbers added up fast—or would have if I hadn't adamantly refused to count my base jumps, almost as a matter of principle.

Usually after a morning jump or two, I rushed out to climb some desert cracks or trained on my backyard wall. My psyche for hard climbing had suddenly returned in full force. I didn't question it, I simply ran with it. I'd missed it. I set myself the goal of free climbing one of the hardest cracks in Moab, the two-hundred-foot Concepción, which was off by itself in a beautiful, isolated canyon. I went out alone the first day and aid climbed up it to fix a rope on it, then a few times a week I used a rope solo system to work on the free climbing from bottom to top, puzzling out the hard sections. It would be difficult for me to complete the climb from ground to top with no falls, placing my protection gear in the crack, but as I got stronger and more familiar with the difficulties, I began to think it would eventually be possible.

I loved walking through the desert canyon alone, spotting the striking crack from the trail, and spending time with it uncovering its secrets. I preferred my solo system to the more standard way of climbing with a partner holding the rope. My system was not nearly as efficient if my goal was to finish the climb as soon as possible. It took longer for me to figure out the hard sections because my rope solo device didn't allow me to go down easily. Rather than going up and down to learn the cruxes, I climbed the whole crack from bottom to top each time I went to it. But my goal wasn't to finish Concepción as soon as possible. Mostly I liked being out in the canyon by myself, climbing on this awe-inspiring crack that motivated me so much, enjoying solving its puzzle and becoming stronger doing so. When I thought I had a chance at climbing it from bottom to top without falling, I would ask someone to come out and belay me. But not before. For now, it was my special place, and I loved it.

I was climbing every day and could finally jump as much as I wanted from the Moab cliffs with nothing to hold me back—no need to pay for a plane ride or to hang around at a drop zone. But I soon started to miss the feeling of flying with the air under my wings. I was addicted to wingsuit flying, which can't be done from the low Moab cliffs. I yearned for flight, even while I was base jumping or climbing, like a libertine craving three different lovers.

A town of five thousand residents, Moab is sustained by tourism. Clint, the child of two devoted skydivers, had grown up on drop zones with his parents and brother and had started jumping himself at the age of twelve. From excelling in skydiving, he moved to base jumping and naturally ended up in Moab. Looking for a way to stay in the base jumper's paradise, he decided to open a skydiving center to offer tandem jumps to vacationing visitors.

Clint had built his drop zone around a Cessna 182 with a high-powered engine, a top-hinged side door, and no seats, a perfect jump plane for a small-town tandem operation. He also had rental space in a hangar at the Moab airport, a pilot, and two tandem instructors. Two customers at a time could ride up in the plane, crammed together with the tandem masters and the pilot in a space the size of a compact station wagon. The pilot had the only seat, wedged between the instructors and their large, two-person rigs. The customers sat between the tandem masters' legs, all of them facing the tail of the plane. The first time I'd climbed into the Cessna, pressing up against everyone's legs and shoulders, it had reminded me of clowns piling into one of those tiny cars at a circus. Clint himself had taken me on my ill-fated tandem jump years before and was chagrined about my dramatic dislike of the experience, so he was shocked when I showed up at the hangar with my wingsuit and skydiving gear, asking if I could somehow squeeze into the Cessna. Apparently I didn't dislike jumping so much after all.

Fun jumpers alone could never keep planes in the air, and without tandem jumpers the sport would never survive. Skydiving is expensive purely because putting a plane in the air is expensive. The cost of fuel is calculated by the minute, when an engine is running. Jump planes cost anywhere from $50,000 to $2 million, and tandem rigs are upward of $15,000. Insurance, airplane, fuel, and gear maintenance are fixed costs, and then you have all the costs of any business, such as staff, rental space, and advertisement. Tandem customers pay about $200 for a jump. Fun jumpers pay about $25. Only the tandems can keep the planes flying. At a big drop zone like Mile-Hi, the Otter can carry twenty passengers. Four tandems still leaves enough room for twelve fun jumpers on a load, so it's an excellent symbiotic relationship between them. And it's the tradition and the ethic in the skydiving world to make some space for fun jumpers, who keep the sport evolving. Without fun jumpers there would be no pool of future tandem masters and camera fliers to keep the industry supplied with a labor force. But two tandem customers create the same revenue as twenty fun jumpers, and twenty regular jump tickets is still just barely enough to cover the cost of fuel to send the plane up to altitude. So

Walking back from the landing area with Fletch at Skydive Moab

without the tandems there wouldn't be any fun jumpers. At least not in most places.

Skydive Moab's Cessna 182 could carry only four passengers, so Clint's goal was to book pairs of tandem passengers to make every load profitable. Still, sometimes people showed up alone or in a group of three, and then the plane had to go up with two empty spaces. From a business perspective, it had to happen, but it was less than ideal. Desperate to fly, I asked Clint if I could get on the plane when there were single customers. He agreed to let me pay as a regular fun jumper, barely covering the cost of the extra fuel that my weight added on the load, and get on with singles. This was easier in theory than in practice. If fun jumpers at big drop zones are second-class customers, I was a third-class customer at this tiny operation, just because of economics. If another person suddenly showed up at the airport wanting to make a tandem jump, I would get bumped from the single load I'd driven out there for. If someone unexpectedly didn't show up, changing the group from odd to even numbers, I would get bumped. If I was late, the plane would go without me. If I was on time, I might have to wait around for an hour because the tandem customers wanted to go up in groups of two and then one, instead of the other way around. And my wingsuit flights were much shorter here than at a big drop zone flying an Otter. The smaller engine of the Cessna took us up to ten thousand feet rather than thirteen thousand.

But if I was willing to accept all those minor deterrents and stay in constant contact with Clint or the pilot, ready to drop whatever I was doing at any moment, I could skydive several times a week in Moab. Since the jumps were few and far between, maybe four a week if I was lucky, they weren't a real drain on my pocketbook. I'd come to need the feel of air under my wings almost as much as I needed the feel of rock under my hands. I'd put up with almost any inconveniences to ride to altitude in the Cessna.

The pilot, a Quebecois jumper named Mario, was quiet but hard not to notice with his chiseled face and gentle, clear gray eyes. I'd heard the name many times from the Moab jumpers and had assumed that Mario would be Italian. Sandy-haired, he had just the remnants of a French

Canadian accent, none of which matched his name at all. He laughed when I finally asked about it and told me that Mario was a common name in Quebec, making me realize that I knew almost nothing whatsoever about Canada and its French-speaking province, though it was just a few hundred miles north of where I'd grown up in New Jersey and Maryland, studying French all through grade school, high school, and university.

Mario had been base jumping exactly as long as I had been climbing and had spent his life skydiving and base jumping, working in every aspect of the sport to the point of owning a drop zone in Quebec and learning to fly the jump planes. But he obviously had a special love for the desert, exploring the canyons and discovering new jumps. He had spent chunks of time in Moab over the years, working with Marta on building base rigs for Vertigo, testing and modifying skydiving gear for base use, and jumping his experiments off the cliffs out of sheer, insatiable curiosity. The desert was in his blood, as much as flying was. Flying Clint's jump plane was a good way to build hours in his pilot's logbook while spending more time in Moab.

Mario exuded an air of utter competence without a trace of arrogance, an unusual trait I'd never encountered in a person. In just a few conversations with him, I was struck by his courteous and respectful nature. Mario seemed to have a friendly or positive word about everything, and though he observed more than he spoke, he gave his opinions simply and directly when asked, with no agenda or hyperbole. He seemed like the most straightforward, well-adjusted person I'd ever met. I wondered if that was a Quebecois quality.

On my first day at the drop zone, I'd climbed up onto the step of the parked Cessna, wondering how I would get out the cramped door in my wingsuit. It was about half as tall and half as wide as the large doorway of the Otter, and the airplane wheel stuck out below the door with a flexing metal step shielding the tire. I wondered how I would get out the door in a stable position without whacking my face on the step as I flew out. Mario walked up to the plane as I pondered the small opening. "If you use the doorframe to climb out, you can stand on the step and grab the strut, and then just let go," he said.

I put on my wingsuit and climbed in and out a few times, knowing it would be more of a struggle with airspeed grabbing at my wings. I sat on the floor next to Mario's seat with my back to the dashboard, the tandem team sitting next to me. I watched Mario concentrate as the Cessna picked up speed and then gently lifted into the air. I loved the feeling of liftoff, the automatic feeling of elation in my chest. I watched the desert landscape from the window, all the familiar canyons and cliffs looking like a small-scale model in bas-relief.

Mario flying the Cessna

At ten thousand feet, Mario turned some knobs and the engine noise dropped a level, then he reached over me and released the door latch. The door popped open, held up against the wing by the rushing air. A little restricted by my arm wings, I grabbed the doorframe, got a foot out on the step, and used brute grip strength to fight the wind and pull onto the strut. I looked over at Mario and smiled, and he nodded and smiled back. I let go of the strut and slipped into the air like a fish dropped back into water, into my brief moment of precious flight.

Flying over the desert was much better than flying over Colorado farm fields. Now that I'd gone from skydiving all day every day to just a few jumps a week, each flight felt even more special. I would drop everything and speed out to the airport if I could get on a single tandem load.

Somehow, juggling my focus between three different pursuits was working for me. Turning my mental energy toward climbing Concepción, I realized that I had been sharpening my visualization skills through base jumping and wingsuit flying all winter. All of that visualization with base had resulted in perfect exits, every time. It worked. But a base exit required only about four seconds of mental work to visualize—the concentration was pretty easy because it was so short. Concepción was two hundred feet long, steep, and angling, and it opened gradually from a tiny seam to an off-width-size crack at the very top. For Concepción, I lay in bed every night, imagining the feel of every handhold and every foothold on the entire two hundred feet of the crack, visualizing my body doing each specific move I'd deciphered, in one continuous ascent.

Freeing Concepción,
Moab, Utah *Jim Hurst*

Usually I fell asleep or got distracted before I had got up even half the climb. I had to work hard to keep my focus long enough to practice the entire climb in my mind.

Another problem created by the unusual length of this crack was the need to carry enough gear to protect it, which was a lot of extra weight. Climbing is highly dependent on a good strength-to-weight ratio, and hanging twenty-five metal camming units from my waist, all of which I would also have to place into the crack and clip the rope into, was not an advantage. I solved the problem by placing only two cams for protection in the last eighty feet of wider crack rather than the eight or ten that one might normally use, to eliminate heavy pieces on my harness through the difficult thin climbing on the lower portion of the route. The physical training, visualization, and full-commitment approach worked. On my first attempt to lead up Concepción with a rope and gear, I free climbed it with no falls.

Only two other people had ever been able to free Concepción, and the climbing community took notice. I was in the best crack-climbing fitness of my life. I was also rapidly becoming solid with my base jumping, and gaining confidence with my parachute skills. As winter turned to spring, I jumped all around Moab and went back to the Little Colorado Canyon, this time flying my wingsuit off the eighteen-hundred-foot cliffs. And I returned to Castleton several times, climbing up the North Chimney alone, using a thin rope to pull up my base rig so I could jump off the summit, no longer in fear of impaling myself on the juniper trees.

Free soloing and jumping Castleton struck me as the most perfect thing I could do. It was perhaps the most majestic tower in the desert, a four-hundred-foot pillar of sandstone set way up on a thousand-foot pedestal of dirt and scree, with a flat summit that could be accessed only by climbing and left only by sliding down ropes or jumping. Jumping was a lot better than laboriously rappelling down ropes, in my book, but waddling off the edge with a lot of bulky climbing gear stuffed inside one's clothing detracted from the experience. Climbing up with nothing and flying off with nothing was the ultimate aesthetic, as well as undeniably practical, I thought: the best way up and the best way down.

And I liked nothing better than something so simple, so practical, and so adventurous.

The steep, switchbacking trail up the long red talus cone ended below the north side of Castleton Tower, providing an imposing view of the sheer wall. From there, climbers could circle the tower, deciding which face to ascend. The North Face route climbed a spectacular crack system that split the face from ground to summit. The dark, sharp-edged sandstone was iced in large sections with white calcite. Huge slabs of this rock lay around the trail, obviously having sheered off the wall. The calcite coating had hardened in drips and channels, creating features that could

Castleton Tower, Moab, Utah *Krystle Wright*

be used as handholds and footholds on the wall. But the calcite was slick and smooth, nothing like fine-grained sandstone, providing a contrast that could be startling when climbing. The North Face was undeniably the most beautiful route on the tower, but certainly not the easiest, and was known to be disconcertingly slick or wide at times, steep and extremely exposed. No one had ever free soloed this beautiful crack line. It didn't take more than a few trips up the easier North Chimney, just beside the striking North Face, for the seed to get planted.

Every time I looked up at the sheer cracks on the clean North Face, I felt a small pull. What could be better than free soloing Castleton and jumping it? Soloing the most beautiful, difficult route on the tower and jumping it. My summer on the Diamond had brought my free soloing to another level. And training for Concepción had left me in better crack-climbing shape than I'd ever before been. I was gaining experience with base, and extreme currency through jumping every day. Jumping Castleton had become a regular outing. I had a system now for approaching a hard free solo, the method I'd used on the Diamond, and I knew it worked. Once I'd started, I couldn't stop thinking about the North Face. My brain began outlining the steps.

In late April, Mario stopped by my house. He knocked on the door in a bright blue motorcycle jacket, and when I opened it, I was startled by his electric-blue eyes. He wore glasses or sunglasses when flying, and I'd never noticed just how blue his eyes were, or even that they were specifically blue and not gray. Maybe the afternoon light was catching them in just the right way, but right now there was no way not to notice. I wasn't used to blue eyes, having grown up in a family of Greek descent. They made me strangely unsettled.

"I took the dirt bike out to check out that feature I mentioned yesterday, the one that looks a lot like the Tombstone, sitting pretty high up on talus. I was wondering if it might be possible to take a wingsuit off it. I remember you were interested, so I took some pictures." Mario took a digital camera out of his pocket. "It's called the Cash Register. It looks too short for a wingsuit jump, and the overall height isn't as much as I was hoping for. But it is a very nice feature." He seemed at ease in his own skin to a degree I'd never seen in a human, only in animals.

"Oh . . . thanks, I'd love to see," I said. "Come on in. I was wondering, actually, if you know how to jumar?"

I'd met plenty of base jumpers who'd assured me they could jumar, using metal ascenders, or "jugs," to climb a rope rather than climbing up the rock itself. My definition of being able to jumar came from Yosemite big-wall speed climbing or alpine climbing in Patagonia and Pakistan, and I had consistently been unpleasantly surprised when taking jumpers up a tower or a wall. Invariably, they took at least thirty minutes to jumar a rope rather than three minutes, arriving exhausted and dragging at the next ledge. I had learned never to believe a base jumper who said he could jug.

"Yes, I have Jumars, and I can climb a little," Mario said.

For some reason, I believed him. "Well, I want to climb the North Face of Castleton a few times and jump it, and I'm looking for someone who wants to go up there, but the route is pretty hard and you'd probably want to jug the rope rather than climb it."

"I'd be happy to go up there anytime," Mario said.

"I'd like to go tomorrow."

"What time?"

The next day I was shocked to discover that Mario could actually jumar. Athletic and efficient, he seemed totally comfortable on the rock and with the climbing equipment. And he could also belay and manage ropes and clean gear after being shown just once. I was starting to sense that he was one of the most competent people I'd ever met. In French they call that a *débrouillard,* which can somewhat be translated as a person who can deal. I valued that quality a lot, especially in a climbing partner.

I led the three pitches of the North Face, placing my gear sparingly as I'd done when assessing the Diamond routes for free soloing and lingering in the crux sections. Each pitch had one hard, steep section that I would have to make solid if I wanted to climb without a rope. Mario jumared with his base gear on his back while I hauled up my rig.

It was beautiful and sunny when we reached the summit, with almost no wind. I'd done a few other base jumps when Mario had been in the group, and I'd noticed his habit of gearing up and then standing quietly to the side, evaluating the wind and the site almost like a scientist or a desert fox, saying little unless someone asked him to explain something. He never seemed in a rush, listening purely to his instincts and the place. I wasn't surprised when I learned that Mario was a legend in the base community. He was B.A.S.E. #320, and he'd been jumping since the late eighties, everywhere from the Venezuelan jungle to Norwegian walls. He'd developed equipment and techniques, opened hundreds of new exit points, was constantly active in every form of jumping, and had never been hurt—the greatest badge of honor for someone who'd pioneered for so long.

Sharing the Castleton jump with Mario was a totally different experience. He stood at the pointed arête, with his hand out over the edge, feeling the slight wind. "It's just updrafts," he said. "The talus cone faces directly south here, getting baked in the sun." He spat down the wall a few times, watching the droplets fall all the way to the base. "There's nothing. We may get some turbulence from the heat over the talus, but there is no wind. It's perfect." Mario described the wind and the air as though they had visible form. He didn't find them mysterious or treacherous at all, but simply elements to be observed and understood, like everything else. This world in which wind and air could be seen like water was another dimension, one I didn't know at all.

I jumped first, flying out over the talus cone, landing softly on the dirt trail. I watched Mario's canopy open, then turn sharply left. He was going the wrong way, behind Castleton, and then he disappeared. Perplexed, I stared up, wondering where he would land in the rugged terrain back there. Suddenly, his parachute reappeared over the notch where Castleton connected to the neighboring formation, the flat place where climbers left their backpacks and shoes before starting up to climb. He was flying a corkscrew around the tower. I started to laugh out loud in delight as he finished the curve and flew down the talus cone toward me. As he approached, he grabbed his front risers and pulled down hard, forcing the canopy into a fast dive. His legs were cocked in a running position, like the wheels of a plane coming in to land. He dropped the front risers and pulled down on the brake toggles to level off just above the ground, toes skimming over the dirt, then ran out the speed as his feet touched down, like a jet decelerating on a runway. Though I'd never seen a base jumper do this, I'd seen it plenty of times at a drop zone. He had just swooped his base canopy.

Mario flying around Castleton Tower

Mario grinned at me, radiating exuberance as his parachute billowed softly down to the ground beside us. I felt as if I'd just seen an elite climber walk up to a cliff, effortlessly waltz up the hardest route there, and then do a handstand at the top just for fun.

"You flew around the tower! That was crazy!"

"No, not so crazy. I wasn't committed until I wrapped around the north side, but by then it was obvious I had the altitude. I've been wanting to do that for a while," Mario said, his entire face lit.

I looked back at the tower, a deep red spike against the blue desert sky.

For the next week and a half, Mario became immersed in my Castleton project, as he seemed to do with anything he turned his attention toward. We climbed the North Face three more times and ran up the easier North Chimney together a couple of times just for the jump. Though the climbing on the North Face was hard enough that he needed to ascend the ropes instead of following my leads, Mario showed no concern or skepticism about my plan to climb it without a rope. He clearly understood why I would want to do it and respected my method of going about it. He was also fully enjoying the opportunity to jump Castleton so many times in a row and gain more experience with climbing systems.

On the fourth trip up the North Face, I brought only three pieces of gear. I climbed up and down the most daunting section of the third pitch, a section where I had to paste my feet on a bulge and reach high for a face hold on steeper rock. Once I had that, the angle eased off and I could get back into the security of the widening crack. But I knew those two moves on the bulge would be intimidating without a rope. The last time I'd climbed the route, just a few days before, I'd felt 90 percent sure I could climb it safely without falling. After this climb, I felt more than 100 percent sure, maybe 110 percent. I was ready.

When we reached the top, a strong wind came up from the west. We sat for a while, waiting and watching, but it quickly became obvious that we couldn't jump today and would need to rappel down with the ropes. I decided to hide my rig in a crevice, covered up with rocks. After a slight hesitation, I put my hiking shoes in with it. The next time I came here, I could climb with nothing. Walking down the trail barefoot today would be worth it. My base rig and shoes would be up here waiting for me. It couldn't have worked out better.

I checked the weather and the wind forecast for the next few days. I needed both good climbing conditions and good jumping conditions, and I also needed the right amount of rest. The weather was not looking perfect, but the forecast made it seem like the winds might be just good enough to do it in two days. I decided to rest for two days and then go for it.

On an overcast and cloudy morning, I started up the talus cone. I'd woken up with a faint scratchy feeling in the back of my throat and wasn't sure if it was just nerves or the actual start of a cold. I decided to ignore it. I wanted to climb while everything was fresh in my mind, and I'd also made plans with my friend Pete to shoot video today while I climbed. I'd done the same on my last solos of the Diamond, feeling that I'd like to have tangible memories someday.

Pete was a Boulder-based filmmaker and a strong climber who was always ready to hike or climb a mountain to capture footage. The day before I free soloed Pervertical for the first time, I'd called him out of the blue to ask him if he'd like to hike up and shoot from a distance while I climbed. With no hesitation, he told me he'd be there, even though it would require a 2:00 a.m. start to hike all the way up Longs Peak, and he'd need to find someone to go up with him. Though I couldn't see him, Pete was stationed almost a mile away on a high overlook with a long lens and a friend shooting stills as I started up the face at 7:00 a.m. When I climbed it again, he shot from a short distance away on the wall, hanging from a rope, while another friend took photos. And when I'd climbed Concepción, Pete was there with two friends, to capture my ascent on film. I'd noticed that even if he was hanging above me on a wall, he had the unique ability to become almost invisible while I was climbing, so he was not a distraction in any way. As long as I didn't have to see or interact with anyone, I didn't mind having someone I knew to be competent hanging out of my field of vision with a camera while I climbed at my limit. I'd grown accustomed to putting in the extra effort to take photos or video, as part of being a professional climber. And I knew that these climbs were something special. My grim feelings about climbing and the climbing world were fading, and the practical part of me was aware that making the effort to shoot these climbs with Pete was a step toward steadying my wobbly career and taking it back.

As I walked up the steep hill, looking at the clouds, I spotted two small, dark shapes high up on Castleton, way off to the side of the North Face. They must have got up early to be up on the wall right now. I noticed the little scratch in my throat again, a little bothered by the slight dent in my energy level. I decided to focus instead on the nice feeling of walking up the hill, carrying nothing but my shoes and chalk bag. It was so easy to walk without the weight of gear or ropes or a base rig.

I listened to music on my iShuffle, walking to the mellow beat. I had some doubts. Maybe today wasn't the day. I felt a touch sick, and the clouds looked threatening. A slight breeze came up. It was only seven, early for wind to come in. Maybe the weather forecast was wrong. It would be a real shame to make the climb and not get to make the jump, the second half of the arc of travel. I reached the base of the North Face and sat below the long, clean dihedral. A fist-size crack started in front of me and stretched up a large corner for a hundred feet. At the top was the first crux of the climb, leaving the fist crack and stepping my feet out onto the white calcite as I grabbed the underside of a sharp flake, shuffling up and right into a much thinner crack.

I looked at the sky and looked up at the wall, felt the sides of my throat with my fingers, swallowing a few times. It's always so hard to know how you feel when you are deciding to go up. In the past, I've nearly always felt almost sick before a big climb or worn out from a sleepless night before it. When I stood below El Capitan, dwarfed by the three-thousand-foot wall, preparing to free climb it in a day, my stomach was in tight knots. I knew that if I fell at any time in the twenty-four hours of difficult climbing, I would probably be caught by my rope, but I would not succeed in my dream of freeing the wall in a day. The pressure would grow with each pitch that I finished, and I felt almost sick with anticipation, doubt, hope, and excitement as I racked my gear and tied into the rope. It's a strange moment, the last moment before setting off on a dream route, putting hands on the first holds, stepping off the ground and onto the rock, knowing that the decision has been made. From that moment, everything in the world will be about the climb, for however many hours or days it takes.

I put my back to the start of the North Face route, leaning against the smooth, skinlike sandstone of Castleton while I taped my hands with white athletic tape, as I always did when climbing cracks. It would be a while before I reached the top. The wind and clouds might pass. Walking down seemed like a terrible option. I was here. I'd thought about this moment for days. I was 110 percent ready, and if I rested for another day or two, I would lose that readiness. Especially if I came down with a cold. I didn't feel as energetic as I wanted to feel, but when had I ever felt perfect before starting up a climb like this? I smoothed down each layer of the tape, making sure it was stuck perfectly to my skin with no wrinkles, not binding too tightly on my wrists. I pulled the tabs on the backs of my rock shoes to get my heels in and stood up, reaching to remove my earbuds, then stopped. I liked the relaxing vibe of the music, the way it kept my thoughts from wandering to places they didn't belong. A crutch, maybe, but I would use it. I had a stick of gum in my pocket too. Along with lip balm, it was my lightweight alternative to carrying water. I put the gum in my mouth and started chewing, feeling nonchalant, teenaged.

I put my hands in the crack, watching the bright white tape slide into the dark sandstone. I flexed my fists and felt the familiar catch of the flat planes against the backs of my hands. I slotted my foot in high and stood. My other foot left the ground.

Free soloing the North Face route, Castleton Tower *Damon Johnston*

I climbed rhythmically up the long corner, making sure that each hand and each foot was solid and buried in the crack. At the top of the crack, the white calcite flake hung down, sealing off the crack. I grabbed the sharp underside of the flake with one hand and buried my other deep in the back of it and stepped my feet out onto textureless calcite lumps below it, leaving the security of the crack. As I crossed my left foot over my right leg, walking my body to the right, my right foot stepped on my loose pant leg. I'd forgotten to roll up my pants before I started climbing. My shoe skated on the fabric, and both hands instinctively clamped down with an adrenalized death grip as I quickly replaced my foot on a smooth knob of calcite, nudging my loose pant leg aside with my toe. I climbed quickly across the flake and into the security of the steep, thin crack above it, locking down hard with my arms as I topped out onto the big, flat ledge. Immediately I sat down and rolled up my pants. I felt drained. Two more hard sections awaited me, one on each pitch above. I couldn't afford to make any more mistakes like that. I sat for a long time, with my back to the wall, looking out at the desert towers and walls out in the distance. The sky seemed to be clearing slightly. I stood up and put my hands into the crack, stepped my feet off the ledge, and started up the second pitch.

I sat on another good ledge below the third pitch for a while. I'd run this section over in my mind all night last night, the moves where I had to leave the crack and climb over the bulge before getting back in, the section where falling off seemed the most possible. I sat until I felt sure I was completely relaxed, mind clear. I knew I could climb this. There was nothing to fear. I stood up slowly and started to breathe deeply. I crossed over a few loose blocks at the end of the ledge and stepped into the wide crack. I hung off my flexed hands in the bulge and then committed, pushing my body out and up with my legs, reaching high for the small, right handhold, getting my left foot levered up into the crack. I pulled myself in with my leg as I pulled hard with my right hand, felt the flow of relief as I buried my hands in the rock, and wriggled in as the crack got wider and wider. Now I would definitely never fall. Pleasure filled my body as my hands reached the flat edge of the top.

On the summit, I felt a mix between relief and satisfaction, a good feeling. The clouds had cleared and the wind had gone quiet. I'd been right to press on, through the doubt and uncertainty down below. I pulled my rig out from its crevice and put on my windbreaker. I zipped my climbing shoes and chalk bag into the front and stepped into the base rig, cinching the straps down as I walked toward the southwest arête.

I knelt at the exit point and spat to make sure there was no wind down the tower. The clouds were preventing even the updrafts I'd felt on sunny days. It was perfect. I could just make out my red-and-yellow flag far down below on the trail, lifting lightly from right to left. It was time. I stood at the pointed edge, head high and shoulders back, took a deep breath, and stepped off the edge, shoving hard with my left foot. The arête rushed below me and the big square boulders grew fast. I threw out my pilot chute, the canopy banged open, and Castleton receded behind me. I landed softly, gathered up my parachute, and walked out to my truck. I had done it.

Of all the climbs I'd done and would still do in my life, all the first ascents, big walls, and alpine routes, this climb of Castleton seemed certain to remain my favorite. No one had free soloed the North Face before, but that wasn't what made it stand out to me, the cachet of being the first to do something. That had never been a big motivator for me. I had also never liked stunts, or anything that struck me as contrived. Free soloing a spire that can be ascended only through technical climbing and descending by parachute, completely eliminating the rope, seemed to me like the most practical and elegant thing possible. I loved what I had done on the North Face of Castleton, this "free solo base climb" if it had to be named, because to me it seemed to be a combination of the perfect climb, the perfect jump, and the perfect tower. From beginning to end, it was perfectly beautiful and perfectly practical.

The experiences on Castleton with Mario had been perfect too. He made me feel grounded yet filled with energy, with his warm smile and candid blue eyes that sometimes were gray. I liked the way he saw the world as an endlessly enjoyable place filled with puzzles to be solved, and the way he gave his full attention to whatever he was doing and free rein to his imagination at all times. He was an unusual blend of engineer, adventurer, and dreamer, both passionate and meticulous. Above all, Mario struck me as simply a good person, the kind of person who makes others want to be better just by being himself. I didn't feel recovered at all from the sorrow of my failed marriage and hadn't even yet figured out how people organized divorces. But I couldn't help but notice that being around Mario felt wonderful.

The first thing Mario said when I told him I'd made it was that he'd had an idea for Pete's footage, to make it even better. He suggested that I go up Castleton again, by the easy North Chimney, which I could scamper up quickly, and jump it again for an aerial shot. He would fly the jump plane past the exit point at the precise moment I was ready to jump, with the cargo door open for the video camera to stick out. I'd clip a radio to my chest so he could talk to me as he approached. It would have to be perfectly choreographed by all of us, with just one chance to line everything up perfectly in a single second to get the shot. We all loved the idea. I hiked up the next morning and quickly climbed the North Chimney to the top, tugging my base rig up behind me on the thin rope. As I stood on the summit, cinching the straps on my rig, I heard the buzz of the 182 approaching from the west. I stood on top of the southwest corner, watching the plane come near, waiting for the exact moment it would pass by as Mario's voice came over the radio giving me a count-down. I pushed off the edge just as the Cessna shot past me, shockingly close. I tossed my pilot chute out, and my canopy banged open. The plane banked and headed back, looping back and forth around me, so close that I could see the big video camera lens pointing out of the open cargo door on each pass. I didn't have to see Mario's face to know that he was enjoying this immensely.

I turned toward my flag, over the runway that now seemed like an enormous and easy landing area, and touched down gently in the slight headwind. The engine grew loud as the plane buzzed low, whooshing dra-matically right over my head, then swooping up steeply and heading off to the west, growing quieter as I laughed and waved. It was silent again. I stood there, looking into the sky, and smiled. I felt so happy, so light.

Pushing myself in my activities was part of me, so I never questioned my motivation to do "extreme things." But I could see the different emotional states my climbs expressed. I could admit to myself now that free soloing the Diamond was born in large part of despair and grief, though it had ultimately lifted me free of them. Free soloing and jumping Castleton was completely different. It felt like a celebration of a new life. It was hard to believe that just a year ago I was at the lowest point I'd ever been. Things will always change—it's the one thing we can count on. I knew this deeply now because I'd lived it, and that seemed to be the only way for me to truly understand a thing. The world was opening like clear sky all around.

Chapter Thirteen

ℋit Me One More Time

Jumping the Roan Plateau, Rifle, Colorado *Mario Richard*

Time had returned to its normal, mercurial rhythm as spring flowed into summer, shifting and swirling like water. Jumping drank me in completely. I traveled around Utah, Colorado, California, and Arizona, flying my wingsuit off cliffs both legal and illegal, antennae, and airplanes, or jumping without it if the cliffs were short. The more I jumped, the more I wanted to jump, with an insatiable thirst that only intensified with each deep draft. Perhaps jumping is an addiction, but it seemed no different from the first ten years of climbing, when climbing is all you want to do all the time.

The biggest problem with the States is our general lack of limestone. America's limestone cliffs tend to be both rare and hard to get at. Italy, Switzerland, Norway, Austria, and France are basically dripping with walls and mountains of the stuff, like a countess covered in diamonds. For both rock climbers and base jumpers, limestone is just as coveted. America has a few pockets, mostly in remote parts of Wyoming, Colorado, Utah, and Nevada, and mostly shortish and of mediocre quality or else hard to access. Climbers have to be motivated to venture out into the wilds, sniff out the usually disappointingly small cliffs, pry off the loose chunks of rock, and drill in bolts for protection. Base jumpers have to be equally motivated to orienteer to the top of the few tall cliffs that can be found way out in the desert, and to be either skilled or optimistic enough to maneuver down to the rugged, rocky landing spots below them. No cable cars, paint-marked hiking trails, or cow pastures frame these faces. So the geology around Rifle, Colorado, is nothing short of a miracle, an unexpected trove of limestone that is fully accessible, good for climbing, and good for jumping.

I'd driven along I-70 between Rifle and Moab countless times, looking at the looming limestone ridgeline beside the highway. The Roan Plateau, sixty-seven thousand acres of wilderness around the town of Rifle, is controlled by the Bureau of Land Management, which means no restrictions against climbing or base jumping, or anything really. Thanks to hunters and outdoorspeople, and to the oil and gas drilling all over the plateau, dirt roads wind up and around seemingly everywhere. For climbing, the Roan cliffs are worthless since the outer skin of limestone is crumbling off the steep faces. For jumping, they are ideal—six hundred vertical feet of overhanging, crumbling limestone situated atop another thousand-plus feet of steep terrain below them.

Just off highway I-70, at the West Rifle exit, the road leads past the one-street town of Rifle with its handful of motels, cafés, and liquor stores. It continues past a few small ranches, an unexpected golf course, a reservoir dam, then curves and climbs along green pastures of white-faced black cows and palominos. Scrubby ridges line the valley as the incline steepens. The road narrows, past rows of cement water troughs at the trout hatchery, then takes an abrupt left curve so sharp you could miss it and launch straight out into the creek valley. The road suddenly turns to dirt, and things slow down. Green, leafy trees, cattails, and wild rosebushes line the creek and shelter the road. The cliffs form a continuous wall of rock on each side, bending and curving along the canyon, steep and undulating, pale orange streaked with gray.

Climbing at Rifle, Colorado *Jimmy Chin*

In this quiet canyon, rock climbers have discovered a lifetime's worth of difficult, technical limestone climbing, and many Rifle climbers have devoted their entire lives to climbing only on these walls, with astonishing results. Even a long sport route is usually no more than a hundred feet in length, so the cliffs are more than doubly as tall as they need to be. The quantity, variety, and difficulty of the short, bolted climbs here are impressive. Even more impressive is the ease of access to the routes. Several main climbing sectors have been developed in Rifle, and climbers park in small dirt areas in front of the sectors and are faced with about a twenty-second walk to the bottom of the routes. For me, Rifle had always been the ultimate rock-climbing paradise. I would never achieve greatness there, as the short, gymnastic face climbs were almost the polar opposite of my particular strength as a climber, and I invariably left almost as soon as I'd built the notorious Rifle-specific fitness base. But I loved it there, that small haven from the outside world, where life was simple and pure. When Moab started to lose the coolness of early spring, my thoughts always turned to Rifle.

Rifle is a haven for dogs too, a place where almost every climber is accompanied by a canine. And it turned out to be perhaps the best place in the world for a retired dog. At Rifle, I could climb as much as I wanted, and even at her slowing pace, Fletch could handle the twenty-second walk to most of the climbs. Mornings and evenings at the campsite were relaxing, Fletch lying in the grass near the creek, occasionally getting up to sniff something nearby. I couldn't ignore her growing arthritis, as her limp was becoming more pronounced.

If climbing was woven into my DNA, Fletch was one of the helices. In the past, she had been almost a role model for me, a rare creature in being even more independent than I was. Now she seemed to need my presence, as well as a lot of help getting up the front steps and in and out of the truck. For years I'd firmly believed that since Fletcher was mostly cattle dog, she would surely break the longevity record supposedly set around the turn of the century by Bluey, a heeler who had herded cows up until his death at age twenty-nine and a half. Now I wasn't so sure. Things had changed fast just in the last few months, and Fletch was only thirteen. Celebrating her thirtieth birthday was starting to look like a pipe dream. In the past I'd always wished I could spend more time climbing in Rifle. Now, with Fletch's parameters having shrunk so dramatically, I completely dropped the idea of going anywhere else. In Rifle, we could be together, at the cliffs all day and camping all night. And then there was the Roan Plateau, an impressive and remote jump site, an hour's drive away on the bumpy dirt roads but just a few miles as the crow flew.

Mario was flying the jump plane in Moab most days, but managed to get two days off in a row as soon as I mentioned the Roan cliffs to him. He'd driven on that stretch of I-70 many times, and the cliffs were impossible not to notice. We drove out, following scribbled instructions I'd got over the phone from a friend who'd discovered the site. The truck bounced and rattled up dirt roads, gradually climbing higher over precipitous switchbacks. The scrubby sagebrush and pale dust gave way to aspen groves and yellow flowers as we gained altitude. The directions were precise yet still confusing, with several turns and loops at complicated junctures, causing us to backtrack several times. The forty-five-minute drive had become well over an hour by the time we crested the plateau and drove to the cliff's edge. It would be easy to launch right off, Thelma and Louise style.

The Roan Plateau

Aspen leaves trembled in the slight breeze, and green fields of grass and flowers swept around us, the rock walls stretching down underneath, pale and sheer, to a long talus field. The place was completely deserted. It gave me chills to see the pale rock curving around us below. Fletch settled comfortably into the soft grass as we walked out along the edge of the cliff. Large, flat plates of rock were stacked on top of each other, held in place by a mortar of dried clay and littered with small, flat, shale-like fragments. They clinked and tinkled under my boots. It wasn't hard to imagine an entire shelf suddenly giving way and hurtling off the edge into the air. We stood on a solid-looking ledge and looked down at the rugged, contoured landscape. The Roan Plateau stretched all around, scrubby sage and rock chips underfoot, with wildflowers and aspens blooming wildly. The exfoliating walls curved below, an enormous am-phitheater of limestone perched atop a thousand feet of shifting talus. Jagged rock formations and scrubby trees made up the complicated land-scape that fed into a ravine at the very bottom. Everything poured down to a dry, tight canyon, like a huge arena.

I couldn't see anywhere flat or open for landing and couldn't spot the orange windsock that my friend said he'd set up in the single spot that was safe for landing. Mario pointed out one small place of a slightly different color that looked as if it might be the landing area. I'd made a practice of walking around the landing area before going up for a jump. Here, I couldn't even see the landing area in the complicated terrain, a couple of thousand feet below. Only one of us could jump because the other person would have to drive back down the dirt road, out around to the front of the plateau to the highway, and then up more dirt roads to pick up the jumper. The jumper would have some scrambling to do in the meantime, picking a way down the tight, scruffy canyon until it opened out on the road. Overall, it was an extremely intimidating place, nothing at all like anywhere I'd jumped before. I was more than happy to take my turn as the driver.

Mario didn't look intimidated; he looked keenly interested. Trying to figure out the best spot to jump and where to land in this convoluted landscape was merely an engaging exploration, like the ones he'd been doing for twenty years. He sat at the edge, observing the area, taking in the shapes and the contours, absorbing the air and height. I could almost see the gears clicking in his brain. Finally he got up and walked back to the car for his base rig.

"I think it looks good, there's really no wind. Is it all right if I jump?"

"Of course," I said. "Honestly, I don't really want to jump right now anyway. It's strange not knowing the landing area. Well, not even being able to see the landing area."

"It is intimidating! It's a big place." He stepped into his leg loops and cinched them tight.

"So you'll walk out and I'll drive around and figure out how to drive in to where you'll come out. It'll probably be an hour, at least."

"That's fine, I'll need to find the walk out anyway."

"Do you have your radio?"

"Yes, we should turn them on now, and also in about an hour in case we need to communicate when you're driving in."

Mario stood at the edge in his rig and helmet, backed up a few steps, and ran out into the air, launching way out with a forceful push, his legs bent wildly as he rode the air. I watched him drop from life size to doll size and become a bright red square of nylon, flying out over the gray slopes. He seemed to stay airborne forever, flying around the sides of the steep canyon walls, over rock outcroppings and small forested areas, then finally zeroing into the small spot he'd picked out from above. The canopy floated down, barely big enough to see from up here, and Mario's voice came over the radio, almost gasping with excitement.

"Woooooohhhhhhh. Whoa. Unbelievable. Just unbelievable!"

"Nice one!" I laughed happily. "How's the landing area?"

"Small. It wouldn't take much to clean the place up, but there are lots of rocks around. Very three-dimensional. The windsock is here, but it's pretty torn up." He breathed out with a long, shivery sound through the plastic radio. "I'm just soaking it in right now!"

Mario often had a lovely way of phrasing things, perhaps due to being born a French speaker with English as his second language. He once commented that skydiving is all about emotion. He was right, I thought, intrigued. Skydiving serves no practical purpose whatsoever. When an airplane hangar is quiet and empty, it's as though nothing ever happened there. But in the height of a jumping day, the air is filled with energy and intensity. Motion is in every space and time. In the airplanes, in the landing areas, emotion is thick and tangible. People are lit up, buzzing with feeling—fear, joy, satisfaction, desire. It's the same for every person at every drop zone, whether first-time tandem passenger, veteran fun jumper, or pilot.

Certainly, this infectious emotion was why Mario had dedicated his life to jumping. He was an intriguing mix of precision and passion, his feet on the earth and his head in the sky, and he was perhaps the most genuine individual I'd ever met, right up there with Fletch. Being around him just made me want to be around him more. It was a strange experience because I was starting to realize I'd never had it before, at least not with a person. I didn't feel recovered at all from my failed marriage, and romance seemed as if it should be the last thing on my list. Somehow, though, it had pushed its way up toward the top. I've never questioned emotion. I've lived my life for it. It wasn't hard to see that over the last several months, I'd been falling in love as much as I'd been falling into air. I wasn't sure what to do about it. But there it was.

I smiled at the radio. "Okay, so see you in about an hour, I'm taking off now." I looked down at the small red spot of Mario's canopy, trying to impress the obscure landing area into my brain so I could find it next time I stood up here.

Fletch and I drove down and around, following a frontage road beside the highway into the graded dirt roads of a drilling operation to get as close as we could to the bottom of the plateau. Mario emerged from the canyon, sweaty, dirty, and glowing. We circled right back up the dirt roads to the top of the Roan and camped in the aspen grove by a small fire as the stars filled the sky and the small round leaves trembled in the darkness. In the morning, it was my turn.

After making a few more visits with Mario, trading shuttles for each other, I returned with an Australian jumper and his girlfriend, then begged rides from climber friends at Rifle on their rest days. We jumped from the cleanest, nicest exit spot at the center of the wall, where the vertical drop was about five hundred feet, taking a short, Moab-style free fall of two or three seconds before opening the canopy. Falling into that enormous rock bowl, and piloting the parachute to a safe stop in the rugged landing spot, was exhilarating and addictive. I was gaining confidence in my canopy skills, and it was a great feeling.

The Roan took some organizing because of the long, four-wheel-drive shuttle trip that it required. Soon I got a call from Ted, a local skier from Aspen who had started base jumping too. The Roan was his local cliff, and he was excited to hear that someone else was jumping there regularly. He invited me for a jump together, with the added bonus that we could get dropped off and picked up by a friend of his who wanted to see us jump.

A professional freestyle skier, Ted was used to moving fast and taking big air, and his approach to base jumping was just as accelerated. He'd been jumping at the Roan from its highest point with a tracking suit. The suit looked like a normal pair of rain pants and a jacket, but it had special venting to inflate in the air, like a scaled-back wingsuit. I had a tracking suit though I'd almost never worn it because whenever a cliff was big enough to track I wore my wingsuit instead. Six hundred feet wasn't enough altitude to accelerate into a full, terminal-speed track. The Roan Plateau was right in the middle, altitude-wise, a strange height for that reason—a little too short for a terminal jump, a little too tall for a subterminal jump. But it was just enough to feel the suit inflate and get almost a tease of forward speed before it was time to deploy, like an extremely compressed version of a terminal jump.

Ted had a full array of gear, from motocross body armor under his tracking suit to a video camera mounted on his helmet. He was geared up and ready in minutes. As soon as all cameras were rolling, he took off running at full speed from the cliff, launching aggressively into the air. I watched as he dropped out, getting smaller and smaller, alarmingly close to the talus slope before his parachute finally emerged.

I pushed the radio button after his canopy had touched down in a tiny spot of color. "How long was your delay?" I wasn't sure how long I should free fall. Probably not as long as that.

"Yeah! That was awesome! Let me check my footage, and I can tell you exactly!" In a moment, his radio came back on. "Seven seconds!"

I looked over at Ted's friend. "Looks like I'm ready. Thanks for the ride. We'll see you down there." I ran off the edge. I counted the seconds in my head, feeling as if I were falling forever, and threw out the pilot chute right at five. I flew over the slopes and ravine and landed next to Ted, flushed with excitement. Wearing the tracking suit and taking the longer delay changed the jump completely. I was hooked on the Roan, even more than before. As we hiked down the ravine, we agreed to come back as soon as we could arrange another driver.

Within a few days, we were on top of the Roan again. Ted's fiancée had driven us up, along with a friend we had in common, Chris. Tall, gangly, and puppyish, with messy dark hair, Chris reminded me of my brother both in looks and in easygoing friendliness. His being young and playful was misleading, as he had years of experience jumping as a tandem master in Hawaii. I looked over at Ted and Chris, geared up and ready, and said, "I think I'm going to go." I never jumped first. Last was my preference.

"Have a good one, Steph," Chris said.

I backed up, the nylon fabric of my tracking suit swishing together, my boots crushing over small cactus lobes. I took a breath and ran down the dirt slope, into the air. Pale gray limestone filled my eyes as I shot straight out and down. The talus was growing fast. I counted in my mind as I fell—"One thousand one, one thousand two, one thousand three, one thousand four"—and felt the arms and legs of my suit start to inflate as I gained speed. I could see the rocks on the slope below me, growing.

I stretched my arms and legs straight back, pointing my toes hard. I was starting to move forward—". . . one thousand five, one . . ."

My brain stopped counting and my eyes started to do it instead, knowing in some way I couldn't explain how close I was getting to the ground. I was just on the edge of tasting flight, just passing the zone of subterminal speed into terminal, 120 miles per hour, just feeling my suit inflate and start to turn the fall speed into forward speed. The milliseconds stretched and snapped, like rubber bands. The rocks were getting big in my eyes. I grabbed my pilot chute and threw it into the air.

The pilot caught the air and pulled the two curved pins free of their loops behind my back, stretching the bridle straight and yanking the folded parachute out of the container. The parachute unfurled in the air, slowed by the mesh slider that zipped down the lines to my shoulders, easing the force of opening. Still, my body snapped with the sudden deceleration, my legs flinging around like a rag doll. I looked up at the canopy, startled at first to see the unfamiliar colors, although I'd packed it myself. It was a Dagger, an old parachute that had belonged to my ex-husband. I always jumped a Flik, a more boxy parachute known for its docility and ease of maneuverability in tight landing areas. But I had the Dagger and an extra container, and I decided it was time to start using it as a second rig, specifically for taller, slider-up jumps like this one. That way I wouldn't have to take everything apart all the time as I switched between the short Moab jumps and the taller Roan cliffs. I didn't like taking my parachute lines apart and reattaching them all the time to take the slider on and off. It seemed like an opportunity to make a mistake and cross something up, causing my own rigging malfunction. I didn't consider that I hadn't flown the Dagger much, and that it was regarded as a fast, ground-hungry parachute because of its slightly tapered shape.

The parachute flew forward, the steep, rocky slopes running down below me. I seemed abnormally low, and I felt that I was sinking rather than flying straight forward. The feeling intensified, and I looked up at the canopy, straightening my arms up as much as I could to make sure I wasn't pulling down on the brake lines somehow. I was definitely sinking. The rocky, tortuous terrain was growing around me. I had to clear this level of the talus, and then it would drop off to the next tier of rocky slopes and trees funneling into the ravine. I wasn't sure I could make it. Landing here would almost surely be painful.

My mind flicked backward. Ten seconds ago, a thousand feet ago, a lifetime ago, I was standing on the cliff with Ted and Chris. Ted and I strapped on body armor and our tracking suits. I looked over at Chris, lightly clad in a base rig, T-shirt, and sneakers. "Chris, you don't even have a helmet?"

"I had no idea this place was so gnarly," Chris said lightly. "Well, hopefully it works out."

I looked at him doubtfully. "Okay. Well, maybe I should go first so you can see where the landing is, since you've never been here."

"Only if you want to. I'd be psyched to take photos anyway. I kind of like going last. It's not as scary when I'm just taking pictures of everyone," he said playfully.

"I should go first. It is really hard to even find the landing when you haven't been here before. It's nice to see someone down there, to see where it is the first time. I'll go," I said. "What do you guys think about the wind?"

I felt some wind pushing against my face. We hadn't got up here early today; it had to be at least ten. I wondered what Mario would think about the wind, if he would think it was safe to jump.

"It's always windy here," Ted replied.

"I think I'm going to go," I said.

"Have a good one, Steph," Chris answered.

Time looped and circled, pinched and swelled.

I was in the air. That moment was gone, ten seconds past at the top of the Roan, a place I could never go back to. I'd taken my choice. I looked up at the canopy again, confused. It didn't seem to be moving. I felt a headwind pushing against me, slowing my forward drive, but the parachute seemed to be sinking at the same time, as if I were pulling down on the brake lines to force it to drop down into the jagged stretch of ravine coming up below me. That was the last thing I wanted to happen. I saw the back of the canopy curved down slightly, though my arms stretched straight to the sky above my head, not pulling the brakes at all. The lines were too short, the length custom-shortened for someone with much longer arms. I hadn't even thought of that when I started to use it. The canopy was essentially sinking itself. I looked again toward the landing spot, starting to appear farther away and higher. I might not make it.

I tried to make my body small by pulling my legs up to my chest as I passed low over the end of the talus slope, lessening my surface area against the headwind, trying to penetrate. I didn't have an alternative landing option in the gnarly, jagged terrain between me and the regular spot. Three-dimensional was a perfect description of this landscape. It was almost disorienting, trying to navigate. The landing spot, about the size of a small living room, hemmed in by cliff walls, hillsides, and a steep drop-off, was perched up and off to the side of the ravine. I had to make it because I was almost guaranteed to get hurt if I didn't.

My heart pounded hard as I flew. I seemed to lose an equal amount of height for the distance I slowly gained forward. It was like flooring the gas pedal of a four-cylinder pickup truck on a steep mountain pass, pointlessly leaning into the dash to make it go. I willed the parachute to move as it crept forward. It looked as if I might make it. But then again, maybe I wouldn't. I couldn't tell.

It seemed I'd been under canopy for hours, fixating on the small dirt opening. I couldn't understand why this was happening. I'd jumped this site six times already, and the parachute flights had gone perfectly. I was getting better at flying, I thought, gauging distance, contours, and height, maneuvering the brake lines to bring myself down softly where I wanted to be. Right now I felt like a helpless victim to the nylon wing over my head. I wasn't in charge. I was just praying I'd get there.

The small, rocky landing area came into sight just ahead. Suddenly, the headwind disappeared. To my shock, I lofted upward just as I started moving forward at a normal speed. I'd made it to the landing area, and now I was floating too high above it, with my parachute actually rising upward. I'd never experienced this before, hadn't even known it was possible. But apparently it was. I needed to make turns, bleed off altitude, and work the parachute down. I couldn't just fly straight in because I would overshoot the landing and fly into a hillside. I started to maneuver instinctively, making S-turns over the landing zone. Suddenly it was as if I'd traded in my reliable old truck for a Ferrari. Instead of sashaying gently from side to side, losing altitude, the Dagger responded like I was revving the engine, sharply diving into each turn and picking up speed. Even as I struggled to slow my velocity, I realized that choosing this unfamiliar canopy had been a huge mistake. With every turn and sink I made to stay on target, I was picking up speed that I couldn't lose. Coming in for landing with so much speed could be all right in the soft, grassy runway of a skydiving drop zone. Coming in this fast to the sunbaked, rock-strewn patch would most likely result in smashing myself. I was too close to the ground for the parachute to recover and slow down. I fought panic. Time snapped into hyperdrive. In the final seconds I knew I was going to slam into the sunbaked clay, sloping slightly uphill in front of me. There was no slowing down, no way to escape the future that was speeding at me, just three seconds ahead, when everything would be different.

Breaking my back had always been my greatest fear. I consciously tried to relax my body and pull down on the brakes as hard as I could, flaring in the last seconds. My back, I thought. I twisted to the right just as I slammed into the incline, taking the hit on my right flank instead of directly on my lower spine. I didn't feel any pain, just an incredible feeling of impact. In my mind came the thought *My pelvis is broken.* I didn't know how I could possibly know that. I lay on my back on the hard dirt, my head slightly downhill in the helmet, slammed. I heard Ted's voice over the radio.

"Are you all right?"

I fumbled in my pocket for the radio. "I think I'm okay. Just give me a second."

Suddenly my whole body hurt. I wiggled my feet. I could move my feet. I bent my toes, feeling them. I could feel my toes. An enormous wave of relief swept over my entire being. It didn't matter what had happened. I could move my legs. I wanted to get to my feet immediately, to know for sure I didn't have a spinal injury, to prove it by standing. I knew that was the wrong thing to do. Articles on backcountry medicine and a few wilderness medicine classes had impressed on me that after a hard impact to the back or head, a person should stay still until they can be immobilized and taken to the hospital. A small spinal fracture could turn into a serious spinal cord injury if displaced.

"Steph, are you all right?" Ted repeated.

"I think I'm okay! Just give me a second!" I felt stunned. Horrified. Not sure of anything.

I struggled to my feet, got dizzy and nauseated, and went right back down. But I could feel my legs and feet. I had stood up. I hadn't crushed my spine. I felt like I had just won the lottery. I knew I shouldn't have stood up. But I also knew I had, and all I could think was that I was incredibly lucky. Maybe I hadn't broken my pelvis, maybe I'd be fine in a minute.

I watched the parachutes lofting down as first Ted and then Chris appeared beside me.

"I'm really sorry," I said. "I think I'm okay. I might be able to walk out."

My mind ran over the hike out of the ravine, the short drop-offs to be jumped down, the steep, sliding dirt hillsides to be traversed. It took at least a half hour to descend to the flat creekbed and meet the dirt road. We should get going before the adrenaline wore off and I really got hit by the pain.

I tried again to stand and crumpled back to the ground. For the next hour or so I lay on the ground, nursing the delusion I was going to hike out. I could stand, for about two seconds, until the pain made me nauseated and I collapsed down. Chris and Ted disappeared for a private conference and came back with the not-so-shocking news that it was time to call a helicopter.

"Do you have insurance?" Ted asked.

"Yeah, I do."

"Should we get the base gear off you?" Chris asked.

"No, my insurance is good, I'm covered."

"Are you sure?" Chris asked.

"I am. My brother has the same insurance, and he just crashed at a bridge in Oregon, and he had air rescue and surgery and everything, so I know it's good."

Chris and Ted stuffed the canopy under my hips for padding. The pain was coming on hard. Ted stood in the most open spot with his cell phone, talking to rescue dispatchers and giving our GPS coordinates. Chris sat beside me, holding my pilot chute above my face to keep the sun out of my eyes. He chatted with me about nothing, trying to distract me. It was nice of him, both of them, to be helping me like this. I'd totally ruined their jump, their whole day. We should all be walking out now, scrambling down the ravine, laughing and talking about our jump. I felt so ashamed and incompetent. I'd screwed up completely, from the moment I decided to use a parachute I didn't know at this rugged, technical site, to the moment I decided to jump in subpar wind conditions, to the moment I hadn't had the skill to pull it off despite everything.

I was used to being good at the things I did, and I had no tolerance for incompetence or recklessness, especially in myself. That intolerance was why I was alive and had never had an accident in twenty years of pursuing the most dangerous and committing forms of climbing. I thought nothing of going alone up and down a huge mountain, or with a trusted partner, because I had total faith in my ability to get back no matter what might happen. I might have spent more days and nights alone in the wilderness than with partners, and I understood the consequences of everything I did. I knew how to keep myself safe. I was smart, strong, and experienced, and I knew how to deal. But that world was different, and I'd never understood that as fully as I did now. I blamed myself in every way for being here, utterly helpless, lying flat on my back on the dirt, unable even to move out of the sun's glare. If I were alone right now, I'd have to crawl out, down the steep ravines, the drop-offs, the talus, and the scrubby hillsides. I wondered if I could have done it. It seemed daunting, nearly impossible now, lying here with the dull pain radiating up from the center of my hips.

I thought of all the times I'd done this jump alone, exchanging rides with Mario or getting dropped off by climbing friends who could barely see me from the top of the cliff and didn't even know the way to this landing area from the road. That had been a bad idea, reckless even, or maybe just naive. I marveled at my stupidity. I'd made so many mistakes. But I could use my legs. I was pretty sure my pelvis was broken, but that would heal. I'd got lucky, much more than I deserved, I thought. I was thankful for it.

Three hours went by until the chopper approached. A paraglider had crashed one ridge over, with severe injuries, another victim of strange late-morning winds and pilot error. They went to get him first. The blades beat the air, breaking the stillness above as the helicopter zigzagged, searching for us. Ted stayed on the phone, trying to explain our location, but they couldn't even pick us out in the canyon until Chris started waving my bright orange pilot chute as a beacon, the pilot chute Mario had lent me. Ted stayed on the phone with the dispatcher while she relayed information back and forth. They'd finally spotted us, but the pilot wasn't sure he could land in this terrain. We waited. I imagined being carried out of the canyon on a stretcher, bouncing excruciatingly as the poor rescuers tried to lower me down the vertical sections. I didn't want to think about it.

The helicopter beat down, landing in the one small dirt spot that was free of rocks, just big enough to put the skids down. The blades whipped the air, filling the quiet with sound. The paramedics jumped out and used my parachute like a hammock to hoist me onto a bodyboard. Suddenly everything was urgent, loud, and rushed. My hair blew all over my face as they loaded me in, closed the doors, and we lifted into the air, rising out of the canyon. I was so thankful to be in the helicopter. It was strange to be so helpless, to be rescued, to be unable to get myself out of a place I'd put myself in. I thanked the paramedics over and over.

I'd fractured my sacrum in three places and torn some intercostal rib tissue and done something to my elbow that caused a burning pain whenever I touched it. I was amazed to have got off so lightly. The doctor told me that my muscles had contracted so hard on impact that the contraction itself had caused my sacrum to fracture. The X-rays had also revealed an old, now healed, fracture on the front of my pelvis, a souvenir from my other crash landing at Castleton Tower. I'd never even known about that break, but in retrospect, it made sense. They don't do anything for pelvic fractures anyway, except load you up with painkillers, so it didn't really matter that it had gone undiagnosed.

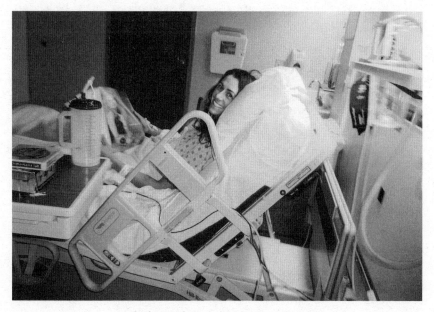

In the hospital, Grand Junction, Colorado

Chris arrived in the ER of the Grand Junction, Colorado, hospital carrying Fletcher in to see me, and Mario drove out immediately from Moab. For the next three days, he flew the jump plane all morning and drove the two hours to the hospital to visit me and then back again. When the morphine drip and catheter came out and I proved I could take a few steps down the hall with a walker, they sent me home with a staggering supply of narcotics, and the directions "Do as much as you can. Sacral fractures are extremely painful, but the more you do, the faster you'll heal." Everything hurt, a lot, but not that bad considering. I was permanently ecstatic not to be more seriously injured and felt that I had been handed a gift from the universe with something so mendable. I saved the narcotics for future emergencies. They seemed like a good thing to have in the jump kit.

Mario took care of me in a way I'd never been taken care of before. He flew the jump plane every morning and came straight to my house by noon. He brought me food, helped me up and down from bed, rented me a walker from the drugstore, and after a few weeks had passed, he put a futon in the back of his Honda Element and drove me out to Dead Horse Point to see the sunset, waiting patiently beside me as I used his shoulder and a crutch to slowly limp the few yards out to the viewpoint. I felt strange having someone there, making everything easier for me. Helping me. It was even stranger to realize how much I liked it. In just a few weeks, I came to depend on him. He actually seemed to enjoy taking care of me. Mario was so solid, giving me the same full attention that he gave everything else he did.

He took care of Fletch too. By now, she had big, comfortable dog beds in every room, and traveling between them was much of her daily activity, kind of like hobbling around the house from bed to sofa was mine. She didn't seem to want to go outside as much, until Mario enlarged her dog door after he observed that she had a hard time ducking down to use it and then built her a ramp to get down the porch steps. I'd noticed her hesitating at the door, but I hadn't figured out why. He added side rails to the ramp and extended it to reduce the slope when he noticed that she seemed hesitant about going down it, then glued carpet on it to keep her from sliding. When everything was done, I felt guilty and thoughtless because I saw that she had been going outside less only because it had been getting too difficult until Mario fixed things. I was starting to wonder how we'd managed without him. It was funny, in a way, when I thought of all those years that Fletch and I had crossed the country back and forth together, living out of my truck, not depending on anyone for anything. She was the only creature I knew who was more independent than me. Now we needed someone, and it felt like a miracle to have that someone there for us.

Mario taking Fletch to the crag

The world was so different, so much bigger and yet smaller. In the first week, I was able to move slowly through the house, taking calculated steps with the walker in front of me. Each step was a considered movement as I made sure I didn't slip or push the wrong way. It took a long time and an acceptance of some pain, but I made my way from bed to bathroom to kitchen. Small distances and obstructions became significant issues to be handled. The three steps on the front porch were a major project, one I had to work up to. I forced myself to graduate from walker to crutches to ski poles until I could make it down the porch steps and out to my truck so I could drive the quarter mile to the pool, where I could swim or just walk weightlessly in the water and get a break from pain. The journey took almost the whole day.

I'd never liked swimming much, but now I looked forward to getting up each day and being in the water. Physically, I felt much like Fletch appeared to be feeling with the arthritis slowly taking possession of her spine and shoulders, making her journey from bed to food bowl slow and considered. Except I would get better, and she wouldn't. It made my heart hurt. It also showed me how lucky I was. I didn't think much about jumping or climbing or anything I couldn't do. Everything I could do struck me as a gift, an undeserved miracle of good fortune, and it filled me with appreciation. Every day was full with figuring out how to negotiate around my injuries and enjoying the novelty of doing things I wouldn't normally do. This injury was actually fun, or at least extremely engaging. My feelings about everything had changed in that last second before impact, when I thought, Not my back. I couldn't get over how incredibly lucky I was.

Exactly five weeks after the crash, the bone doctor told me the fractures had mended. Just like that, I was free to climb, skydive, and base jump again, to love every shred of life out of all the things I was so lucky to be able to do. I was deeply thankful.

In the last few months, I'd given in completely to my unquenchable thirst for jumping, charging full speed ahead, jumping everything that seemed even close to the parameters of my quickly gained experience, pushing myself rather than holding myself back. I'd been like an addict with free access to drugs, and now I was experiencing the consequences firsthand. As usual, the only way for me to learn a lesson was to live it myself. For a time when I'd first started to jump, I'd been almost indifferent to the thought of losing my life. Now I had come out of that dark feeling. The world seemed bright, glorious, and spilling with promise, as it always had before. But my thoughts about death had changed slightly. Now death struck me as something inevitable, the guaranteed result of living itself, not something that could be dodged or skipped. Just another thing that simply is. Like gravity.

But before now, I'd thought of base jumping as being a lot like free soloing, as a pursuit where small mistakes can result in fatality. Generally speaking, free soloists who fall die. Period, the end. It's tragic for everyone else, but for the climber, it's a simple game—if things go wrong, it's just over.

I understood now that the comparison was not good. It's possible to make enormous mistakes and have little skill and still walk away from a base jump. As a free soloist, you probably won't even get off the ground unless you're highly skilled, and if you make a mistake, you'll almost certainly die. It's possible to make mistakes and die on a base jump, of course. But more likely and more typically, messing up a jump and not getting lucky that day results in getting hurt, often badly. I thought about everything that had happened, all the mistakes I'd made, and I wondered how I hadn't seen it before. Getting hurt badly meant losing my freedom, for me an outcome worse than death. I'd been stupid, or at least inexperienced, in many ways, and knowing it shifted my perspective about base jumping completely. I'd been given a cheap lesson, and it would not be wasted on me.

Chapter Fourteen

Half-Empty

Fletch at the Tombstone parking lot

Winter came to the desert, in a sudden hush. The frenzied days of fall seemed like another life. The endless stream of visitors had all gone home or to warmer places, and once again I had time to think and feel, to return to solitude and quiet. The days were short and brilliant. White snow frosted the red cliffs, blue shadows fired the orange rock. Fletch and I sat in front of the woodstove in the long evenings, watching the flames wrap the wood. I listened to the crackling and to Fletcher's deep-sleep breathing, comforted by the sound of air flowing through her little body.

All three of us—the fire, Fletch, me—creating heat, breathing air, living.

Fletch was fourteen, and I knew that my dreams of celebrating her thirtieth birthday were just that. The X-rays showed arthritis in her spine, back legs, front shoulders, and elbows. She wasn't hearing quite as much. She wasn't seeing quite as much either. Her nose seemed to work perfectly, though, and she definitely had all her taste buds.

I remembered when we ran together in the desert for hours. Fletch would run and run, darting everywhere, chasing lizards, chasing rabbits, giving a great big f%*@ you to the ravens, whom she always had some kind of vendetta against. I remembered her legs flying across the slick rock, her entire face stretched in a glorious, ecstatic smile. Walking was slow and hard now. Those sturdy little back legs had become floppy and prone to wipeouts, and my heart caught when she struggled to her feet. I wondered what I'd do on the day she couldn't make it back up. In this, as in everything else, Fletch had a spirit so strong it put me to shame. I watched her closely in these quiet winter days because she was showing me yet again the right way to live—never giving up, doing the best she could, with a smile on her face. Fletch was a happy little creature. She loved the moments of her life.

Fletch at home in the yard

The morning after Christmas, I lifted Fletch into my truck and drove down Kane Creek Road to the Tombstone, as we did nearly every day. I planted my wind flag and helped her out into the dirt parking lot. Exploring the yard and traveling up and down her ramp to her dog door and into the kitchen to keep a close tab on her food dish had become enough exercise at home. But she liked her outings, liked seeing my canopy fly toward her and touch down. We could do it together. When I set her on the dirt, she stood a little shakily at first, like a fawn, and looked timid. This, from my little dog from the Navajo res lands, who used to know she owned the world. It grabbed at my heart. I ignored her, like she liked, and started my own investigations, looking on the ground for heart-shaped rocks, feeling the winds move, watching the flag dance. I knew already the winds were too variable and swirly to jump. I didn't jump in that kind of wind anymore. I'd learned.

Fletch got interested. She made her way to the scrubby, dried grasses and nosed through the brush. Gradually her radius widened. We strolled around together, noticing things. The breeze flipped and circled, playing with the flag and swirling around the canyon like water.

The flag dropped flat. Suddenly the wind was out, switched off.

The Tombstone was all rich winter light, the face smooth and perfect, glowing orange. I thought about stepping off the edge and feeling my body loose in the air. The wind swept my face from each direction, then spun around giddily, brushing me and flipping my hair. The flag leaped up, flicked from side to side, dancing. The air darted around invisibly.

This was obviously the wrong time for jumping. But Fletch was winding down from her tour. I watched the flag flick around some more. Little lulls came, when it fell straight down and stayed flat for a few seconds. I lifted Fletch into the car, into her circular dog bed in the passenger seat, and cracked the windows so she'd have fresh air but not get too cold. She curled up, ready for a nap after all that excitement. I picked up my rig and started up the snowy trail.

Wind pushed into my face as I turned the first corner, into the canyon that leads to Back of Beyond and the top of the Tombstone. It was still a half hour to the top. At some moment, the wind would rush away as fast as it rushed in. It would go away to the next place, leaving silent calm behind it, an entirely different world. It was good to walk to the top, even if the winds were wrong at the parking lot. It could still happen. I liked walking up the snow-covered slabs near the top, stamping my feet to make them stick. Behind me the La Sals were bright and pointed, the softly draped slopes like skirts of white velvet.

When I reached the top, I sat in my spot, where I always sat. The flag was still crazy-dancing down below. The wind was slicing up the wall and from side to side. I crawled to the edge of the Tombstone and spat down the face, just to see what it would do. My saliva flew up and left, while the air blew my hair back. I sat back. I looked at the desert walls lining the canyons that forked out beyond me. I felt the wind.

It was good to be here, on top of this rounded rock wall, surrounded by snow and sandstone. It was good to feel the wind, take the cold air into my lungs. It was good to hear the birds shoot past, riding the air. It was good to think about the feeling of falling through the air, talus rushing into my eyes.

I imagined the jump, those clean seconds of time. I wanted to jump. Tomorrow the wind would be in Colorado or Kansas, leaving the desert calm and safe, and the Tombstone and I would still be here together, for the rest of my life. There was no hurry. I had been very stupid, I thought now, leaping off things and into things when the time wasn't right. Somehow my deep intelligence with climbing hadn't translated to anything else. I knew better now. I didn't want to get hurt anymore. I'd decided strongly that I wouldn't get hurt again. The wind rippled my jacket and made my eyes tear a little. I stood up, satisfied. It was good to walk down, to Fletch.

As summer approached, my internal clock started to sound. The heat was coming to the desert, ready to set in like an oppressive force, sapping all energy and motivation. In the summer, it was impossible to be in direct sun. The days seemed endless, bearable only for a few hours at dawn. The arrival of June had always meant it was time to migrate, to escape from the desert heat until September. Fletch had always been fine with friends if I'd left on a summer expedition or went into the mountains. Now there was no question of leaving her. She had a hard time walking and needed to wear a diaper when she was sleeping or in the car, thanks to the spinal arthritis. She needed me and seemed happiest when I was within her sight. She didn't like to be alone at all now. She seemed to understand that she was vulnerable and that she needed help. Coming from such an independent little creature, this new dependence was incredibly touching, but also a heavy burden. Things had become hard physically too, with lots of lifting, carrying, and cleaning. Forty pounds wasn't heavy, but picking Fletch up all day long was starting to take its toll on my lower back. Although taking care of her was tiring and emotionally draining, there was nothing else I'd rather be doing. I wanted to be with her all the time, making sure she was comfortable, making sure she was safe. I wondered if this was how Mario had felt when I was hurt, when he'd looked after me so devotedly, and realized it must be how he felt all the time because he was always looking after me in thoughtful ways.

Fletcher's crag wagon at Rifle

For Fletch, going to Rifle seemed even better than staying in Moab. At Rifle, I could spend every second of the day with her. She'd have no steps or ramps to negotiate. I put a dog bed in the bottom of my garden wagon and some safety straps, so I could pull her up and down the dirt road between climbing sectors and then carry her to the bottom of the cliff I wanted to climb, where she sat comfortably on a blanket. In the evenings, we sat together by my truck eating dinner and watching the dark fall. I put a clean Depend pad in Fletch's cloth doggy diaper—a system I'd come up with as dribbling had turned to soaking—before we got in the back of the truck to sleep, cuddling her against my chest. At home she refused to get on my bed, but in my truck we always slept together.

Even more to my surprise, I realized that I didn't want to get too far from Moab for the summer because Mario was there flying the jump plane. I found myself missing him after just a couple of days away at Rifle, which seemed almost ridiculous to me. In the past, I'd thought nothing of setting off on my own for months if my ex-husband wanted to climb somewhere I didn't, happier on my own. Now I drove back to Moab every two days when it was time to take a rest day from climbing. I missed Mario. Like Fletch, I seemed to have become dependent on him, feeling better when he was nearby. Though I seemed to be inexplicably exhausted all the time, Mario was endlessly energetic, seemingly incapable of not being productive. When Fletch was home, he worked on modifying a baby jogger into a dog wheelchair with a small harness system, hoping to make it easier for her to walk. She'd started to drag her back feet and was getting a chronic scrape on the top of her left foot. I kept it bandaged and put a dog bootie on it, but it got worse. I was starting to become a regular at Dr. Sorensen's.

Fletch downed every meal with her characteristic gusto. She didn't have the wide, face-stretching grin she'd always worn, but she still smiled. But what if I was just prolonging her life, making her suffer? It was so hard to be sure what was right. I didn't know what to do. I'd never had a dog before. I'd believed I would have Fletch with me for the rest of my life. Somehow the idea of her growing old or dying had never entered my mind at first, and when it did, it just seemed ludicrous. I didn't want her to suffer, but I couldn't imagine being without her. I wondered if I should put her to sleep. I'd never thought about it before.

"You'll know when it's time," friends told me.

But how? How would I know?

"You'll just know," they said, a maddening response. She didn't seem to be suffering unbearably, but it was so hard to tell with Fletch. She'd never complained about anything. She'd always been more stoic than any other creature I'd ever seen, almost as a point of dignity. Just before Scott relinquished her to me, she'd been hit by a car and dragged herself home to him, bleeding from huge gashes in her back legs. He and the vet had picked her up, and she never made a sound. Only days later did they realize she'd also broken ribs, in the same spot people had been lifting her. Maybe she was hurting too much now, but it was impossible to tell. Only her limp revealed any clues to me. She wouldn't limp if it didn't hurt. It was easier to throw myself into the daily details of taking care of Fletch. That was easy to understand. I knew how to take care of her. At night, I lay in the back of my truck with Fletch curled up against my stomach, breathing rhythmically, and wondered what to do. She depended on me for everything.

In the past, big decisions had always seemed clear, so easy to know. I'd instinctively trusted my heart and implicitly trusted those around me. I'd lost that habit of pure trust, especially in my decisions. My choices had led me into every place I'd been, and I no longer assumed that I would always choose right. This deep doubt spilled into my feelings about professional relationships. At this point I had to either put all my energy back into being a professional climber or switch gears completely and find a new path and new employment. Climbing was woven into my being and I didn't want to leave it. I started working with a new clothing sponsor, with the encouragement of two good friends who worked at the company. At first I had a hard time not thinking about the past. I wanted to trust, to be as carefree as a new puppy, but I felt more like a shelter dog who wags uncertainly and starts forward, then dodges back at the sight of a raised hand. It was scary stepping into a new relationship after having felt used and discarded in the not-so-distant past. The company was changing quickly, was in deep transition, and as months passed, I saw integrity and professionalism being not just voiced but practiced at every crossroad. I was objective enough to see the difference between where I'd been and where I was now. This was a good place, a place where people did the best they could and stuck by their word, made decisions that balanced professionalism with humanity. I didn't have to be ruled by the past.

Mario was also teaching me to trust simply through sheer trustworthiness. In the last year, I'd come to depend on him to a degree I'd never before depended on anyone. He was unfailingly gentle and true, and no matter what happened, he was there with me.

I remembered my decision to take Fletcher, almost thirteen years ago, when Scott, her original human, had decided to take an electrician's job at McMurdo Station in Antarctica. For him, it was the chance of a lifetime, and one of the perks was a stopover in New Zealand after the contract was finished. He planned to stay in New Zealand for a year or maybe more, since he never had any trouble finding work anywhere he went. It wasn't fair, he thought, to ask someone to watch his dog for years and then come home and take her back. The right thing to do was to give her to someone. Scott could afford to be choosy since he was inundated with petitions to take Fletch, who made an indelible impression on everyone who met her, even people who'd never liked dogs before. But since I was already sharing her with him, he told me that I had the first choice. I was living in an Oldsmobile, I left the country for at least four months a year, and I spent a good portion of my time in national parks, where dogs are outlawed as much as weapons. I didn't see how I would make it work. I thought of all the ways in which it seemed like a hopeless plan. Then I thought about not seeing Fletch anymore. Being without her was unthinkable. It turned out to be the best decision of my life.

At first, this self-possessed, strong little creature was my role model. I watched her and learned how to move through the world gracefully, naturally, and with dignity. Over time she became my soul mate, who showed me the meaning of pure love. Simply through example, Fletch taught me how to live the life I wanted to live, how to be the person I aspired to be. She became part of me, not just my soul mate, but my soul itself. It's hard to explain how much I loved her.

I would have given anything to have Fletcher with me forever, healthy, vibrant, and not in pain. I wanted to do the right thing, but I still didn't know what it was.

In Rifle, I loaded and unloaded Fletcher's wagon from my truck and pulled her from one place to the next. I changed the bandage on her foot every morning and night, cut up vegetables to mix into her dog food, washed her cloth diapers in the stream and hung them over bushes in the sun, and anxiously leaped up to follow her when she got up to wobble around. Climbing was simply what I did to fill the time in between. And I was supposed to climb; it was my job, after all. So I climbed.

We had a routine of two days at Rifle and two days in Moab, with a lot of driving, a lot of lifting Fletcher in and out of places, and a lot of washing. The sore on her foot was growing, despite my changing the bandage twice a day and three attempts by Dr. Sorensen to staple the skin shut. I'd tried to put a cone on her neck to keep her from chewing the bandage open, but it seemed so uncomfortable when standing and walking were already difficult endeavors. Every time I took my eyes off her for a minute, she chewed into the bandage and pulled the staples out, making the wound worse. She was determined to get the staples out and to lick the ointment off.

"You need to keep her from chewing on it. I can't close it up at this point. You're just going to have to keep it clean. Change the bandages and bring her back every week," Dr. Sorensen told me. Her circulation wasn't good in the back legs, and we had no choice but to hope it would somehow heal. I bought rolls of purple and pink stretch gauze at the desk, and powdered antibiotic.

The morning had started off badly. We'd camped by the creek, and I was sitting in the sun eating cereal with soy milk and raspberries. Fletch was lying in the grass nearby, her breakfast finished and her foot rebandaged and wrapped in purple gauze. I finished the cereal and looked over. She was gone, which didn't make sense because she couldn't walk far or fast. I rushed over and saw her lying in the creek. A steep hillside led to the water, and she couldn't have walked down it. Somehow she had tumbled or slid down the hillside and was now caught in the shallow water, half sitting, half standing. I had no idea if she'd been there for thirty seconds or five minutes and, dismayed, I ran down to carry her out. She was chilled and shivering, her thick double coat of fur soaked. Why on earth had she gone down to the creek? She didn't even like water. She had plenty to drink in a bowl right next to her, and it was the first week of September, no longer blazing hot. I toweled her off, replaced her soaked foot bandage, and sat her beside me in the sun, feeling deeply unsettled. I'd relaxed my guard for just a minute, and the next thing I knew, Fletch was in the creek. She could have drowned. Or frozen to death. I sat right beside her while she dried.

Last morning at Rifle

I tried to move ahead with the day, carrying Fletch to the warm-up wall and tucking her into fleece blankets at the cliff. She seemed worn-out, abnormally so, and started shivering again. I put her in the car, where it might be warmer and more comfortable in her dog-bed seat, but she anxiously tried to stand up as I shut the door to leave her. I was starting to feel completely unsettled. We needed to go home.

I drove down the winding roads, past the green fields and the wide reservoir. Fletch lay in her round bed on the passenger seat, her head resting on my thigh. I stroked the soft fur between her eyes, following it back to her pointy ears, over the beautiful patterns of white, rich brown, and black on her forehead. She felt different. She felt limp. A quiet feeling of alarm rose inside me. We got out onto the flat stretch of I-70 and the feeling intensified, threatening to become panic. I stroked her head and shoulders. Tears trickled down my face. I'd never seen her like this before. She was worn out. We both were. Clearly she'd done as much as she could, but she was done.

I drove in a blur. I didn't know what was going to happen. I couldn't imagine anything without Fletch. The thought of it was a bleak mine of emptiness that scared me to look at. My breath got ragged, the start of deep, shuddery sobs. I smashed back the panic to keep it from Fletch. She didn't move, every muscle in her body lax, her ribs gently rising under my hand. My eyes and nose flowed as I held quiet, rubbing at them with the back of my wet sleeve, breathing through my mouth. It didn't seem real. I drove without seeing anything, without caring, feeling a choking weight inside my chest and Fletch's smooth fur between my fingers. Every thought that entered my head triggered a fresh flow of tears. I tried to empty them from my mind, to make it blank, get some control. I had no idea if we'd crossed the Colorado-Utah border. I wanted to stay here with Fletch beside me forever, just keep driving in this limbo zone where nothing had to be finished. When we got home, it would be over. How could this be the last time? How could this be possible? The miles smeared by inevitably, like time, like tears.

I pulled into the driveway and went around to Fletcher's seat. I gathered her up. Her forty pounds felt heavy, heavier than usual. She was so limp. I carried her in to her dog bed in the living room, the one with arms around it like a sofa. Strips of old carpet ran from that bed to her other bed in the bedroom, and to her food dishes and the dog door. Mario and I had tiled the floors a few months before, driven to the project now that the carpet kept getting soaked from Fletch's diapers, not taking into account that tile would be harder to negotiate with arthritic joints. So we had covered the new tile with walkways cut from all the smelly carpet we'd pulled up. Fletch lay still, her head resting on her paws. She looked so tired. It was time—there was no way to mistake it now. She didn't seem to be in pain or misery. But it was time. I'd wait for Mario to get home. In the morning, Dr. Sorensen would come. He'd told me he would come to the house if we needed to put her to sleep.

Last evening at home *Lisa Hathaway*

I curled myself around the bed, petting Fletch, whispering to her. Lisa came over to say good-bye. Lisa had lost dogs before, but for me this was a new, earth-changing experience. I teared continuously, listening to Lisa's reassuring voice, telling me that Fletch had had a perfect life, that she would be okay. I'd had so many friends die over the years, climbing, jumping, getting sick, having accidents. I'd almost become immune to that loss. Or I thought I had. Lisa and Fletch were my two most constant companions in my adult life, the ones I'd grown up with. Now Fletch was leaving me. It was so hard to grasp.

Lisa was gone and Mario was there. I'd put small bowls of food and water nearby, but Fletch didn't lift her head. She lay still, resting on her paws, not moving, breathing gently. She'd never refused food before. I cut some small pieces of cheese, one of her favorite treats. She perked up slightly and ate a small piece. Mario and I looked at each other, almost ridiculously pleased. She ate another, then another, looking more interested.

"Let's take her out to the grass," Mario said. "She loves lying in the grass."

Carefully, he carried her out, and we sat with her on the green lawn. Fletch lay still, with her head lifted up from her paws, and then suddenly she vomited. I looked at Mario, stricken. She threw up some more, just the small pieces of cheese we'd given her and clear fluid, and her head dropped down. She rolled partly to her side, her chest rising and falling quickly. "Oh, no, oh, no," I said, heaving sobs, stroking Fletch's head. "I'm sorry, girl, I'm sorry, I'm sorry."

Fletch lay on her side in the grass, taking fast, shallow breaths. Tears poured down my cheeks, heavy, gasping sobs welling up behind small moans. I couldn't pull myself together. I curled around Fletcher's back and shoulders, trying to comfort her, to calm her. She panted, sounding exhausted and helpless, then suddenly tried to push herself up with her front legs. Her shoulders and head raised just a few inches and then dropped back down. It became a horrible rhythm, seemingly beyond her control. Panting, trying to push up, dropping down. Panting, trying to push up, dropping down. It was past five, and Dr. Sorensen's office was shut until morning, and I had no way to help her. I was racked with guilt. She shouldn't have to do this. I should have decided, should have called him before this started to happen. I stroked her and held her, and she panted, pushed up, and dropped down. It went on for hours, until dark fell. I just wanted it to stop. I wanted her to rest. She kept on, laboring, seeming to move without conscious thought.

We carried her inside the house, to her bed at the foot of my bed. She'd always refused to sleep in the bed with me. I put blankets and pillows on the tile floor, and Mario and I lay beside the dog bed with Fletch. We didn't talk. Tears flowed from my nose and eyes as I spooned with my little dog, feeling her mechanical breaths against my chest, the push of her legs as she ineffectually tried to push up. Mario lay on the other side of her, quietly. He'd taken such good care of her. He'd never known her in all her glory, when she was the strongest, bravest little res dog, when she dominated dogs three times her size without even breaking a snarl, when she charged coyotes in the desert, when she got lost in a thunderstorm and turned up herding sheep at a rodeo, when she ran beside me for hours, her grin stretched so wide it split her face in half. I was so tired. I listened to Fletch, panting and pressing in the dark. I never imagined this place where Fletch was laboring, gasping, dying. I was so tired.

I woke up suddenly. Fletch was coughing. I curled my fingers through her fur, the thick ruff at her neck. She was quiet. I looked at the clock, the numbers glowing red: 1:02. I lay in the dark, my eyes open. She was gone. I whimpered, the sound creeping out from my chest, cutting off my breath, making me pull deep, shuddering gasps of air through my mouth to refill my lungs. I shook Mario. He held me as I cried until I was just too tired, then we got off the floor and into bed. Fletch was in her bed, where she always was. I fell asleep, my back against Mario's chest.

The light woke me. I lay in bed, watching the orange glow on the cliffs outside the window. Fletch was in her bed, at the foot of mine, the way she always was. I stayed still, feeling it. This was the last morning she'd be there. I'd have to get up. We'd have to take her away, bury her. She would be gone. I didn't move. We couldn't bury her in the yard. What if someday I didn't live here? I couldn't leave her here if I was gone.

Mario woke up.

"I don't know where to bury her," I said.

He was quiet, then said, "It might be better to have her cremated."

"I want to bury her. Somewhere. At the Tombstone. We could bury her in the landing area, and then we'll be there with her all the time, when we jump."

"Babe," Mario said gently, "it's summer. And it's really hot and the ground is baked hard. It might turn into a bad thing trying to take her down there and dig. I think it might be better to have her cremated."

"How do you even do that?" I asked, feeling helpless.

"Vets do it. We can take her to Dr. Sorensen's, and they can do it."

I got out of bed. Fletch was lying on her side. I took off her diaper. It was still clean. She felt stiff, her muscles rigid under her soft fur. Mario was right. He went into the other room and called the vet's office.

"They say if we bring her right now, they can do it this morning. We can have her ashes this afternoon."

"Right now? I'm not ready, we can't go right now." Tears rolled down my cheeks.

"Okay, we'll take our time, but if we can bring her this morning, they will be able to do it today instead of keeping her there. I think it's the best thing."

Mario wrapped his arm around my shoulders. I leaned against his chest and cried until I ran out of breath again. My nose was so clogged I couldn't breathe through it. Mario went out to his car and cleared the floor in the back. I wrapped Fletch in a blanket and carried her out to the car. I sat on the floor, holding her as Mario drove, looking up through the windows, hoping we weren't there yet. We would get there and then I would have to give her to them. I held Fletch, stroking her ears. I'd wondered if it would be strange holding a dead animal. It was still Fletch. She felt just like Fletch, only a little stiffer. She still smelled warm, like herself. I just wanted to hold her, to keep her. I felt as helpless as a four-year-old, clinging to the toy that mattered more than anything else in life.

Mario pulled into the driveway in front of Dr. Sorensen's office, which adjoined his house, with horse pastures all around. He opened the door.

Immediately I lost all my courage. "I don't want to give her to them!" The thought of bringing Fletch inside and giving her up forever was more than I could bear. Sobs racked my chest again.

It didn't seem possible to hurt this much. Everything that had happened in the last year or two, the emotional pain, the physical injuries, it had been nothing compared with this. "I think we should bury her. . . ." I trailed off, clutching Fletch to my chest, feeling the solidity of her little body.

"Babe, you might like having her ashes. I think it's the best thing."

I knew he was right. I stood in the driveway and forced myself through the office door, pressing her fur against my arms and cheeks. I could hardly bear to give her to them, to the kind people who'd taken such good care of her. I laid her on the metal table, where Dr. Sorensen had scratched her ears and said, "What a good dog," as she'd patiently allowed him to give her shots or stitches. Sobbing and gasping, I turned away. More than anything else in the world, I just wanted to keep her. But I couldn't. I couldn't keep her. I walked out the door, Mario's arm around my slumped shoulders. She was gone.

The door flung hard, torn by the wind. The trees thrashed, the tears blew from my eyes, my hair whipping wildly. It stung my wet cheeks, snatched ropes of runny liquid out of my nose. I got into the car and slammed the door against it, feeling drained. We drove back slowly, without Fletch. I didn't know how I was going to do it. How could she be gone? Everything I'd ever thought was important was nothing. I'd give anything to have her back, to have her with me for the rest of my life. There was no way to change it. There would be no getting her back. Ever. It was absolutely final. Fletch was part of me, my alter ego. And she was gone.

I sat in the living room. Mario quietly rolled up the ragged strips of carpet and disappeared outside. I moved around the house uselessly, looking at Fletcher's beds. It was the worst day of my life. I wondered if I would feel like this every hour of every day forever. I picked up her beds and carried them onto the porch. Mario was stacking wood planks beside the driveway.

"What's that?"

"I took down her ramp," he said. "Let me take the beds. I'll put them in storage."

"Wait." I went inside and picked up Fletcher's food bowls and the stand to keep her from leaning down to eat, all of her colorful harnesses with her name and phone number written in Sharpie, her travel food bag that had gone everywhere with us. "Can you take these too?" When he was gone, I looked around. My house was cozy but minimalistic, decorated sparingly. A framed photo of Fletch was in every room. Those would stay.

The day dragged on, hours to be got through, the wind scraping branches on the roof. Mario came back and drove me to the vet's office. Dr. Sorensen's wife handed me a grapefruit-size plastic bag full of light gray ash, and a card. I'd given them my heart, and I was getting back a plastic bag of dust. Tears blurred my eyes.

"I'm really sorry," she said sincerely. "We all loved Fletch. She was a sweet girl and you took very good care of her."

It was so easy to believe in non-attachment, embracing loss. It was so much harder to live it. As usual. Everything had changed, and nothing would ever be the same again. Somehow there must be good in it. There had to be.

I smiled painfully as tears ran down my cheeks and dropped into the neck of my shirt. "Thank you."

I sat in the passenger seat, the plastic bag on my lap, as Mario drove home.

The next morning, I woke up and Fletch wasn't in her bed. She was gone. I didn't move, feeling. The dawn light was soft, the leaves of the mulberry tree green and shiny outside the window. A tear trickled down the side of my cheek and rolled into my ear. I was dehydrated, my stomach sharp and empty. The grief was softer. No day to come would ever be as bad as yesterday, as the day Fletch died, I thought. It just couldn't be. That was good to know. I looked over at her ashes, sitting near the foot of the bed, near her spot. A small shape moved, startling me. A black cat jumped onto the covers, purring. It strode up beside my legs and stood above my shoulder, jauntily. It was real. It must have come in through Fletch's door on the kitchen porch and ventured down the hall, right up onto a bed full of large creatures. That took some nerve.

I rubbed its tiny pointed ear and stroked its high cheek, in the spot cats like. It rubbed against my hand, purring, winding against the comforter tucked around my body, then abruptly curled into a tight ball beside my hip.

"Mario," I said, turning toward his shoulder, knowing he was still asleep. He too was solid and warm, breathing smoothly. "There's a cat. A little cat."

He says his name is Mao

Chapter Fifteen

Learning to Fly

Lauterbrunnen Valley, Switzerland

Without Fletch, I had a surprising amount of time. The tiny black cat meowed so loudly and frequently to be petted that I finally named him Mao. He didn't seem to require much other service aside from a bowl of dry cat food that he delicately nibbled at when he wasn't devouring sparrows and mice.

After a few days of wandering aimlessly around the house, I'd started checking flights to Europe. Summer was over, but fall wasn't quite in, and ticket prices had dipped with the end of the official high season. Mario found a pilot to cover for him at the drop zone. We decided to go.

To climbers, Yosemite is simply "the Valley." For base jumpers, "the Valley" is Lauterbrunnen, a fantastically picturesque mountain pastoral of green fields and Swiss farm chalets. The limestone walls of the valley lead higher to the snowy glaciers and rugged faces of the Eiger, the Mönch, the Jungfrau, and the Schilthorn. With cliffs ranging from fifteen hundred to five thousand feet and trains and cable cars running up the sides of the mountains like Swiss clockwork, Lauterbrunnen is quite simply a base-jumping mecca.

In Yosemite Valley, park rangers taser base jumpers and throw them in jail for flying from the big granite cliffs; in the Swiss Valley, jumpers are just tourists and mountain athletes along with everyone else.

For as long as I could remember, for better or for worse, Yosemite had been the Valley. Lauterbrunnen, the Valley of the flip side, was another world: a magical paradise, the promised land, a place almost too good to be real.

My trips to Lauterbrunnen had been in the late fall or early spring, piggybacked onto speaking invitations at mountain festivals in Italy, Britain, or France. It was nearly always possible to jump from the "small," eighteen-hundred-foot walls of the Valley year-round, but it had always been too snowy to climb up to the most enticing, high peaks when my trips had presented themselves. I'd hoped to finally travel to Europe this summer in the high season, but when Fletch started deteriorating in the spring, my world had shrunk and there was no thought of leaving her. Suddenly, now she was gone.

Mario and I flew to Zurich and then switched from a double-decker, high-speed train in Interlaken to the small, toylike train for the last few kilometers up to Lauterbrunnen. We each had a bag full of warm clothes and our base jumping packs filled tight with base rigs, wingsuits, and helmets, wearing our boots to keep the bags within the luggage limit.

The train rolled slowly up to Lauterbrunnen, curving beside the dusty gray-blue stream. Trees and steep ridges stretched above the windows, the glaciers starting to come into view as we gained elevation. I felt tired and jet-lagged, but happy as the familiar landscape moved past the windows, feeling the pleasant anticipation of returning to a familiar place. It was morning, and in just a couple of hours we'd be settled into Lauterbrunnen and riding up the cable car to make a jump off the classic High Nose exit point, just as I always did as soon as I arrived in the valley.

I leaned against Mario's shoulder, and he put his arm around me. It felt good to be sharing the odd limbo space, of being neither in the place we'd left nor the place we were going to. This space had become familiar too. I was always riding on a train, passing things and being passed by things, steadily moving forward, sometimes to new places, sometimes to places I'd been before. People changed, seasons changed, and the outside world just kept moving slowly past the windows. I thought about Fletch. Somehow I'd never truly understood permanence before, in much the same way as I'd never fully understood change. Most of the things that had disappeared from my life had just gone in different directions. They still existed, but their trains were going down different tracks, traveling away from mine. I wasn't expecting them to come back my way, but I also knew they were out there, moving. You never knew when the tracks might meet in some future place. Fletch hadn't chosen a different route or a different journey. She wasn't riding down a different track. She was gone. Life was entirely new, never to be the same again.

The train curved slightly, and sun hit my eyes just as the tullelike waterfall appeared, filmy against pale gray walls. Beyond it, a bulge of rock jutted out from the top of the eighteen-hundred-foot limestone cliff, the High Nose, a specific point that jumpers had named, just as climbers named the sections of walls they climbed. The scene opened up like a painting before us, almost too beautiful to be real. "We're here, babe," Mario said, leaning down by my ear, his voice full of the birthday-morning promise I'd come to rely on. "It's the Valley."

Lauterbrunnen is a little valley below enormous mountains, with an age-old tradition of farming and mountaineering. The handful of farmers who have lived here for generations keep perfect green fields, healthy and happy cows, sheep, pigs, goats, and chickens. They make big, hard wheels of cheese, alpkäse, which they keep in dark storage on shelves in their barns, and ride vintage tractors around the narrow road that loops up and down the valley.

The Swiss engineers have built an astonishing network of via ferratas, cable cars, trains, and buses around, onto, and actually through the mountains. They drilled a train tunnel through the top of the Eiger. They built an enormous round restaurant on top of the Schilthorn, rising out of snow. Everything runs on a perfectly regulated schedule, to the second.

Spending a day in Lauterbrunnen provides instant insight into how this tiny country, bordered by nations that have feuded over land, religion, and money for centuries, has been able to maintain untouchable neutrality and fiscal command. These people are capable of anything. Who would even try to mess with them?

The Swiss smoothly integrate new uses of the place as they arise: skiing, helicopter transport, paragliding, downhill mountain biking, base jumping, wingsuit base, skydiving, and Swiss-army target practice. Everything is managed beautifully, tidily, and profitably. Of course. It's Switzerland.

In the States, most of the spectacular, accessible high cliffs are illegal for base jumping, for no reason I could ever uncover other than that national park administrators think jumping is scary and, admittedly, just don't like base jumpers. For the ultimately pragmatic Swiss, who can make miracles from manure and carve train tunnels through the Eiger, human flight seems to be just par for the course, hardly something to be perturbed about.

In Lauterbrunnen, as in all Europe, flying is just another form of tourism and mountain adventure, accepted and respected. For base jumpers, Lauterbrunnen is kind of like Disneyland, but with the real Eiger and the Jungfrau staring you in the face as you ride the small, beautifully maintained cars along the edges of sheer cliffs and mountains. To stand at the edge and launch into the open air, to feel your wings inflate as you begin to take flight, is a surreal experience for the human body and mind, no matter how many times you do it. It's hard not to fall into the grip of strung-out, addict-style frenzy, rushing from bottom to top until dark falls, especially for an American who can't quite believe the place is real and that people are actually allowed to fly. Thanks to the trains and cable cars traveling from the valley floor up to the cliff tops, a motivated jumper can make at least five jumps in a day in the Valley, slowed down only by the time it takes to repack a parachute and run back to the train station. A lazy jumper can easily make three jumps, without even rushing.

Exiting from the via ferrata jump, Lauterbrunnen

The Valley jumps, though undeniably some of the most user-friendly on earth, feel a bit intimidating at first for wingsuit flight. Ranging from fifteen hundred to two thousand feet, they are not the tallest cliffs, and the low-ish height requires you to be totally on, with good exits and reactions for pull-time. But it would be hard to find nicer landing areas, even at a skydiving drop zone. The valley floor is a patchwork of lush grass divided into green pastures. The locals have even installed windsocks in the fields below the most popular jump spots.

If you are a base jumper and you follow a few simple rules, you can leap off the cliffs in Lauterbrunnen until the cows come home and land next to them in their pastures. The Swiss impress me for many reasons, but above all because they seem to regard the world as full of puzzles to be solved, rather than calamities to be battled. For an American jumper, arriving in Lauterbrunnen for the first time, this approach to life can create severe culture shock. When you come from a place where base jumping is often outlawed simply because someone might not like it, it's almost mind-bending to watch how the Swiss effortlessly reconcile all user groups with no fuss whatsoever.

In the middle of Lauterbrunnen is a helicopter base, for air rescues and construction. The choppers fly all day long. When base jumping became popular in the Valley, the helicopter pilots expressed concern because they didn't want to be surprised by suddenly appearing parachutes when they were coming in to land or take off. Rather than pointing to this potential airspace conflict as grounds for outlawing jumping, the heli base requested that base jumpers make a phone call to the helicopter office before jumping, to make sure the air is clear.

The Swiss army requires frequent target practice, since all Swiss men over the age of eighteen may be called to service at any time. The shooting range is close to one of the common landing areas for base jumpers. Yet it wouldn't occur to the Swiss to outlaw a user group because it conflicts with another, even in the name of national military service. Instead, the target practice times are scheduled and posted in the local pub, and jumpers just don't jump in that spot during target practice.

A local paragliding company offers tandem paragliding rides to tourists. The cliff under their launch site became a popular spot for base jumping. The paragliders were concerned about the safety of their customers because they could possibly hit base jumpers in the air when they appeared off the cliff. The problem was solved by requesting base jumpers to wait until 4:00 p.m. to jump at that site, when the tandem business is done for the day and only experienced paragliders will be in the airspace.

There is no fuss, no disagreement, no cry for outlawing anything, no targeting certain user groups as being different or "crazy" or risky, no exclusionary rules that cost time and money to enforce. The Swiss simply evaluate potential conflicts, propose a simple solution, and all carry on with what they were doing.

Compared to the way I'd seen base jumping handled in the States, this kind of practical, conflict-free management seemed kind of weird. It certainly wasn't exciting. It was all so . . . reasonable.

This feeling of freedom and levelheadedness was just one of the reasons that Lauterbrunnen had quickly become one of my favorite places in the world, right up there with the Diamond or Rifle or Moab. Added to the staggering beauty, the jumpable cliffs in every direction, and that I could show up there alone without a car and fly all day every day, Lauterbrunnen could hardly get much better. Unless the Swiss franc crashed.

Mario and I had jumped in Lauterbrunnen together, and I'd made three other trips on my own over the last two years. Every time, I'd hoped to fly from the Eiger, and every time fresh or accumulated snow had made it too treacherous to hike and climb up the thousands of feet of limestone slabs to reach the exit point. The "mushroom" of the Eiger isn't an easy jump to get to. The train rides up to the side of the mountain are singularly expensive, close to $80 to get to this one jump and then back to the valley. And from the last station, it's another two to three hours of vertical hiking to reach the bizarrely detached pillar that perches alongside the shoulder of the mountain. Jumpers have stretched a thirty-foot tightrope from the Eiger to the top of the pillar. To reach the small, bulbous summit of the mushroom, you have to clip a carabiner to the chest strap of your base rig and slide across the rope, looking down at thousands of feet of air below your feet.

The payoff is big, though. Instead of flying for thirty seconds off the eighteen-hundred-foot cliffs in the Lauterbrunnen Valley, a wingsuit can stay airborne for two or three minutes off the Eiger mushroom, soaring through almost five thousand feet of altitude. It wasn't a jump I'd be doing four times a day, like the High Nose, but I yearned to experience it. And for a climber, the Eiger itself is shrouded in legend. Even just to climb on it by scrambling up the backside would be like meeting Rein-hold Messner. I had to jump the Eiger, at least once.

Late September was the cusp of fall, when snow could drop at any time in the high mountains and make them too difficult to access for the rest of the season. But we were lucky this time. The Eiger was gray and mostly clear of snow, and summer had a few final days in it. Less than twenty-four hours after we'd stepped off the train from Zurich, Mario and I stood on the edge of the Eiger, tucking jackets into pants against the cold of higher elevation. Still well below the actual summit of the mountain, we stood several thousand feet up on the shoulder, where the thin rope stretched to the top of the mushroom, seemingly miles above everything else around.

I put on my gloves and my hat and zipped my windbreaker up all the way to my chin. I could hardly believe we were finally here. A gleaming black bird popped up on updrafts at the edge and skimmed above my head, banking hard straight toward Mario. Mario reached out his hands, almost touching the bird as she curved back and swooped at him again, playing on the breeze. I watched her with delight as she dipped her left shoulder slightly in a turn, wings spread fully. I knew what that felt like. She caught the wind again and popped forward and up, gaining altitude toward the Eiger's cold, gray summit, far above us. That feeling I would never know. I watched her shrink to a dot, and then she was gone.

I stepped into my wingsuit, tightened my leg straps, and zipped my legs shut. We both left our arms unzipped for the rope crossing, sliding across the exposed gap to the top of the mushroom pillar. This small point felt like the top of a slender desert spire, no larger than a pool table, but here we were thousands of feet up, looking down at miles of scree and talus, dotted with patches of snow and ice. It was very much the Eiger, cold despite the sun, big, exposed, and alpine.

Mario and I stood side by side at the edge of the mushroom. I looked down at the gray wall and the vast terrain below it. The contours flat-tened out from above, showing no indication of slope or angle, making it look like an outrageous horizontal distance to reach the green expanses beyond the talus. It was also impossible to know if those green areas were flat or hilly, for landing. I wondered how far I would fly, where I would end up when I'd dropped low enough to open my parachute for landing. Looking out over the huge stretch of rock, earth, and trees, rubbing my hands to keep the feeling in them, I had more questions than answers.

"Do you think we can make it that far?" I asked.

"Yes, definitely," Mario said. "It looks like you can fly straight out and there's that area by the forest that looks open, or you can angle more right and head toward the train station if you think you can make it farther."

"True." I gazed out at the forest of tiny-looking pine trees. "I think that station is Alpiglen—that's where people talk about landing. It looks far, though!"

I felt confident in my suit. I was flying a Vampire 3, the latest, fastest wingsuit available. Phoenix Fly was in a never-ending quest for better flight, and Robi, who brought out a newer, better Vampire every year or so, was already dropping hints about the prototype V4 he was testing. Though I had almost no interest in cars, climbing equipment, or clothing as long as they got me from point A to point B without wasting my time, I was unable to resist flying the best possible wingsuit. As soon as a newer, better suit was available, I simply had to have it. Since part of the problem with wingsuits was the wait time of several months for custom orders, I could easily sell, to someone who didn't want to wait, an old suit at a decent price once I'd upgraded.

Mario had been flying a wingsuit since they'd started to become commercially available in 1998. He had owned one of the first suits that Robi had designed for Birdman, the earliest wingsuit manufacturer, and Mario had base jumped it off giant cliffs in Norway when the idea of taking a wingsuit off a cliff was still pretty out there. Though Mario kept a virtual fleet of parachutes for every possible type of canopy flying, his true passion, he'd purchased exactly one more wingsuit in the ten years since his first purchase, and he was still flying it. I found that mind-boggling. It was kind of like driving a beat-up Honda Civic when you could easily sell it and get a brand new Lamborghini for not much more money. I pestered him ceaselessly to buy a Vampire so he could fly as high and fast as

I could, because flying side by side was the best thing of all, and we both had to work hard to match our flights in such different suits.

Mario in the Firebird

But Mario seemed to get a kick out of teasing out the best possible performance from the sturdy old Firebird. And seeing him fly was a good reminder that having the best wingsuit is only part of flight performance—ultimately, it still comes down to the pilot. Watching Mario fly that clunky, outdated suit as if it were a vintage Porsche was amazing, but it didn't give me much information about my own flight potential. I was light and lanky in a high performance wingsuit. I would definitely fly out farther than he would off the mushroom, and I would have to make my own guesses about where that would be even if I watched him go first.

We spent a long time discussing the height of the wall, scientifically dissecting the angles and distances as we always did. We arrived at the same conclusion that our eyes had given us. Mario would take the shorter, direct line toward the clearing he'd spotted, and I would take the diagonal line out right and fly to Alpiglen. Standing at the sharp edge of the Eiger, sharing the analysis and the experience, alone on this vast mountain, was wonderful. Mario made me feel solid. He had no ego or selfishness, and virtually no fear. He was innately calm and generous, as much so at the edge of a cliff as in a living room. I trusted his judgment completely, not just because he was a respected and accomplished innovator in the world of jumping, but because I knew his decisions were ruled by intelligence, equanamity, and sheer love of flight.

"Do you want to go?" I asked.

"I'll go, and you can see how far I make it. Watch my canopy flight so you can see what the wind is doing."

Though watching Mario's flight wouldn't tell me much about how far I'd get in my wingsuit, it would tell me about the wind, even just by seeing the tiny red square landing in the distance. I always liked jumping last. I preferred to observe everything I could from the other parachutes in the air, and I also liked taking pictures with my small camera as each person left the edge. Most of all I liked the calming moment of standing alone at the exit, with no one else there when I stepped into the air.

Mario adjusted his goggles and buckled his helmet under his chin. "Okay, see you down there." He tugged down the zips of his arm wings and loosened his chest strap slightly. I smiled at him, feeling something rise up inside. It was happening. Mario smiled back, his pupils wide and dark, making his eyes turn gray as he looked straight into mine. "Have a good one, babe," he said, then kissed me gently on the mouth and shot straight off the edge.

I leaned forward to see the orange fabric of his wings flutter in the dead air until he reached terminal speed and the suit grew rigid, shooting forward out of the long dive. Mario was beautiful to watch in flight, whether piloting his body, a parachute, or an aircraft, as much at home in the sky as I was on rock. He streaked out across the mass of snowy gray limestone, shrinking to a dark dot over the green slopes way out below, seeming to fly forever, until finally his parachute blossomed open tiny and bright, right above the clearing he'd pointed out. I noted the wind direction by watching it land, a red dot that folded to the ground. He was down, safe and exhilarated, I thought, feeling the warmth of his happiness even from a mile away.

As a new jumper, I was incredibly lucky to have Mario sharing his lifetime of knowledge with me as I gained my own experience, leading me by example through intelligent decision-making and always happy to answer in astonishing detail any possible question I might have, about everything from altitude to equipment to conditions. But more than that, I was lucky to have found Mario to share my life. I trusted him completely. He'd shown me that I could, in both the lowest and the highest times. And he showed me daily that he was strong enough to fly with me in whatever direction I might go. Finding each other was a small miracle, one I could never have imagined.

But what I knew best was the quiet of solitude, with the stillness to absorb everything in my own way. The calm silence of knowing that my life was in my own hands. My decisions and my actions were entirely my own now. I was alone on the Eiger, in a world that was only mine, with Mario waiting at the other side of it. Whatever happened next would be completely of my own making. I switched my thoughts now to my jump.

I scanned the terrain again, making my flight plan, looking for the outs in case something went wrong. I thought about flying as far and fast as I could, envisioning myself taking the perfect body position in the air for maximum flight performance. I could almost feel my wings inflate, feel the suit rocket forward, my legs straight and strong, my arms canted back for maximum speed, like Fletch's ears in a full sprint. I pushed my helmet over my head, grabbing the chin guard to wiggle it down all the way, and pulled my goggles over my eyes.

It was coming. The seconds ticked forward toward the moment when it would all begin, when there would be no going back. As soon as my feet left the Eiger, I would be in the air, the rock left far behind me absolutely. I'd be gone from this place, immersed in the beautiful impossibility of human flight. As soon as my feet left the Eiger, the past would be finished. Nothing would ever be the same again. It could be the last flight of my life. It could be the start of the rest of my life. The ticket was bought. The only way to find out where it was going was to go.

I fluttered my shoulders, straightened my spine, and filled my lungs all the way down to my stomach. It was time. I looked up and smiled, then lowered my chin in the direction I would dive, in a steep forty-five-degree pitch from the edge. I breathed out, settled into stillness, and then suddenly pushed off hard, feeling the force of my shoes against the edge as I dove forward into the air, tipped down into the angle of flight. Gray rock rushed around my eyes, then the air caught me, lifted me, filled my wings, and I left the Eiger behind, watching it grow distant behind my legs.

The world spread around in all dimensions, vast with possibility. I stretched my wings, floating up slightly, trading speed for buoyancy as I savored the sensations of flight, seeing, hearing, feeling. I made a slow, easy turn to the right, toward Alpiglen. The earth rolled out beneath me like a terrain map. I watched it dispassionately, eaglelike, free now of questions. High up in the sky, it was so easy to see.

The green meadows lay out ahead, far beyond the cold mountain. I plunged down, tucked my wings, and flew.

Flying over Switzerland

Chapter Sixteen

In the Air

"When life instantly and drastically takes you completely by surprise, the first reaction is confusion. If one minute you're following a normal routine in an airplane, motors roaring, and a couple of minutes later the plane crashes and you're on a raft, lost and adrift in a vast, loud silence, the disorientation is, at best, intense. Then a new world unfolds. You need time to understand and figure out what's happening."

—LOUIS ZAMPERINI, *DEVIL AT MY HEELS*

My story had a fairy-tale ending. Mario and I got married in 2011. After my painful and crushing first marriage, I saw Mario as an angel straight from heaven, the kindest, most loving man I'd ever met, and I actually felt thankful for the hard past experiences that made me appreciate him in every way.

By the time *Learning to Fly* was published in April 2013, we'd just completed the arduous green card process for Mario's US citizenship. Writing the book itself was a major project, a year of writing squeezed in between trips and life projects. We built an octagonal, off-the-grid cabin on twenty acres of land near Indian Creek. We got a puppy, a wild little cattle-dog mix who'd been dumped to starve by a cell tower and was found surviving on cow manure on the Navajo reservation at Montezuma Creek. Mario chose the name Cajun because as he said, she was sweet and spicy—an ebullient, ecstatic little creature—not the most dignified dog I'd ever seen, but definitely the most athletic and exuberant. Cajun was Mario's first dog, and he adored her, taking her everywhere on adventures around the desert, carrying her in a backpack or on his shoulders in places that were too steep for her to climb, and teaching her to run down from the tops of cliffs to meet us after we base jumped. We used our combined skills of climbing and jumping to have unique adventures on multiple desert towers, and we made an independent film about our base climbs on the Moab spires, *The Perfect Circle*. Together we achieved my longtime dream of making a wingsuit base climb, by climbing and flying off a remote limestone mountain called Notch Peak in the west desert, the second tallest vertical cliff face in North America.

In between all of this, Mario ceaselessly explored the Moab cliffs and towers and the La Sal mountain peaks with Cajun, his base parachute, his paraglider, and his speed wing. He tinkered with gear and concepts and quietly opened spectacular new jumps alone and with friends, using his quickly developing climbing skills to pioneer new routes to the tops of cliffs and towers he'd been eyeing for years. He made countless cutting-edge and innovative jumps in his typical meticulous style, getting intrigued by a place or an idea and enjoying the process of exploring it thoroughly. He jumped from a higher cliff to land his parachute on top of the King Fisher tower in the Fisher Towers, and then jumped off it to get to the ground. He flew his parachute in a corkscrew spiral around the Titan, the tallest freestanding tower in the States. He explored the network of mining roads on the Roan Plateau by motorcycle and flew his base parachute off nameless points, through curving canyons and around strange pillars and walls. He made his way solo with ropes and climbing gear to the tops of obscure desert towers and mesas and set up via *ferrata*-style hand lines so he could share them with friends. He jumped from the skydiving plane and landed his parachute on the extremely small, uneven, and rocky summit of Castleton Tower, and to get down he launched his speed wing off the top, with the base parachute zipped into the belly of his jacket. Mario was as comfortable in the three-dimensional environment as most people are on flat land. No one else ever even knew about most of these adventures, and he remained happily occupied in the details of progression until he was satisfied with the experience and then moved to the next idea he'd dreamed up. But no matter what project Mario had going on, he'd always drop everything if I asked for help or if any friend needed a hand from him for anything. I'd never seen someone so driven, and yet so nonself-absorbed.

And in between all these other projects, we started a business together in Moab called Moab Base Adventures, the first company in the world ever to offer tandem base jumps from cliffs. For Mario, it was the ultimate extension of his passions—pioneering in the air and creating a way to share this magical experience with people who could otherwise never feel it on their own.

Mario had spent over a year building, modifying, and testing his equipment and, just as importantly, developing a careful method of training and preparing people for the tandem base jumping experience. To anyone who asked if it was safe, he immediately responded "No, it's not safe. Base jumping's not safe. We're jumping off a cliff."

But Mario did believe that while tandem base jumping would inherently never be safe, he'd succeeded in bringing the risk to an acceptable level, a level that would allow people who were willing to put their trust in him to have an otherwise unattainable experience. I was there for every jump, starting as the passenger on his first two tandem base jumps, and I felt that Mario was the one person in the world who could take people off a cliff "safely." His innately calm and reassuring manner made it possible for people to put their full confidence in him in the most intense moments of their lives.

And for many of the people who came to jump with us, taking a step off the cliff with Mario was a life-changing experience. One woman who had been sexually assaulted years before and had never been able to fully recover from it, despite building both a successful career as a physician and an impressive résumé of many athletic achievements, wrote to him several months after her jump to say that, for the first time in her life, she felt strong and free. Another man lost a significant amount of weight in order to make his first base jump with Mario. He trained and lost even more weight to come back for a second jump from a cliff, which required a steep two-hour hike with some sections of rock climbing, an ascent he never would have been capable of on his first visit. He wrote afterward to say that for him, the experience was the equivalent of climbing Everest, and that as a result of his two jumps with Mario, his entire life had changed.

Being the channel for people to have these experiences was life altering. It was a lot of work, and it was extremely intense. Mario said from the beginning that he'd never do more than two tandem base jumps per week, even if the business boomed—which it quickly did. With the inherent risk of the sport, he felt that from a mathematical standpoint, there must be a certain number of jumps at which an incident is inevitable, and he wanted to set a limit and keep the number low in hopes of staying within those parameters of inevitability.

Through the business, Mario was also offering courses for new base jumpers who wanted to be thoroughly instructed on the safest techniques for cliff jumping in Moab, and he was guiding traveling jumpers who wanted to be shown to the best cliff sites in the area. I pitched in by guiding jumpers up desert spires, for those who were more experienced and had some climbing skills and wanted a more exciting adventure. The tandem business was getting a lot of attention from the media, including the *New York Times*, *National Geographic Adventure*, and *Outside* magazine, and Moab Base Adventures was taking off in every way.

Life was very busy by the summer of 2013, and as August approached we kept procrastinating on buying plane tickets for the annual Europe summer trip. Things were so hectic this year with the business growing and everything else that it seemed hard to leave on vacation. But wasn't this the whole point of having our own business? To have even more freedom to get out and fly our wingsuits and travel? In early July, I checked flight prices to Switzerland and said, "Mario, we need to pull the trigger—or not go. I could accept either way, but the tickets are just going up, and we need to decide now." We agreed that it could be nice to stay in the States and travel to the northwest to jump Mount Baring and climb at Index in Washington, a trip we were always talking about doing. And finally, without either of us actually deciding, we went ahead and bought tickets to Zurich. We knew that if summer came and went and we weren't flying wingsuits in the Alps or the Italian Dolomites, we'd regret not going.

We arrived in Lauterbrunnen in the first week of August to torrential rain, more than we'd ever seen in Switzerland. We'd decided to tent camp on this trip, and the tent was flooded on the first day. Mario was uncharacteristically exhausted, from teaching and guiding groups of jumpers in Moab up until the very day we left for the airport. After a couple of wet days in Lauterbrunnen, we fled to Brento, Italy, where the weather is always better. Damian and Jay joined us, on their way home from a similarly stormy stint in Norway, and we all stayed in Brento for a week, flying when the storms allowed and watching the weather forecast in the Dolomites, where the weather was equally unsettled.

Mario and I had jumped in the Dolomites on our last two summers in Europe, and it had become one of our favorite places. Our skills, and the sport itself, were advancing exponentially in the last few years. The goal had shifted from simply flying straight out from the cliff into open air, to terrain flying: intentionally turning and diving to get closer to the rocks and trees on the ride down a mountain. More dangerous, of course, but even more amazing to experience.

With just a few days left, the four of us drove to the Dolomites and pooled our euros for helicopter rides to the summits of two lofty limestone spires. The week in Brento had been fun, but the first day in the Dolomites was phenomenal. Damian was wavering on the edge of changing his travel plans and staying with us for a few more unique jumps. Jay didn't have an option to stay: they were traveling in the same car to the airport, and finally Damian decided to stick with the plan and leave with Jay. But we all agreed that we'd meet back in the Dolomites the next year for a good long trip together, and we'd fly everything.

Mario and I had only two days left, because we'd planned to go and visit Robi in Slovenia at the end of the trip. We'd jumped a nearby mountain called the Sass Pordoi a couple of years before, and we needed only one car to access it, which was key now that we were on our own. We could camp anywhere in the forest near the landing area and hike an hour up a trail to get to the cable car that would take us the last 3,000 feet to the top of Pordoi. To top it all off, the landing area was a grassy meadow beside a charming hotel and restaurant. The weather had cleared, and with the short hike and the inexpensive cable car ride, we could easily make several jumps at this idyllic site in our last two days.

We got to Sass Pordoi on August 18, pitched the tent by a wooden picnic table, and set off to the cable car. The enormous summit was just as we remembered, a sprawling limestone mountaintop decorated with whimsical cairns and alarmingly deep crevasses near the sides. Random pitons and bolts dotted the edges, left there by climbers taking different routes to the top. Panoramic views of distant blue and gray dolomitic peaks extended around in all directions, almost too beautiful to be real. A tall metal cross stood at the exit point, guyed up with metal cables.

Curious hikers and tourists clustered around watching as we geared up and stood at the exit, which made for a slightly distracting feel, a little more like a stunt jump than vacation. We made two flights that day, Mario choosing to go through a large notch feature on the side of the mountain, while I flew around outside the notch, not wanting to be so committed until I got more familiar with the site.

That evening we sat side by side at the wooden picnic table, chopping vegetables for dinner, a glass of Italian wine at hand, and paging through the climbing guidebook. A French jumper camping nearby in a small European-style RV came to visit and was delighted to discover that we could chat in French. His name was Jean-Louis; he told us this place was his paradise. He came here every year to climb and jump but was not feeling confident jumping right now, so he was only climbing. He offered to drive us up to the cable car the next day. After these last two weeks of rain and clouds, we wanted to savor the nice weather and the relaxing time of walking uphill for an hour before getting into the cable car. We told him we might take him up on it for the second or third jump.

I woke the next morning on my air mattress, cuddled against Mario. Part of me just wanted to stay in bed, enjoying the feeling of lying close together and waking up slowly, the kind of thing you might do while on vacation. Being in the base jumping business in Moab meant that days started before sunrise; a chance to sleep in for a few hours had become all too rare. But finally we had incredibly beautiful weather, and this was our last day in the Dolomites, and we didn't want to miss out on such a perfect morning. We drank some tea, shouldered our packs, and set off up the hill. As we walked we talked about how nice it all was, and we agreed to stop in at the hotel restaurant for apple cake and coffee after we landed, to take advantage of all the small joys of Italy one last time.

On top, I'd never seen such perfect conditions. There was no wind, the sun was shining, the air was warm yet crisp. A group of birds flew past in a magical cloud as we stood at the exit in our wingsuits, chatting with a group of Italian motorcyclists who had ridden the cable car up for the view. Mario asked me if I wanted him to follow me and shoot video on the flight, as he often liked to do. Although we'd jumped twice the day before, I still felt first-jump-of-the-day jitters, just a little. "No, let's just take it easy on this first one. You don't have to follow me too close," I said.

"Okay, I probably won't," Mario said with a chuckle.

I pushed off the edge, watching the notch that seemed so far ahead as I transitioned into flight, trying to gauge the distance and my height. I did want to fly through it at some point, but I needed to build confidence, and I didn't want to get committed. I decided to head just right of the notch again, and to look more carefully this time to estimate how high I was above it as I passed: another scouting run. Maybe on the next jump I'd fly through, provided I had plenty of altitude to dive down and stay in control. Mario had gone straight through the notch on both jumps yesterday, but he was much more confident with gauging his height and getting close to the terrain. Though I'd become a seasoned wingsuit flyer in the last five years of obsessive jumping, I was still far less confident and far less experienced than Mario. Again, I flew around to the right of the pillar that formed the right side of the notch formation, pleased to see how comfortably high I was above it, and then turned out toward the landing area.

When I deployed my parachute, the shock of opening was abnormally forceful. Stars flashed across my eyes and for a moment I wondered if I'd fractured my neck. I cautiously moved my head around, squeezed my eyes shut hard a few times, and then forced myself to focus on flying a correct pattern around the tall trees surrounding the hotel. I touched down in the grassy lawn, rattled, and looked for Mario beside me. He wasn't there. Confused, I looked around in the air and then back all the way toward the gray mountain, trying to make out the tiny cross up at the exit point. Had he waited so long, still chatting with the motorcyclists?

Jean-Louis rushed toward me with another couple, talking fast in French. "We saw Mario jump right behind you, and he seemed very low. He flew to the notch, and then we did not see him again." I stared up at the mountain, not understanding. I called his radio. Silence. Was there some way Mario could have flown left of the notch, into some huge gully in the mountain I somehow had never seen before, and around to the other side of Sass Pordoi? I looked up at the mountain. It was a solid mass of stone. I'd seen it from above, from below and from all sides. There was no other way left of the notch. I called the radio again, refusing to let go of confusion yet, asked Jean-Louis to repeat what he'd said. "He jumped behind you, right after you, and he was very low. We saw him flying, toward the notch, but I did not see him come out." The radio was silent.

I pulled out my phone. "We need to call a helicopter now." Suddenly the task of making myself understood in any language was too much. I handed the phone to Jean-Louis, and we rushed over to the campsite, to the rental car. Mario had hidden the key under a rock just before we started walking, as we always did according to policy. Otherwise it would be in his pocket. "We need to get to the cable car station, we need to talk to them," I said, fighting to control my rising panic, the anxiety swelling inside my chest. Jean-Louis drove up the endless switchbacks. I couldn't speak. I knew.

The day before, I was buying our tickets for the cable car, and Mario stepped away to take a photo of a man and his son with their camera in front of the station. When I turned around, he wasn't there, and I was gripped by a completely inexplicable panic. Mario and I had never been angry at each other, but I was so upset I almost yelled at him when he came back around the corner. "You can't just disappear like that! I didn't know where you were, and I couldn't find you—you don't have a phone here, and you can't just disappear!" He was startled by my vehemence. I was startled too.

The next morning we made a joke of it when I went to buy the tickets. Mario took my hand gently and said, "I'm going up to the bathroom to put my contacts in, and I'll be up there, and then I'll wait right outside the bathroom for you until you get there."

I laughed and kissed him. "I just need to know where you are all the time!"

Now I ran to the ticket booth, barely able to breathe, and the woman inside recognized me from our last three trips up. She could see we were jumpers, buying one-way tickets up and carrying packs, and had smiled sweetly each time, telling us to have a good flight. I explained that a helicopter had been called, but I didn't see one in the air, and I wanted to make sure they were actually coming, please, could she call again to make sure it was coming? I was trying hard to speak calmly, to stay calm, to be someone she'd want to help. She assured me that the helicopter had been called. They were flying on the other side of the mountain searching, so we couldn't see them. Mario was in a black and blue wingsuit, hard colors to spot in a huge landscape of dark limestone. I couldn't hear the chopper and was nearly out of my mind with anxiety. I knew in my heart that Mario was dead. But what if somehow he was just badly hurt and each second mattered? It was driving me insane not to know where he was, not to be able to do anything. I sat on the curb and watched the empty sky, tears running down my cheeks, down my neck.

My phone rang. Jean-Louis had ridden up the cable car to try to help from the top, to explain to the crew where he'd last seen Mario flying. "I am sorry," he said in English. "They found him. I am very sorry."

It was all surreal after that. Driving eternal switchbacks with a uniformed man to a high, grassy meadow, far across from the Sass Pordoi. Standing at the side of the road there, not knowing why. The landscape was like some kind of movie scene, too beautiful to be true. Not real. The helicopter coming down, a body bag in the grass. Kneeling next to Mario's body, not knowing what to do: how could he be in there? Someone leading me away, the helicopter rising up, everyone gone. Down in the city, in the town office, explaining that both our passports were around Mario's waist, the safest place we had. Two men walked in and handed me his wedding ring, the passports in his cloth hip pouch with the strap sliced neatly off from each side. The sympathetic women in the office, looking at me, waiting for decisions. What language to write his death certificate in, which form to use, which embassies to call, what to do with his body. In America, it was four in the morning. No one answered the phone.

I went outside and sat in the rental car. I couldn't do this. I looked at Jean-Louis bleakly. And then I seized my cheap Europe phone and scrolled to Matt, an American who'd been living in France for ten years for the flying, one of the most together and efficient people I'd ever met.

Matt answered immediately, his voice expectant and happy, "Steph and Mario! You're in Europe!"

"Matt, Mario's dead."

His voice dropped instantly, brusque, military-style. "Where are you?"

"I'm at Sass Pordoi. I'm down in the town at some office. It's near the mortuary. I don't know what to do."

"Who are you with?"

"These nice French people who are helping me, we just met them yesterday. Matt, I don't know what to do."

"Where are you staying?"

"We're camping by the landing area."

"I just got home from Spain. I can start driving in a couple of hours. Get help finding a hotel room, have someone else pack the tent if possible. Otherwise I can get it tomorrow. Don't stay in your tent by yourself. Text me the hotel and the room number when you get it. Keep your phone charged and call me anytime for any reason. I'll be there at midnight."

At five p.m. the skies opened. The window of my room looked directly at the Sass Pordoi, barely visible through a curtain of rain, and I almost couldn't bear the agony of it. Of all of this. Of waiting. Sitting in this room alone, like being in hell. There was nowhere to go. Rain pounded on the roof and I was furious. Why hadn't it rained like this eight hours ago, to keep us from jumping? Why had it been so beautiful? I couldn't bear it. It wasn't fair, it just wasn't fair. This morning I was waking up in our cozy tent, with my head on Mario's shoulder and my leg curled over his stomach, thinking of flying and apple cake and driving to Slovenia. Why hadn't it been me? It should have been me. I was less experienced, less skilled, less good than Mario in every way. Why hadn't I been the one to die? I wished furiously it had been me, and then immediately I thought, no, I would never want Mario to be doing this right now. Mario should never have to do this. But I was angry that I was in front and didn't see him go in. My brain locked on this new unfair thing. I was cheated of the chance to dive down and follow him, why couldn't I have seen him? But I probably would have automatically flown to safety in the second it took to understand, leaving the terrain behind, and now be sitting here hating myself for not choosing to follow him.

I just couldn't understand how Mario could have hit below the notch. He'd flown through it twice the day before with plenty of altitude. It wasn't difficult or cutting-edge for him to make that flight. He wasn't trying to push the envelope, he was simply flying an enjoyable line that he'd already done easily. From what Jean-Louis told me, it sounded like Mario had an unusually bad start into flight and was pretty low when he started flying. But that happens sometimes, and it shouldn't have mattered at all on this jump. Even with a bad start, Mario wouldn't have flown to the notch if he thought he was too low to pass through it. He would have just headed right and flown around it, as I was doing. But the idea that he turned toward the notch thinking he was high enough to pass it when he actually wasn't didn't make any sense at all. Mario understood his altitude and proximity to terrain better than anyone. He'd been piloting every type of flying device almost every day for thirty years. The helicopter medic told me he'd impacted ten feet below the notch. How could he have made such a huge mistake? He didn't make mistakes. It didn't make sense. None of it made any sense.

Suddenly my stomach clenched and I saw us back in the landing area in the sun, yesterday afternoon. We'd just landed from the second jump, and Mario stood beside me holding his goggles in his hands, looking into them.

"What are you doing?" I asked.

"I think my contact might have popped out of my eye. It's strange, maybe it's in the goggles," he said.

In the few months before this trip, Mario had decided to try contacts instead of glasses for the first time, and rather amusingly battled with getting them in every morning, often calling me into the bathroom to help him get the slippery little plastic disk in place. Half the time it folded, slipped off, and got lost, or slid around the side of his eyeball.

I was always mystified at Mario's attitude to his vision. He loved fixing things, keeping his equipment in perfect condition, and never neglected or rushed through any type of maintenance. He gave his full attention to even the smallest and most uninteresting tasks. But the vision in his left eye had been steadily degrading since he was eighteen, and he was always procrastinating about keeping his prescription up to date, as it changed every year. What could be more important for a pilot than vision? Why was he so uncharacteristically lax about dealing with his glasses and his changing prescriptions? In a way, his left eye seemed almost to annoy him, an obstinate member of the team that refused to do its job correctly like everyone else and that tried to seek attention through bad behavior.

Even harder for me to understand were the red-tinted ski goggles that Mario had started to wear for flying in the last year—not just in his wingsuit, but also paragliding and speed flying, sometimes even for regular base jumps in order to keep the wind out of his eyes. I'd tried the red lenses, and I found them terrible. The tint changed my depth perception, especially in the shade or in sun-to-shade conditions, and it even made me nervous about gauging my height for landing the parachute. I insisted on using only clear lenses in my goggles because I couldn't tolerate anything distorting my view at all. But Mario didn't seem to mind the red goggles; he used them for everything. I chalked it up to his greater experience and better understanding of his altitude and depth perception. Obviously he knew whether or not he was comfortable and seeing right, and he always seemed absolutely at ease in the air, even when testing out some sort of strange gear or modification.

Yesterday afternoon I had taken the goggles from him. "Well, if your contact's out, you won't be able to find it. Let me look."

There was nothing in the goggles.

"Maybe check my eye?" he said, "Maybe it slid around, or it's folded?"

I looked at his left eye, at the blue iris, and there was the contact sitting flat over it, perfectly positioned. "Honey," I said, rather shocked, "it's right there on your eye."

"Wow," he said, "it must be changing really fast now. I guess I'll have to get new glasses again when we get back."

It rained and rained, slamming the roof, streaming down the dark window glass. Why didn't I insist we stop jumping, why didn't I say, "Mario, if you think your contact fell out and it's there on your eye, we shouldn't be flying anymore!" How could I not have realized? And the red lenses. I didn't have any vision problems, and *I* couldn't see right in those things. Why didn't I put all of this together and tell Mario I didn't like it, tell him he shouldn't be using those red goggles, he shouldn't jump anymore if he thought his contact was out and it was sitting *right on his eye*?

At high speeds, while flying close to things, depth perception is important. Vitally important, no matter how good you are, no matter how much you understand the visuals. And to have those visuals change suddenly, when you're not even aware they're changing—it's a hidden trap lying in wait. Your brain only knows what your eyes tell it. Now it all seemed so terribly clear. I could never know for sure what happened, but it was the only thing that made sense, at all. And it was too late for me to see it, to stop it somehow. Such a small thing, such a small flaw. A tiny plastic disc, and everything was lost.

The helicopter medic had taken my hands that afternoon and said gently, "it was instant. He didn't suffer." I sat alone in the dark thinking that the luckiest people in the world aren't the ones who are the healthiest or the richest or the smartest or the most beautiful . . . it's those very, very few who get to leave together.

The next day Matt took over. I stared numbly at the walls of the town hall. Matt's equally efficient fiancée, Megan, was on the phone back in the States, coordinating flight changes, invoking Matt's Diamond status to get instant results, and googling airport hotels, while Matt called the rental car company headquarters to arrange a return in Italy instead of in Zurich.

"You'll follow me to the rental return place, we'll drop your car, and then I'll drive you to Zurich. You can fly out tomorrow morning. Look. I know you want to wait for the cremation, but in Italy that can take weeks. They have this crazy situation where there are more people than crematories, and there's a waiting list. You can't stay here that long; you need to go home."

I protested weakly that Mario wouldn't leave me in Italy, that I should wait for him, that I couldn't leave him here alone.

"I understand, Steph, but you can't stay here. It could be weeks. You need to get home, and there's a direct flight from Paris to Salt Lake tomorrow morning that we can get you on."

Not having to make decisions was what I really needed. I got into the rental car, clutching the papers I'd been given, and blindly followed Matt's BMW up and down the curving passes. We were going to drive right past the high meadow where they had set Mario's body on the grass before they took him away again. I turned on the blinker, and Matt slid over ahead of me. I walked to the meadow, into the unreal panorama of 360-degree beauty. The last place Mario lay on the ground. The last place I sat beside him. The last place I saw him on earth. I couldn't move. How wrenching to leave this place, to start going toward the time when it was all gone. Matt let me look, held me briefly, and then nudged me toward the cars. We drove over the pass.

The flight home was interminable, a torture. I was trapped in a box of metal and plastic, surrounded by strangers, with no way out, no way to do anything but think, and no way to stop thinking. My brother and several friends had offered to fly over and fly back home with me. But why should anyone fly all the way to Switzerland, just to turn around and fly back again? It made no sense. I told them all not to come. Now, sitting on the plane alone, I understood that I'd made a huge mistake in refusing company. I sat in the uncomfortable seat, twisting and turning, trying to keep control. Slow tears started and couldn't be stopped, and gradually I dissolved into heaving sobs with my head in my lap for most of that eternal flight, not caring what the other passengers thought, unable to get control of my grief. In the Salt Lake City airport, my brother was waiting at the door. Chris, who'd been there for my crash at the Roan and had become Mario's closest friend in the last few years, had driven up from Moab with his wife, Eula, and Cajun. I looked at Cajun's expectant little face and collapsed on the floor.

For weeks I stayed in bed with Mao curled in a ball by my hip, getting up only to take Cajun on ten-minute walks. Friends called, emailed, texted, wrote. My parents drove ten hours from Arizona. My brother stayed for the first week, fielding visitors. It was too many people. Sleeping was the only relief. There I could see Mario in my dreams, but it was always followed by the misery of waking to this empty place. Cajun moved uncomfortably between the bed and the floor, unwilling to settle into Mario's spot.

I'd been through a marriage that had left me almost broken. Things had happened that I would never tell anyone, that had left scars so deep they would never disappear. I'd lost my confidence in almost everything. And then I'd found Mario, a love I trusted completely. And now he was gone. I couldn't see the point. I thought constantly about going to a cliff and jumping off without deploying my parachute. That would seem to have been an accident, easier for my friends and my parents to accept. Friends who'd lived through this kind of loss promised me that time would help, take the searing edges off the pain; that they were happy now. I didn't even have the energy to hike up to a cliff with the rig on my back. But I visualized it constantly, from the moment of pushing off the edge through the second I kept control and didn't reach back to pull. If this crushing hopelessness never ended, I had a way out. There were plenty of cliffs around. Eventually I'd have the energy to walk to the top of one. I wasn't trapped. Chris quietly moved into the guest room after whispered discussions with Virgil and Lisa.

Realizing I wasn't committed to go on living allowed me to endure the grief day by day, to see what would happen. I asked myself what Mario would do. I started sanding and painting the siding of the house, a task he had planned to do when we got home from Europe. When the house was painted, I painted the window trim and window frames. I tiled the insides of the bathroom cabinets. My parents plunged vigorously into the extraneous home improvements. They drove back and forth from Arizona to reengineer my heating ducts and install a new furnace. They replaced the washer and dryer, built a counter over them and then did laundry with them. Friends tore down the old back deck and rebuilt it, another project on Mario's house list.

I started to go climbing with Lisa, managing one or two pitches before I had to leave. Once I was actually touching rock and moving up I felt okay, but fell back into a silent lethargy on the ground. It was hard for me to be away from home for more than a couple of hours at a time, to be apart from Mao.

Eventually I gained the energy to walk uphill. Cajun and I walked to the tops of cliffs. I jumped with pinches of Mario's ashes tucked into my parachute, waiting at the bottom for Cajun to run down to meet me. I didn't care if the winds were bad. If I wanted to jump, I jumped. I was sick of the unfairness of it all. I was seeing people who jumped recklessly, in poor conditions, who did sloppy, ridiculous stunts or made careless mistakes with gear or execution, and then who walked away without a scratch, while Mario—who'd worked endlessly to be as safe as possible, who was more skilled and experienced than anyone I knew, who was quite simply a better human than anyone I knew—was dead. It was a stupid bullshit activity, because it wasn't fair at all. It was a stupid bullshit life because it wasn't fair at all. I couldn't stand to be around jumpers whom I considered reckless. It was too hard to be around people who had the gall to be alive when Mario was dead. And then of course I felt guilty for being angry that people were alive. It was easier to be alone.

Over time the sharp longing for Mario turned into an ache. Cajun got used to sleeping in bed. I got used to waking up pressed between a dog and a small cat instead of my husband. I thought about all the ways people can die, some of them so terrible. I thought of the possibility of

Mario ending his days alone, sick, in a bed, hurting. And I realized that he had had a very good death. He was healthy, vital, and strong. He was happier than he'd ever been, as he told me every day in those last weeks, and he was looking forward to so many things. The upcoming months were to be packed with new adventures that were coming as a result of all the foundations we'd built. He was flying in a place he loved, with me in front of him. It was instant, with no anticipation. This was a nearly perfect way to die, for Mario. Sooner than he would have chosen, much sooner than I would have chosen. But it was an effortless death, in a moment of joy, in a time filled with both fruition and anticipation. And in a vast sea of unfairness, this one thing was fair. I could accept this. In time I would even be grateful for it.

One day, going through Mario's old photos and logbooks, I found a square printed card with thumbtack holes in the corners. I read what was written on it:

For a long time it seemed to me that life was about to begin—real life but there was always some obstacle in the way, something to be gotten through first, some unfinished business, time still to be served, a debt to be paid. At last it dawned on me that these obstacles were my life. This perspective has helped me to see that there is no way to happiness. Happiness is the way. So treasure every moment you have and remember that time waits for no one. Happiness is a journey, not a destination. —Souza

Mario had never shown this to me, but it seemed as if this idea had directed his life. He appreciated everything, even things that were hard, painful, or tedious. Simply by living, he'd shown me how to choose a life of happiness and how to soar through the sky. This message was a gift he'd left for me to find—the instruction manual he hoped I'd read, since I no longer had him here to do boring things, like reading directions, for me. If I was going to stay alive, I was going to LIVE, and I was going to be happy. Otherwise there was really no point in being here at all. It was time to stop enduring and time to start living. It was time to see if I still wanted to fly.

Just before Christmas, I drove to Skydive Arizona in Eloy, where Mario and I had skydived together every winter. I had a new wingsuit Matt had given me after he'd gotten me home from Italy. Matt, one of the best pilots out there, had an additional passion: modifying and engineering the best possible wingsuits for himself, and he had ultimately started a company called Squirrel to produce his designs. Matt firmly believed his suits to be the best-performing and safest suits to fly, and he wanted me to try one, if I decided to fly again. I told him I might, eventually, but it would have to be white. In just a few weeks, a top-of-the-line white Squirrel Aura, custom-made for me, arrived at my door. I didn't know what it would feel like to fly. What it would feel like to fly without Mario. I didn't know if the joy would be there.

The first plane ride to altitude was wrenching without Mario across from me, his blue eyes sparkling. I cried as I flew over the familiar Arizona desert without him. But I also felt he was there in the air, the place he'd been most at home. I'd already lost so much. If I stopped flying, it needed to be on my own terms, not because I was running away from pain or trying to hide. I stayed in Eloy, buying jump tickets one at a time, every day wondering if I'd leave the next morning for home. Friends arrived, and now I was flying among them in a flock, not alone anymore.

On Christmas day I woke in the desert in the dark, in the back of my Honda Fit, with Cajun curled up next to me. It was much too early for the jump planes to fly. The first load wouldn't go up for hours. I stuffed away my sleeping bag, rolled up the air mattress, and drove to nearby Picacho Peak, a small rock mountain perched on a saguaro-studded hill and surrounded by open desert. A dirt trail led up through the cacti and thorny bushes, and I followed it slowly, Cajun bounding off ahead. Dawn came as I reached the shoulder and wrapped around the back of the peak, passing king saguaros standing tall beside the steep trail. What a beautiful life to live, peaceful and silent, keeping watch over the desert. The sun rising and setting, the days rolling by like waves, one after another.

We climbed the steep rock sections to the top just as the sun rose and made a heart out of small rocks, for Mario. Cajun lay quietly beside me like a grown-up dog, looking out over the desert. We watched the shadows change and shift over the earth. A bird circled above, close at first, then spiraling higher and higher until he flew off to the east and disappeared into the sky. I felt my heart rise. We walked down the mountain, into another day.

It's 2015. It's been two years since Mario died. I've fallen in love again with a kind and beautiful man named Ian, a respectful and talented wingsuit pilot, a friend of Mario's and mine. An industrial engineer turned skydiving tandem instructor, Ian now lives in Moab with me, Cajun, and Mao. Ian was behind me on my first wingsuit base jump without Mario, and he was with me when I landed. We understand what it means, perhaps more than most.

I'm happier than I've ever been, something I would have thought beyond impossible two years ago. I love Ian more every day, and so I can't wish for anything different on the long and curving path that brought us to now. I also wish every day that Mario was still here. Ian understands this paradox, because he feels the same way. We both miss Mario. We wish more than anything that he were here. We feel thankful to be together and to share a growing love. From this I've learned that things don't have to make sense.

Things will not stop changing. You never know what's going to happen, even in the next second. The truth is, we don't decide anything. But we can decide how we feel. That's the meaning of life.

I think we all have a different degree of spiritual development, just as we're all born with a certain amount of intelligence, athleticism, or beauty. Mario was the most spiritually evolved human I've ever known, but he certainly didn't see himself that way. He considered himself a very simple person. He saw magic in everything and good in everyone, and he brought out the best in people. He lived in the air.

I came across something Mario said while I was watching old video clips of him, on a day when I was feeling strong. He was talking about the pull of flying, but to me, hearing him now, he was really talking about the ephemeral nature of life. About my good fortune in having known him.

"It's there, but only in your thoughts, like a souvenir. It lingers, and you're like, oh wow, but it's not there anymore. And I think that what keeps you going back is you can't stay in that state very long, you can't be in the air forever basically, you're always coming back down. And I think what makes it a little bit magical too is you'll go through great lengths to go back and get that couple seconds, couple minutes, couple hours feeling through different ways, because as soon as you step on the ground, it's gone."

When Mario died, a few months after this book was first published, it felt to me at first like a cruel joke. I hated that book. Its fairy-tale happy ending was nothing but a fantasy turned to ash. But now I love the book because it's about Mario. It's the story of someone almost too pure to be real, too good to stay on this earth, and it's the story of how I fell in love with him. Mario tamed me with love and patience just as the Little Prince did with his fox. Mario made me precious through the time he spent on me, and he became part of me forever. He taught me how to fly. He still teaches me. And as long as I'm here, the story doesn't end.

Acknowledgments

Thank you:

To Greg Crouch and Farley Chase for making this book exist and to Mario Richard for existing.

To my brother and parents: Virgil Davis III, Virgil Davis Jr. and Connie Davis.

To Stacy Creamer, Megan Reid, and the team at Touchstone for hours of review and encouragement.

For draft reading: Karen t'Kint, Chad Davis, Virgil Davis, Jimmy Pouchert, Beth Rodden.

For helping: Mario Richard, Lisa Hathaway, Karen Roseme, Patti Haskins, Karen t'Kint, Chris Pope, Brad Lynch, Christian Griffith, Brendan McHugh, Jay Epstein, Alan Martinez, Marta Empinotti, Jimmy Pouchert, Robert Pecnik, Andrew Hyde, Jeff Leads, Beaver Theodosakis, Pam Theodosakis, Ken Meidell, Eric Hobbs, Brett Cardamone, Charles Cole, Laura Sanders, Jacob Fuerst, Adam Peters, Karen Bednorz, Jimmy Chin.

For pure love: Mao and Cajun.

For being: Kevin Reese, Craig Luebben, Emily Berkeley, and Betty M. Fletcher.

Index

Page numbers in *italics* refer to illustrations.

About the Author

Steph Davis is an iconic name in climbing.

Steph's résumé of climbing achievements spans twenty-five years. She was the first woman to free climb the Salathe Wall on El Capitan, and the second woman to free climb El Cap in under twenty-four hours. She has established first ascents around the world, of difficult rock climbs and high-altitude mountains from Yosemite to the Karakorum. Few climbers practice the high-risk style of free solo climbing, using no ropes or protective gear. Steph is the most accomplished female free soloist in the world and is also one of world's top wingsuit base jumpers. She is one of just a few people in the world, and the only woman, combining free solo climbing with base jumping.

From an unusual start as a classically trained pianist with a master's degree in literature, Steph chose to leave law school in order to pursue climbing full-time. She has become one of the most successful professional climbers in the world.

Steph has written two memoirs, *High Infatuation* and *Learning to Fly,* and curates a blog at stephdavis.com about climbing, flying, vegan cooking, training, simple living, and travel. She owns and operates Climb2Fly Productions in Moab, Utah, a climbing and base jumping stunt company.